The YANKEES *Index*

EVERY NUMBER TELLS A STORY

Mark Simon

TRIUMPH
BOOKS

No part of this publication may be reproduced, stored in a retrieval system, or transmitted in any form by any means, electronic, mechanical, photocopying, or otherwise, without the prior written permission of the publisher, Triumph Books LLC, 814 North Franklin Street, Chicago, Illinois 60610.

This book is available in quantity at special discounts for your group or organization. For further information, contact:

Triumph Books LLC
814 North Franklin Street
Chicago, Illinois 60610
(312) 337–0747
www.triumphbooks.com

Printed in U.S.A.

ISBN: 978-1-62937-176-4

Design by Andy Hansen

All photos courtesy of AP Images.

To Grandma Frieda, who let a little boy who liked numbers play with her adding machine on trips to her house in Elmont.

And to Dr. Robert Cole, who taught me the keys to being a journalist, and convinced me that I had a future as one.

To Dave + Darcy—
Enjoy the book!!

Contents

Foreword

Lou Cucuzza Jr. has helped to manage the home and visiting clubhouses at Yankee Stadium for decades, and when old Yankee Stadium was scheduled to close in 2008, he asked every major league player who walked in that season—and every former player—to sign his office door. Derek Jeter signed, of course, and Yogi Berra and Miguel Cabrera and Josh Hamilton and hundreds of others. By the end of the summer, so many autographs coated the thing, made of heavy steel, that one of the clubhouse guys who works for Cucuzza suggested that he create a notebook to identify all of the names, some scrawled and some curled perfectly, for posterity.

Cucuzza had the door wrapped up in outfield padding and bubble wrap, and it rests against a wall in his basement, just another of the many stories to come out of a Yankees franchise smothered in folklore. Babe Ruth pointing at Cubs pitcher Charlie Root in the 1932 World Series, or the stands behind him, before clubbing a homer. Roger Maris hitting his record-setting 61st homer into a sparse group of fans stretching for the baseball. A kid with a glove reaching out of the stands to knock a long fly into the stands in the 1996 playoffs—the Jeffrey Maier play. Jeter goading President George W. Bush into throwing a ceremonial first pitch from the mound during the 2001 World Series, adding a warning that if he didn't do it the right way, Yankees fans were sure to boo him.

The stately Joe DiMaggio kicking at the dirt in anger after an outfielder robbed him of extra bases in the 1947 World Series. Yogi Berra leaping into the arms of Don Larsen after the only perfect game in World Series history. Mariano Rivera sprinting to the mound and throwing himself down in prayer after Aaron Boone ended the AL playoffs with one swing. Billy Martin emerging from the dugout to ask home-plate umpire Tim McClelland whether George Brett had too much pine tar on his bat, and, a few moments later, Brett sprinting out of the other dugout, rage in his eyes. Reggie Jackson pausing a moment at the plate and watching his deep drive carom off the black seats in faraway center field, the perfect punctuation mark to legend. The immortal words that Lou Gehrig spoke into a microphone not long before he died.

There was only one major leaguer who came through Yankee Stadium in 2008 without signing Lou Cucuzza's door, he recalled—Bobby Murcer, the longtime Yankees outfielder and broadcaster who was dying from cancer and passed away. Murcer was so sick and Cucuzza didn't have the heart to ask him to sign. But Murcer's place in Yankees history lives on, from his days as the worthy heir to Mickey Mantle to the moment he homered and circled the bases with tears in his eyes after burying his close friend and teammate Thurman Munson.

The number of signatures on that door is staggering, but it won't tell you the whole story. The real stories are behind the numbers, just as Mark Simon shows in this book.

The signatures on Cucuzza's door may fade eventually, but the tales are eternal.

—Buster Olney

Introduction

As a baseball fan, there is so much to appreciate when it comes to the Yankees franchise.

You don't have to love the Yankees to respect the Yankees and what they represent. The pride is in the pinstripes, as some like to say.

Much of that can be found in the numbers. Numbers make for great storytellers.

Some produce very specific memories. The number 60 evokes the thought of a larger-than-life giant of a man and ballplayer who became the game's greatest immortal. The number 2,130 is about a streak, about giving it your unbounded best every single day until you have nothing more to give. The number 56 is about a streak of a different nature—an unbreakable mark from a man who considered himself to be among the greatest at what he did. The number 3,000 is about a picture-perfect day in the Bronx, and a picture-perfect accomplishment by a picture-perfect star.

Every number tells a story of some sort, and you don't have to have a plaque in Monument Park for your time with the Yankees for it to have meant something. Aaron Small's 10–0 means just as much to him as any number meant to any Yankee. It represents a turning point both in his career and in his life. Dr. Bobby Brown's .439 batting average in the World Series is something he still thinks about every day and night.

The Yankees have an incredibly rich history as the most successful franchise in professional sports. There are many who love them and many who hate them. But even the haters can't deny the greatness of the past and the present. Yankees history is unlike any other team's history. There are overwhelming numbers of great players, great managers, great games, and great moments.

This book is about the numbers and the stories that matter in Yankees history. Each is important in its own right. We're here to share both from the earliest days of the franchise (which didn't just start with Babe Ruth and Lou Gehrig) to the most recent successes (and even a few failures).

The goal is to educate and entertain. Maybe you'll learn something you didn't already know. Maybe you'll see something and it will evoke a memory for you of how you remember that moment, whether you were at the ballpark, watching on television, listening on the radio, or even following as it was live-tweeted. Regardless, if a story made you think about something, or re-think what you knew about something, I feel like I've accomplished a goal in writing this book.

I hope you enjoy the journey.

Dominance: 27 World Series Titles

When Joe Girardi was introduced as Yankees manager in November 2007, he was presented with a uniform that would serve as a reminder of the ultimate goal.

The number on the back was 27, which represented what number the team's next World Series title would be.

The Yankees have since won a World Series, and Girardi subsequently changed the number on his back to 28. But for now, it's that total of 27 championships that represents the greatness of the Yankees' historic past.

"They have more than twice as many as any other team," said ESPN baseball analyst Tim Kurkjian, noting that the Cardinals rank second with 11.

It is a number to celebrate. It's the most championships by any team in any of the four major sports. The next-most by a New York team is eight by the NFL's Giants.

There is a singular expectation when you become a member of the Yankees. The 10,000-plus regular season wins matter. But they pale in comparison to the 27 titles.

Your goal is to win the World Series. You'll hear the owner say it, the general manager say it, the manager say it, and the players say it.

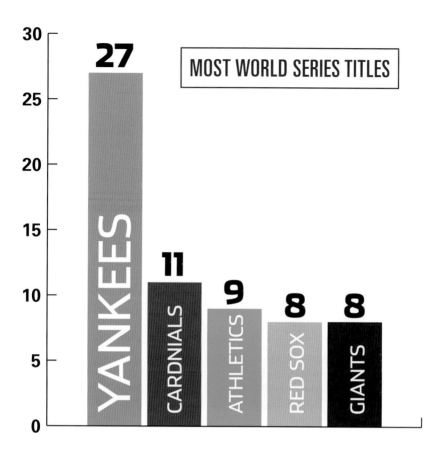

MOST WORLD SERIES TITLES

That's a lot of pressure. There's also the extra pressure that comes with playing in the biggest media market in the world.

"Playing here is at the complete other end of the spectrum than anywhere else," then-Yankee Dave Winfield said in 1987. "In New York, it's life or death. Everything is magnified."

Some players thrive in that sort of atmosphere and those who do become legends. The greatness of Babe Ruth, Joe DiMaggio, Mickey Mantle, Reggie Jackson, Don Mattingly, and Derek Jeter shined in the most important moments under the New York spotlight. They're now icons in the team's history.

How did the Yankees get to the point in which greatness was such a casual expectation? From 1903 to 1919 they were more often pretender than contender. They came close to winning the AL title

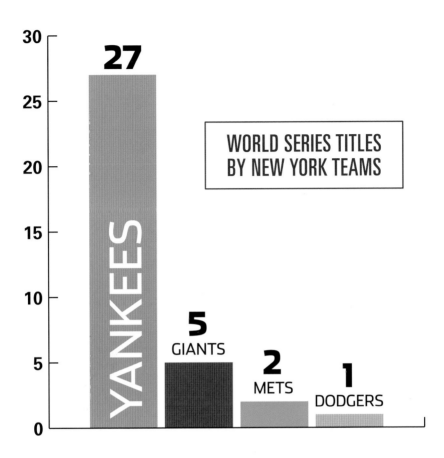

WORLD SERIES TITLES BY NEW YORK TEAMS

27 YANKEES

5 GIANTS

2 METS

1 DODGERS

on a couple of occasions but were not the dynasty that dominated much of the 20th century.

That changed with the purchase of Babe Ruth from the Boston Red Sox, though the Yankees did not win a pennant until 1921 and a championship until his fourth season, 1923, the team's first in Yankee Stadium.

Coincidentally, the Yankees winning that Series stopped another potential dynasty, the New York Giants, in its tracks.

There was an October magic that seemed to follow the Yankees. This franchise seemed capable of all sorts of greatness in the Fall Classic. They were a team of destiny, a team that has won more than twice as many World Series as it lost. And they've had so many memorable postseason moments.

Yankees captain Derek Jeter was an integral part of the Yankees dynasty of the late 1990s and 2000s. In 2009, he'd add a World Series ring for the thumb too.

Three-homer games? Check.

A perfect game? Check.

Amazing ninth-inning comebacks? Check.

The Yankees' home ballpark also provided a comfortable advantage. The team had something it could build around, left-handed hitters who could take aim at the short porch in right field. Ruth was the first great slugger. Many others followed.

The Yankees established themselves as consistent championship material in the late 1920s, but it wasn't until the next decade that they became a dynasty. The Yankees won four World Series in a row from 1936 to 1939 and six titles in eight seasons in all. They would better that over the 18-year period from 1947 to 1964, when they appeared in 15 World Series, winning 10, including five straight from 1949 to 1953.

This was when the Yankees–Brooklyn Dodgers rivalry was at its peak. The Yankees beat the Dodgers in 1941, 1947, 1949, 1952, and 1953 before the Dodgers finally vexed their nemesis, winning the title in 1955. The Yankees came back to win it all by beating the Dodgers the following season.

The Yankees lost their way from 1965 to 1975, not even making a postseason in that time.

MOST CHAMPIONSHIPS BY SPORT

NFL
PACKERS
13

MLB
YANKEES
27

NBA
CELTICS
17

NHL
CANADIENS
23

New owner George Steinbrenner did his part to change that, bringing in best-of-the-best talent in Catfish Hunter and Jackson, which resulted in the Yankees winning back-to-back titles over the Dodgers in 1977 and 1978. Steinbrenner, for better or worse, also brought with him a version of "winning or bust" that was loud and harsh.

The Yankees again suffered a prolonged title-winning slump, partly due to unwise spending in the 1980s and early 1990s but returned to prominence by winning four titles in a five-year span, including three straight from 1998 to 2000.

It's a lot harder to win the World Series than it used to be, with the combination of revenue sharing and three full rounds of postseason play leveling the playing field a little bit. Since that last dynastic run, the Yankees have won only one title, the 27th in 2009.

The Yankees fan has learned to be a more understanding and more patient fan and to be accepting of other accomplishments.

"While winning every year is a fine goal, I've enjoyed plenty of teams and years that haven't resulted in winning the last game of the year," said Jason Rosenberg, who runs the Yankees fan blog It's About the Money, Stupid. "I am disappointed when we don't win, but I don't expect to win every year."

But that doesn't change the goal, for the owner, the general manager, the manager, or the players. There's an appreciation for winning in New York that goes beyond other places.

"What I miss when I'm away is the pride in baseball," former Yankees manager Billy Martin once said. "Especially the pride of being on a team that wins."

And there's no bigger winner than the New York Yankees.

Colonel Jacob Ruppert Buys Babe Ruth for $125,000

When Miller Huggins took over as manager of the Yankees in 1918, the team was lacking in a number of areas. That's why one of his first moves was to try to trade his entire infield for St. Louis Browns star George Sisler.

Huggins didn't land Sisler, but that didn't stop Huggins and Yankees management from pursuing other players. In the off-season following the 1919 season, the Yankees were given the opportunity to purchase a one-of-a-kind player. It became the most notable deal in baseball history.

The player was Babe Ruth, the game's greatest hitter and arguably one of its best pitchers, whose three victories helped the Boston Red Sox win World Series titles in 1916 and 1918.

Ruth hit a major-league record 29 home runs in 1919, the last year of baseball's Dead Ball Era, as he moved into a role in which he played the outfield much more than he pitched.

Ruth's power was far beyond that of his fellow players. Only three other American Leaguers even reached 10 home runs that season. He was referred to as a "Colossus of the bat" a name that would eventually be refined to "Sultan of Swat."

It was a pleasant sight for Jacob Ruppert to see the most iconic player in baseball put pen to paper.

But Ruth had some concerns heading into the 1920 season. Though he had two years left on his contract, he wanted a big raise and a deal more befitting of his talents, at around $20,000 per year. He threatened to hold out if his contract wasn't redone.

Reporters began to take sides. Sportswriter Ty Hettinger said that Ruth should be disciplined for refusing to fulfill his contract. That same day, famous sportswriter Damon Runyon pointed out that Ruth would be a bargain if he was making $100,000.

Red Sox owner Harry Frazee was stuck. He was a theater operator and needed money, both to finance his plays and to pay off debt on Fenway Park. He couldn't afford a fight with a ballplayer who wanted a big-money deal.

Frazee knew that his friend, Yankees owner and president Jacob Ruppert, had the money to make the biggest transaction in baseball history, as the two had conducted a number of deals for players the last few seasons and Ruppert had previously pursued Ruth over the summer.

In a deal that now would be best described as "Steinbrennerian," Ruppert bought Ruth from the Red Sox for $125,000 and a $300,000 loan that secured a mortgage on Fenway Park.

The idea that any such deal between the Yankees and Red Sox would take place now is unthinkable. But back then, circumstances for both sides were such that it was reasonable. The rivalry was in its earliest stages back then.

Initial reports were that Ruth was resistant to the deal. But Ruppert dispatched Huggins to Ruth's home in California and within a day, Ruth was on board.

"New York fandom may rest assured the big fellow is determined to set such a home run record in 1920 as has never before been dreamed of," Ruppert told reporters.

Ruth lived up to that by hitting 54 home runs in 1920, 25 more than the record. The Yankees didn't win the World Series, but they won 95 games that season and established credibility when the sport needed it.

THE IMPACT OF GETTING RUTH

Yankees 90-Win Seasons	Yankees WS Titles
1903–1919: 2	1903–1919: 0
1920–1934: 11	1920–1934: 4

There was no resting for Ruppert. In his biography on the Society for Baseball Research Bioproject website, author Dan Levitt notes "Ruppert, always the perfectionist, wanted not only to win, but to win big."

Ruppert returned to the Red Sox not only for other player purchases, but to pilfer away front-office personnel. He signed away Red Sox manager Ed Barrow, to fill the role of what we now know as a general manager.

Together, the two built a baseball dynasty. Ruppert and his partner, T.L. Huston, also built a new ballpark. The team moved into a new home in 1923, one that became a baseball mecca. The Yankees won six pennants and three World Series in the 1920s and won five World Series titles in the 1930s, though Ruppert was not around to see the last of those.

He died in 1939 at age 71.

"Colonel Ruppert's passing robs his organization of a keen intellect with outstanding business judgment and acumen and baseball of an outstanding and colorful personality," said Yankees executive Larry MacPhail.

Though Barrow was inducted into the Baseball Hall of Fame in 1953, Ruppert was not enshrined for another 60 years.

When the Hall of Fame convened a special pre-integration panel to vote on candidates in December 2012, a number of that panel's members were surprised to see Ruppert on their ballot. Former Yankees GM Bob Watson admitted to thinking that Ruppert was already an honoree.

The committee voted Ruppert into the Hall. He was inducted in 2013.

Babe Ruth's
60 HR in 1927

Nine games into the 1927 season, Babe Ruth was hitting .233 with one home run.

"Ruth Falters During Early Season," read one newspaper headline.

Such was the narrative for baseball's best slugger for a couple of weeks, which seems ridiculous in hindsight. But it wasn't unusual.

"Babe Ruth had more photos taken of him than anyone on the planet and more words written about him than anyone on the planet," said MLB's official historian, John Thorn.

Said baseball writer Cecilia Tan: "He was a cultural phenomenon that went beyond sports or even American popular culture in general."

When Ruth was playing well, the words were kind. When he wasn't, the treatment was rough.

Ruth had set such a high standard in previous seasons (he set the major league record for home runs with 54 in 1920 and 59 in 1921) that if he dared go into a funk, the media was all over him.

Entering May 11, Ruth was hitting .314 with seven home runs and 14 RBIs in 24 games (along with 25 walks). But one syndicated article referred to him as "the big disappointment of the Yankees" and speculated that Ruth's off-season moviemaking was to blame.

1927 AMERICAN LEAGUE HOME RUN LEADERS

Babe Ruth   **Lou Gehrig**   **Tony Lazzeri**

"It is a well-known fact that the powerful Klieg lights used in the process of making motion pictures are not regarded as eye tonic for a home run hitter," read the column. "Perhaps the glare of the winter work has temporarily hurt Ruth's vision."

Ruth, who liked to box, put that talk down with a few baseball-style haymakers.

He hit .373 with 10 home runs and 29 RBIs in a 20-game stretch to close May. That shut the reporters up and put him in line for a historic feat.

Through June, July, and August, Ruth had company in his homer hitting. His teammate, first baseman Lou Gehrig, matched Ruth blow for blow.

The home run chase became the story of the season, as the Yankees pulled away in the pennant race. At the end of August, Ruth led 43 to 41.

What makes Ruth's 1927 season really amazing is how he closed it. Entering September, he needed 16 home runs to tie and 17 home runs to break his previous home run mark.

Ruth's high for home runs in a calendar month to that point was 14 in July 1924, when he played in 37 games. The 1927 Yankees had only 28 games remaining.

Ruth had one thing going for him. The Yankees were set to finish their road schedule on September 7. They closed the season with 21 straight home games, advantageous because the short porch in right field was an inviting target for a left-handed power hitter.

A September 6 doubleheader at Fenway Park marked the turning point. Gehrig homered early in the first game against the Red Sox to go ahead of Ruth, 45–44.

But Ruth matched Gehrig with a titanic blast, one described as the longest homer hit at Fenway. He added two more to retake the lead 47–45.

After Ruth hit two more home runs the next day, giving him a record-tying five in three games, it was clear that he had a chance at something special.

Ruth went three games without homering, but made up for that by homering in three straight after that. When he hit his 50th against the St. Louis Browns, celebrating fans showered the field with straw hats with such intensity that the game had to be stopped.

Ruth's home run chase was interrupted by something unexpected. A disabled man charged Ruth with assault, saying that Ruth hit him during a confrontation on the Upper West Side in Manhattan. Ruth claimed he was in New Jersey at the time of the alleged incident (the case was dismissed a few days later).

BABE RUTH CALLS HIS SHOT…OR DOES HE?

"Did the Babe call his shot, or was it just a mystery plot?"

That's the final line of a poem written by Edward Kirwan, about the most mythical moment of Babe Ruth's career, his home run against the Cubs in the fifth inning of Game 3 of the 1932 World Series.

And it's a great question.

Legend has it that Ruth pointed to center field, letting the Cubs, who had been taunting him, know that he was going to hit a home run. Baseball historians and authors have studied newspaper accounts and video, but no one can say definitively what happened.

What is known is that Ruth's homer was his 15th in World Series play, then a major league record. Ruth twice hit three home runs in a World Series game (the only player to do that multiple times), but it is this home run for which he is best remembered.

Ruth followed with two home runs the day after his initial court hearing as the Yankees clinched the pennant with a doubleheader sweep of the Indians.

In today's game, priority would be given to resting players in preparation for the postseason, but there were no thoughts of that pertaining to Ruth. Maybe he needed a rest, but he didn't take one. He hit only one home run in a six-game stretch, giving him 53 with nine games remaining in the season.

But if you thought hitting seven home runs in nine games was impossible, you didn't know Ruth. He hit his 54th in Game 2 of a doubleheader against the White Sox.

He hit 55 and 56 in his next two games against the Tigers. The latter was a game-winner, and in an odd scene, a young fan came out of the stands to finish the home run trot with Ruth, who ran around the bases, bat in hand.

"The youngster was like the tail of a flying comet, holding onto the bat for dear life and being dragged into the dugout by the Babe, who raced to escape the rush," read the description in the *New York Times*.

After failing to homer in his next two games, Ruth hit his 57th against the Athletics. That meant that Ruth needed three home runs in the final three-game series of the season against the Washington Senators to break his mark.

Piece of cake.

Ruth homered twice in the series opener to match his previous record of 59.

"He makes miraculous deeds appear commonplace," wrote John Drebinger of the *New York Times*.

His 60th was no miracle, just another wallop into the right-field stands the next day against Senators pitcher Tom Zachary.

As the crowd celebrated, Zachary protested, arguing that the ball went foul. He threw his glove down in frustration when Ruth circled the bases.

That epitomized how most pitchers felt that season, arguably the most dominant by a player in the history of the game.

We marvel at the accomplishment now, and Ruth certainly reveled in the even greater celebrity status that came with it.

But to Ruth, hitting home runs was actually a simple endeavor.

"All I can tell them is pick a good one and sock it," he once said. "I get back to the dugout and they ask me what it was I hit and I tell them I don't know, except it looked good."

A lot of them looked awfully good in 1927.

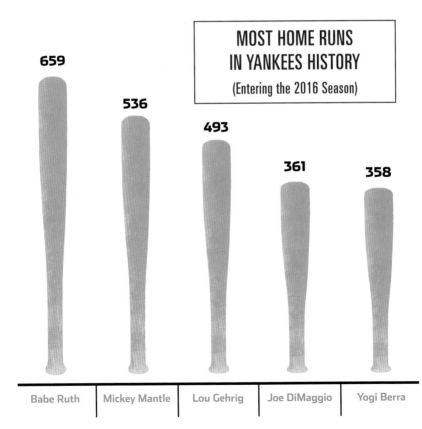

MOST HOME RUNS IN YANKEES HISTORY
(Entering the 2016 Season)

Babe Ruth	Mickey Mantle	Lou Gehrig	Joe DiMaggio	Yogi Berra
659	536	493	361	358

Lou Gehrig Plays in 2,130 Consecutive Games

He was the luckiest man on the face of this earth, but really we were the lucky ones for being able to remember one of the greatest players in Yankees history, Lou Gehrig.

The New York native and Columbia University graduate made his mark with his offensive prowess and durability.

Gehrig made an early impression in the final week of the 1923 season. He homered in his first start against the Red Sox and then had four RBIs in a 24–4 rout the next day.

"He looks promising," noted a writer in the *Fitchburg* (Mass.) *Sentinel*.

Promising indeed.

In 1925, Gehrig got his chance to play on an everyday basis, when he replaced Wally Pipp as the team's first baseman. He took full advantage in what was a rough season for the team (which finished 16 games under .500), hitting .295 with 20 home runs in 126 games.

Gehrig's consecutive-games streak began innocuously—with a pinch-hitting appearance on June 1. The next day, he was inserted into the Yankees lineup and went 3-for-5.

He played in every game for almost 14 straight years.

The media had fun with Gehrig's Ivy League education. After he had two home runs and seven RBIs on July 23 in one of the team's most impressive wins of the year (an 11–7 triumph over the defending AL champion Washington Senators), Harry Cross of the *New York Times* wrote:

> "Not in vain did Lou Gehrig bask in the classic atmosphere of Columbia's fountains of knowledge. Not in vain did he delve deeply into the books in the School of Applied Science. Lou absorbed enough applied science to put it to practical use."

Also notable from that day was that Gehrig hit the first of his 23 career grand slams (only Alex Rodriguez has hit more).

Gehrig made the jump from good to great in 1926 and from great to elite in 1927. While we celebrate Babe Ruth's 60 home runs that season, it should be noted that there was an absurd rule at the time that no one could win the MVP Award more than once, so since Ruth won the inaugural honors in 1923, he was not eligible to win in 1927. Gehrig won the award instead.

LONGEST CONSECUTIVE-GAMES STREAKS, YANKEES HISTORY

Lou Gehrig
2,130

Hideki Matsui
518

Source: Elias Sports Bureau

AL president Ban Johnson was pleased, describing how Gehrig played in a way unlike how he probably would have described any other player—conscientiously.

It would have been interesting to put Gehrig against Ruth in the voting that season. Look at their numbers side by side.

Ruth: .356/.486/.772, 60 HR, 97 XBH, 165 RBIs

Gehrig: .373/.474/.765, 47 HR, 117 XBH, 173 RBIs

The Yankees won the World Series in both 1927 and 1928 with the latter being Gehrig's best postseason.

MOST CONSECUTIVE GAMES PLAYED, MLB HISTORY

Player	Games
CAL RIPKEN JR.	2,632
LOU GEHRIG	2,130
EVERETT SCOTT	1,307
STEVE GARVEY	1,207
MIGUEL TEJADA	1,152

0   500   1000   1500   2000   2500   3000

In a four-game sweep of the Cardinals that avenged a World Series loss two years earlier, Gehrig hit .545 and set multiple records. He's the only player to hit at least four home runs in a four-game World Series, and his 1.727 slugging percentage is the best in any Fall Classic.

True to form, Ruth upstaged Gehrig, hitting .625, along with three home runs in the clinching game.

It wasn't always Ruth that stole the headlines.

On June 3, 1932, Gehrig hit four home runs in his first four at-bats in a 20–13 win over the Philadelphia Athletics. He was the first player to hit four in a game since Ed Delahanty in 1896.

Gehrig was modest and thoughtful in sharing his feelings about that distinction.

"I'm as tickled as a kid with a new red wagon," Gehrig said after the game.

The story was secondary in the baseball world that day, surpassed by legendary New York Giants manager John McGraw announcing his retirement.

In that year's World Series, Gehrig hit .529 with eight RBIs in a sweep of the Cubs. That too was upstaged by Ruth's "called shot" home run.

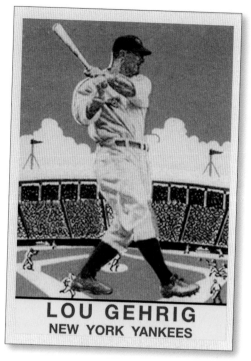

LOU GEHRIG
NEW YORK YANKEES

As Ruth's performance began to decline, Gehrig was still going strong. In Ruth's final year with the Yankees, 1934, Gehrig won the AL's Triple Crown, leading the league with a .363 batting average, 49 home runs, and 166 RBIs.

It was the second time Gehrig led the league in home runs and RBIs. The other was in 1931, when he had 46 home runs and an AL record 184 RBIs (some historians have shown this may actually be 185).

"[Gehrig] is probably the most underrated of the inner circle Hall of Famers in the Live Ball Era," wrote baseball historian Craig Wright, who authors the newsletter *Pages from Baseball's Past*. "It seems impossible that anyone could play 10 seasons with Babe Ruth and possibly be the better player, but Gehrig did that [from 1925 to 1934, Gehrig had more Win Shares—a stat that measures overall performance]."

All the while, Gehrig continued to play every single game.

MOST RBIs, YANKEES HISTORY

Lou Gehrig	1,995
Babe Ruth	1,992
Joe DiMaggio	1,537
Mickey Mantle	1,509
Yogi Berra	1,430

"Why do people make such a fuss about a fellow sticking to a good steady job," Gehrig said. "I like to play baseball and the Yankees seem to want me in there, so why shouldn't I play every day?"

Yes, a couple of times he kept the streak alive through creative means. In 1934, he suffered a back injury against the Tigers and had to leave a game. The next day, barely able to stand, he hit leadoff, singled, and was immediately pulled from the game.

The man known as "The Iron Horse" recovered pretty well from the injury though. Over the next 23 games, he hit .427 with 12 home runs.

In 1938, Gehrig played in his 2,000th consecutive game. "As I look back over the seasons, the thing that impresses me most is the realization that I always have tried to do my best and that I have helped the Yankees to win," he said.

That season, the Yankees won their third straight World Series, but it was clear that Gehrig was starting to fade, whether due to age or the affliction that more severely developed the next season.

In 1939, it was obvious that something was wrong with Gehrig. He stumbled at first base and had a hard time doing anything that required muscular effort. In his first five games, he managed one base hit. He played his last game on April 30, going 0-for-4 in a loss to the Senators. Two days later, he told his manager he could not play that day. He never played in a major league game again.

On July 4, 1939, Gehrig delivered his famous speech at Yankee Stadium, in which he said, "Today, I consider myself the luckiest man on the face of the earth." The speech is considered one of the most memorable moments in baseball history.

Two years later, on June 2, 1941, Gehrig died at his home in the Bronx. He was 37 years old.

A nation mourned.

"There was only one Gehrig and there isn't likely to be another," wrote *Brooklyn Eagle* sportswriter Tommy Holmes.

Fortunately, the Gehrig legacy has lived on in the proudest, most positive way it could.

Lucky for us.

WALLY PIPP: TWO-TIME AL HOME RUN CHAMPION

Wally Pipp is most remembered as the Yankee whom Lou Gehrig replaced at first base. What's often forgotten is that Pipp was a very productive player.

A dozen different Yankees have led the American League in home runs, and among the names are those you would expect: Lou Gehrig, Babe Ruth, Joe DiMaggio, Mickey Mantle, Roger Maris, Reggie Jackson, and Alex Rodriguez.

But it's Pipp who was the first. He hit 12 home runs in 1916 and nine in 1917, both high totals for the Dead Ball Era.

"Few men in baseball swing as heavy as Pipp," read one newspaper article.

Pipp could also bunt with the best of them. In fact, he's the Yankees' all-time leader in sacrifices as well.

But that's something overlooked given how well things worked out when he was replaced.

1927 Yankees: .714 Winning Percentage

The 1927 Yankees weren't just a great team. They were ridiculously great, consistently great, and great when it counted most.

When the *Los Angeles Times* did a series on the teams that are the gold standard in sports, the first team profiled was the 1927 Yankees.

This is a team that gets referenced not just in baseball terms, but in popular culture as well. In 1998, one article reviewing the history of the show *Seinfeld* described year four as its "1927 Yankees season."

This Yankees team was an iconic team. They are the best of the Yankees teams that featured Babe Ruth and Lou Gehrig. They went 55–22 in their first 77 games and 55–22 in their last 77 games to finish 110–44. Their .714 winning percentage remains the best in franchise history.

The Yankees were determined to avenge a loss to the St. Louis Cardinals in the 1926 World Series and they had the tools to do so. They bulldozed through anything that got in their way.

A signature win came on June 8, when they trailed the White Sox by five runs in the bottom of the ninth but rallied to tie (on Tony Lazzeri's third home run of the game) and then won in the 11th. James Harrison of the *New York Times* wrote, "He met the greatest ovation that a Yankee athlete has faced since Miller Huggins was knee high to a bat bag."

Huggins, the team's manager, was small in size (5'6", 140 pounds) but knew how to get the most out of his players.

Huggins was not someone who relished credit for what he did. When asked by John Kieran of the *New York Times* what makes a great manager, he said simply, "Great players make great managers," meaning that if a manager has a talented roster, he can look smarter than he is.

They went **55–22** in their first 77 games and **55–22** in their last 77 games to finish **110–44.**

The Yankees opened up a sizable lead in the American League, but the Washington Senators came charging hard around the midway point. The Senators won 10 straight to get within 9½ games of first place entering a July 4 doubleheader at Yankee Stadium. The Yankees obliterated them with power, winning 12–1 and 21–1.

The pennant was never in doubt after that. The Yankees won the American League title by 19 games over the Philadelphia Athletics. Ruth's 60 home runs were more than any other American League team. Gehrig's 47 were more than four clubs.

BEST WINNING PERCENTAGE, YANKEES HISTORY

.714	.704	.702	.695
1927	1998	1939	1932

Though Ruth and Gehrig stood out far above the rest, they weren't the only offensive stars on the team. Center-fielder Earle Combs matched Ruth's .356 batting average and tallied 231 hits. Tony Lazzeri batted .309 with 18 home runs and 22 steals. Bob Meusel hit .337 with 47 doubles and 24 stolen bases. It's no surprise that this lineup is often referred to as "Murderers' Row," even though the term was not originated to describe them specifically.

"Baseball never had anything like these Yankees before," said Brooklyn Robins manager Wilbert Robinson, whose roots in the sport dated back to the 1880s.

The Yankees not only hit home runs. They avoided allowing them. The 42 home runs yielded by the pitching staff ranked second fewest in the American League. The staff was led by future Hall of Famers Waite Hoyt and Herb Pennock. The Yankees also had something that wasn't common at the time—a closer. Rookie Wilcy Moore earned 13 of his 19 wins in relief, and he would have had 13 saves if the save rule had existed at the time.

The Yankees' World Series opponent was not the Cardinals, but the Pittsburgh Pirates, who edged St. Louis out for the NL pennant. Pittsburgh won a World Series in 1925 and had young stars in future Hall of Famers Paul and Lloyd Waner. But the Pirates were not able to stop the Yankees juggernaut.

MOST HR BY AL TEAM, 1927 SEASON

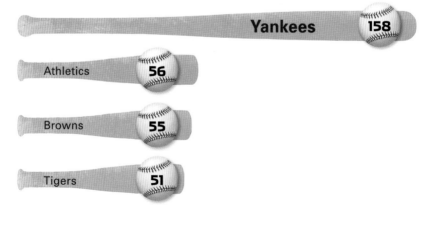

Yankees 158

Athletics 56

Browns 55

Tigers 51

WAITE HOYT'S 0.00 ERA IN 1921 WORLD SERIES

The Yankees teams of the 1920s were known for their Murderers' Row offense, but they could pitch a little bit too.

The staff ace for most of those teams was Waite Hoyt, who did something in World Series play that has not been done in a single Series since.

In the 1921 World Series against the Giants, Hoyt threw 27 innings and allowed no earned runs. He won the first two of his starts but lost the third 1–0, allowing an unearned run. The Giants clinched the title in that game.

Hoyt was the second pitcher to throw that many innings without allowing an earned run in a Fall Classic. The other is legendary pitcher Christy Mathewson.

Hoyt excelled throughout his World Series career with the Yankees, with whom he won three championship rings. He later became a well-known broadcaster and was inducted into the Baseball Hall of Fame in 1969.

The Yankees won 5–4, 6–2, 8–1, and 4–3. The Pirates led at the end of two innings in the four games. Ruth had a pair of home runs and seven RBIs. Gehrig had four RBIs.

The Pirates may have had a case of the jitters. In Game 2, the Yankees scored key runs on a wild pitch and a hit batter. The winning run in Game 4 came via a walk-off wild pitch.

At the time, the American League and National League were fierce rivals, and AL president Ban Johnson sent a telegram to the Yankees stating, "We like to destroy the enemy in that manner. Four straight victories will have a wholesome effect upon the public mind and strengthen the position of professional ball."

That isn't exactly what happened, but the 1927 Yankees definitely left their imprint upon the game.

Their dominance will be talked about today, tomorrow, and long into the future.

1939 Yankees Hit 13 HR in Doubleheader

The Yankees doubleheader with the Philadelphia Athletics on June 28, 1939, shared headlines with a Joe Louis title fight that took place that night at Yankee Stadium.

Each was a case of a champion pounding a hapless challenger. But while Louis' match was stopped in the fourth round by a sympathetic referee, the Yankees mauled their opposition with no one to stand in their way.

The Yankees put on their greatest one-day display of power by walloping 13 home runs in a sweep of the Athletics in Philadelphia.

With a day's rest behind them and playing in their comfort zone of the daytime, the Yankees went to work against starter Lynn "Line Drive" Nelson. Yes, that was his nickname. It would have been more appropriate on this day if he was nicknamed "Deep Fly."

Nelson's day didn't last long. He allowed more hits (9) than he got outs (8). Four of the hits were home runs, including three by Joe DiMaggio, George Selkirk, and Babe Dahlgren.

Reliever Bill Beckmann, a 32-year-old rookie, had the misfortune of entering next. He faced 11 batters and eight scored, including DiMaggio, who hit a home run over the left-field roof. The Yankees added nine runs, including two more homers, against mop-up man Bob Joyce, and won by the overwhelming score of 23–2.

Before the second game began, there was a notable meeting at home plate between legendary Athletics manager Connie Mack and Lou Gehrig, who had ended his consecutive-games streak earlier in the season, but was well enough to deliver the lineup to the home-plate umpire. The crowd gave Gehrig a loud ovation, a preview of what he would receive in the Bronx on Lou Gehrig Day the following week.

Perhaps inspired by their captain, the Yankees jumped out to a big lead. Leadoff man Frankie Crosetti homered, the first of five home runs the Yankees hit in a 10–0 win.

The 13 home runs in the doubleheader stood as the most in a two-game span for 60 years, until broken by the 1999 Reds, coincidentally also in Philadelphia, against the Phillies. Thirteen still stands tied for the AL mark for most in two games, since matched by the 2003 Angels and 2007 Yankees (against the White Sox).

The eight home runs in Game 1 remains tied for the team's single-game mark. The 2007 team matched it 68 years later against the White Sox. The 23 runs from Game 1 ranks third in team history, behind the 25 the Yankees scored against the Athletics in 1936 and the 24 they tallied against the Red Sox in 1923.

With the two wins that day, the Yankees improved to 48–13. It took 62 years before another team started that well through 61 games (the 2001 Mariners did).

THE DAMAGE DONE
The Yankees in the June 28, 1939, Doubleheader

Runs: 33

Hits: 43

Home Runs: 13

Strikeouts: 2

You could make a case for the 1939 team being the greatest in Yankees history, though it certainly faces a strong challenge from 1927, 1961, and 1998. These Yankees went 106–45 and thanks to games like these, outscored their opponents by 411 runs, the greatest run differential in major league history.

This team had both a powerful offense, led by 24-year-old DiMaggio (who had 126 RBIs in 120 games) Hall of Fame teammates Bill Dickey and Joe Gordon, Red Rolfe (who led the league in hits and runs), and great pitching depth (seven pitchers won 10 or more games, something done by only two other teams—the 1914 Athletics and 1976 Reds). They out-homered their opponents 166 to 85 and allowed 3.7 runs per game in a year in which the league averaged 5.2.

> *You could make the case for the 1939 team being the greatest...*

Defensive metrics, applied retroactively, also indicate that this was a terrific defensive team, particularly up the middle with Crosetti at shortstop and Gordon at second base. J.G. Taylor Spink, publisher of the *Sporting News*, described the work of the Yankees infield as "machine-like perfection."

The Yankees won their fourth straight World Series by sweeping the NL champion Reds, as rookie Charlie Keller paced the team with a .438 batting average, three home runs, and six RBIs. The most-remembered play of the Series came in the 10th inning of Game 4, when Keller bowled over Reds catcher Ernie Lombardi trying to score, and while Lombardi laid dazed, DiMaggio, who got the hit that scored two runs on the play, scored as well.

"In a game in which the human element is a vital factor, [the Yankees] have come closer to perfection than any other club in the first 100 years of baseball," wrote Fred Lieb in the *Sporting News*. "Perhaps in another 100 years, the feats of this team will have become legendary. Fans still unborn, thumbing through record books will ask 'Could a team have been that good?'"

We're not at 100 years yet, but the answer remains a resounding yes.

Joe DiMaggio's
56-Game
Hitting Streak

When we talk of unbreakable records, we can divide them into two types—the kind of records that can't be broken today because of the way the game is played (no pitcher is going to match Cy Young's total of 751 career complete games) and those that can be broken, but are so rarely challenged as to seem improbable.

Joe DiMaggio's 56-game hitting streak from the 1941 season falls into the second category. Anyone can have a hitting streak. But not everyone can have a *long* hitting streak.

"It would take a lot, but it's conceivable," said Lyle Spatz, chairman of the Society for Baseball Research, Baseball Records Committee.

It *would* take a lot. Consider the following:

Since DiMaggio broke the record, no one has gotten closer than a dozen games of the mark. The only one to get within 12 was baseball's all-time hit king, Pete Rose, who hit in 44 straight in 1978. Rose is the only one to reach 40 games since DiMaggio.

Arguably the six best hitters for average who played after DiMaggio's streak ended are Ted Williams, Tony Gwynn, Stan Musial, Wade Boggs, Rod Carew, and Ichiro Suzuki. The only one of those to have a 30-game hitting streak was Musial, whose longest was exactly 30 in 1950.

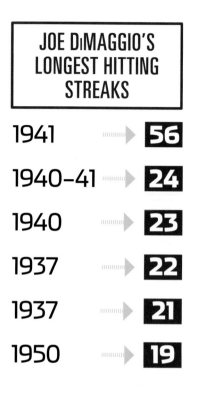

JOE DiMAGGIO'S LONGEST HITTING STREAKS

Year	Streak
1941	56
1940–41	24
1940	23
1937	22
1937	21
1950	19

Only four players have gotten to 30 this decade. Andre Ethier reached 30 games in 2011 and Dan Uggla got to 33 later that season. But that's not even really *that* close.

"It was a fun run," Uggla told reporters afterward. "But all things have to come to an end some time."

Only one Yankees player has gotten halfway there since DiMaggio's streak ended—Joe Gordon, who had a 29-gamer in 1942.

It is amazing how impressive DiMaggio's hitting streak was in that context, and it is also amazing how well DiMaggio hit during the streak.

DiMaggio hit .408 and had 91 hits in the 56 games. He had 15 home runs, 55 RBIs, and only five strikeouts. Amazingly, after the hitting streak ended against the Cleveland Indians on July 17, DiMaggio put together a 16-game streak. In 73 games, he totaled 120 hits and six strikeouts.

There wasn't a pitcher in baseball capable of getting DiMaggio out consistently that season. Consider this: He had 69 at-bats against the four non-Yankees who finished in the top five in ERA. In those, he hit .377 with 10 walks and no strikeouts.

When DiMaggio broke Wee Willie Keeler's single-season mark by hitting in his 45th straight game (which he did with a home run against the Red Sox), UP sportswriter Harry Ferguson joked that Red Sox manager Joe Cronin started a lineup that included Jesse James, Robin Hood, Ali Baba and the 40 Thieves, and John Dillinger, because only a burglar lineup was capable of robbing DiMaggio of hits.

Joe DiMaggio almost always made good contact on his swings.

"[Cronin] had it figured this way:

1. If you pitch low to DiMaggio, he will get a hit.

2. If you pitch high and outside to him, he will get a hit.

3. If you (A) fast ball him (B) slow ball him or (C) curve ball him, he will get a hit," Ferguson wrote.

When DiMaggio outfoxed that defensive alignment by hitting the ball out of reach, he said, "I'm going to try to keep right on hitting. After all, that's what I'm supposed to do, record or no record."

He had *361* home runs and only *369* strikeouts.

Today's hitter faces a challenge in terms of hitting approach. Most hitters are encouraged to swing for the fences rather than for hits.

But DiMaggio was someone who could slug without striking out. He had 361 home runs and only 369 strikeouts. He may not be thought of as one of the game's top sluggers, but his .579 career slugging percentage ranks 10th all-time.

Those who saw DiMaggio attest to how remarkable a player he was. Hall of Fame managers Connie Mack and Joe McCarthy, as well as the legendary Ted Williams, all refer to DiMaggio as the greatest player they ever saw.

DiMaggio was also a winner. He played in 10 World Series and the Yankees won nine of them. He had the World Series–winning hit that clinched Game 4 of the 1939 Series against the Reds. And he hit a game-winning home run against Hall of Famer Robin Roberts in Game 2 of a four-game sweep of the Phillies in 1950.

DID YOU KNOW? Over a 73-game span in 1941, Joe DiMaggio had at least one hit in 72 games. He totaled 120 hits and 6 strikeouts.

**Longest Hitting Streaks by Yankees
Since DiMaggio's 56-Game Streak**

Joe Gordon (1942)	29
Derek Jeter (2006)	25
Don Mattingly (1986)	24

"You know, some fellows play a whole lifetime without even smelling the roses," DiMaggio said in a 1980 interview. "That's quite an accomplishment to be with a bunch of guys that were able to perform and bring you home with all these pennants and World Series."

DiMaggio had two advantages over today's players in compiling his streak. There was no reliever specialization in that era, so teams did not bring right-handers out of the bullpen to face him as often as they might now.

Also, baseball was not yet integrated, which prevented DiMaggio from facing what was truly the best competition (his worst documented career 0-for is 0-for-8 against Negro League–legend Satchel Paige).

We close with this note: A 2009 mathematical study done by Josh Witten concluded that the chances of the streak being matched are 1 in 350,000 (in a 2,000-game career).

In other words, don't expect it to happen any time soon.

DiMaggio, Keller, Henrich Form the First 30-HR Outfield

The 1941 season is best known as the one in which Joe DiMaggio had his 56-game hitting streak.

But there is a secondary notable statistical accomplishment from that season.

It's the year that DiMaggio, right-fielder Tommy Henrich, and left-fielder Charlie Keller comprised the first outfield in which each regular hit at least 30 home runs. That's a distinction that has only been done once since (by the 1963 Twins).

The 1941 outfield has been called one of the best of all-time by baseball historian Bill James. All three players were in the prime of their careers, none older than 28. They hit 3-4-5 in the lineup, with Henrich and Keller sandwiching DiMaggio. Keller finished second in the AL in home runs with 33. Henrich placed third with 31. DiMaggio ranked fourth with 30. Each had a good eye at the plate. The three combined for 118 strikeouts and 259 walks.

DiMaggio had the hitting streak, won the MVP, and further cemented his legendary status that season, finishing with a .357 batting average, 30 home runs, and 125 RBIs.

Henrich and Keller were integral to the success of a team that won 101 games and defeated the Brooklyn Dodgers in the World Series.

Henrich came up first in 1937 and hit .320 with 42 RBIs in 67 games. Injuries limited his playing time over the next three seasons, but he showed modest power and was viewed as a strong leader.

In 1941, Henrich had the most powerful season of his career, with 31 home runs, 85 RBIs, and 106 runs scored.

"Henrich is the answer to a manager's prayer," wrote George Kirksey that September. "He's easy to handle, tends strictly to business, always hustling and is willing to risk his neck, if necessary, to win a ballgame. Henrich's value to the Yankees never has been appreciated fully by the public-at-large and many persons tab him as the most underrated ball player in the American League."

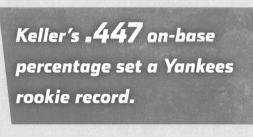

Keller's **.447** on-base percentage set a Yankees rookie record.

Keller was heralded after two phenomenal seasons with the International League's Newark Bears and was a hyped prospect upon making the Yankees roster in 1939.

An article in the *Brooklyn Eagle* said, "Keller is the rookie of the year. It has been almost the unanimous opinion of baseball men who have seen him that Joe DiMaggio and Joe Medwick are the only major league outfielders who can hit with him."

Keller thrived when he got his chance. He had a triple, home run, and six RBIs in his first major league start, though it was overshadowed by being the day Lou Gehrig ended his consecutive-games streak at 2,130.

Over a 32-game stretch later that season, Keller hit .424 with 56 hits, 31 walks, and 34 RBIs. His .447 on-base percentage set a Yankees rookie record and is the second best by a rookie in AL history (Joe Jackson had a .468 OBP in 1911). Keller was a World Series hero, hitting .438 with three home runs in a win over the Reds (Henrich was injured and did not play).

By 1941, Keller was a star, posting career highs in home runs and RBIs.

The three were all fortunate to be in good health when October came around. The most famous part of that World Series involves all three of them.

The Yankees trailed the Dodgers 4–3 in the ninth inning of Game 4 at Ebbets Field.

The Dodgers appeared to have a series-tying win when Henrich struck out with two outs in the ninth. But reliever Hugh Casey's potential last pitch was muffed by catcher Mickey Owen. Henrich raced to first base safely, giving the Yankees new life.

DiMaggio kept the rally going with a single, bringing up Keller with two on and two outs. Keller muscled a double on an 0–2 pitch, scoring Henrich and DiMaggio to put the Yankees ahead. They won 7–4 to take a 3–1 advantage in the Series and clinched the title with a victory in Game 5, helped by a Henrich home run. Keller was again a Series star, batting .389 with five RBIs.

Henrich played one more season, but missed the 1943 through 1945 seasons while serving in the U.S. Coast Guard during World War II. Upon returning, Henrich did something he'd never done in his earlier days, lead the American League in triples, which he did twice. Henrich made five All-Star teams in his career and was dubbed "Old Reliable" by Yankees broadcaster Mel Allen because he repeatedly delivered in big games.

The biggest of those hits came in Game 1 of the 1949 World Series, when he snapped a scoreless tie by hitting the first walk-off home run in World Series history. He retired a season later, finishing with a .282 batting average and 183 home runs.

In retirement, Henrich, whose passion was music (he used to listen to Beethoven after Yankees games), worked as a coach and broadcaster. He enjoyed a long, successful, post-baseball life. He died at age 96 in 2009.

"Tommy was a darn good ballplayer and teammate," Yogi Berra said. "He always took being a Yankee to heart. He won a lot of championships and did whatever he could to help us win."

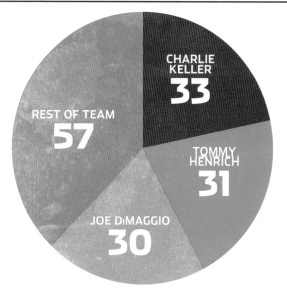

1941 YANKEES HOME RUNS (151 TOTAL)

CHARLIE KELLER
33

REST OF TEAM
57

TOMMY HENRICH
31

JOE DiMAGGIO
30

Keller had two more outstanding seasons in 1942 and 1943, with the Yankees adding another championship in the latter year. He served as a Merchant Marine, which cost him the 1944 season and most of 1945. He starred again in 1946 and seemed on his way to a Hall of Fame career.

In 1947, Keller was beset by a back injury, one that cost him his effectiveness at the plate. He also played for the Tigers, but was never a full-time player again, retiring in 1952.

"Charlie Keller, had he not been injured, would have been one of the greatest power hitters in the history of baseball," wrote James in *The New Historical Baseball Abstract*.

Keller made the most of his success in retirement. He became a successful horse breeder at his Yankeeland Farms in his home state of Maryland. He raised a family, and his son Charles Jr. played four seasons of minor league baseball. The elder Keller died in 1990.

Together, Henrich and Keller combined with DiMaggio to do something that was unprecedented and left its mark on Yankees history in a big way.

Mickey Mantle's
1956 Triple Crown:
.353, 52, 130

Mickey Mantle won the 1956 Triple Crown on Opening Day.

Well, not exactly, but it must have felt like he did.

One of baseball's most legendary figures set the tone for a legendary season in his very first at-bat, with a home run against Washington Senators starter Camilo Pascual.

This wasn't just a home run. It was one of Mantle's legendary mammoth shots. This one traveled nearly 500 feet to center field, bouncing off a roof across the street.

In the sixth inning, Mantle struck again, with a similar drive, this one a little shorter in length. He finished the day 2-for-3 with two walks, two home runs, and four RBIs. Yogi Berra actually had the better game (four hits, five RBIs), but Mantle's hits, as well as a couple of nice catches, made the biggest impact.

"Without a doubt, it was one of the most outstanding showings ever made by a major leaguer in the history of our national game," wrote sportswriter Dick Kelly of the *Hagerstown* (Md.) *Daily Mail*. "It would be no surprise if he captured the triple crown—batting, home runs, and runs batted in titles—as well as the league's Most Valuable Player honors…. There are many people who believe that

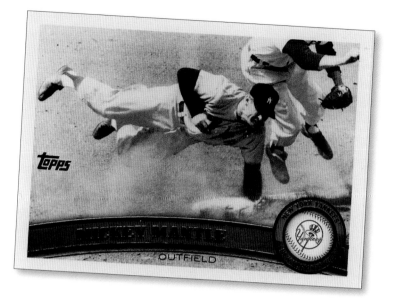

Mantle will become the greatest player who ever lived…. If the mighty Mantle can stay healthy all season, don't be surprised if he shatters Babe Ruth's all-time home run record."

If Mantle felt the pressure of such proclamations, he didn't show it on the field. Through six games, he hit .455 with four home runs and 13 RBIs.

Mantle kept a Ruthian pace going for most of the season. On May 30, against the Senators, Mantle was 4-for-8 and hit two extraordinary home runs. The first of those is estimated by the Mantle family website at 620 feet (perhaps exaggerated) and came within 18 inches of flying out of Yankee Stadium.

At the end of that day, Mantle was hitting .425 with 20 home runs and 50 RBIs in only 41 games. Each year since his career began as a 19-year-old in 1951, Mantle had been hyped by the media to be a future legend of the likes of Babe Ruth or Lou Gehrig. And though he'd performed splendidly and admirably (particularly considering the knee injury he suffered in the 1951 World Series), it never seemed like he was quite fulfilling his potential.

Until now.

"The boy has come of age," teammate Jerry Coleman told the *New York Times*.

This was the season that elevated Mantle to legendary status. He couldn't quite maintain the batting average (he hit *only* .324 the rest of the way) or RBI pace (he had 80 in his last 109 games), but he was a reasonable threat to Ruth's home run mark until tailing off in September.

Mantle was also clutch, hitting .444 with runners in scoring position.

He also had a major league leading six hits in the ninth inning or later that either tied a game or put the Yankees ahead.

The best of those came against the Senators. In the second game of a doubleheader sweep, Mantle hit a game-tying home run in the seventh inning and a game-winning homer in the ninth.

MOST HR FOR YANKEES, CAREER BEGAN POST–BABE RUTH*

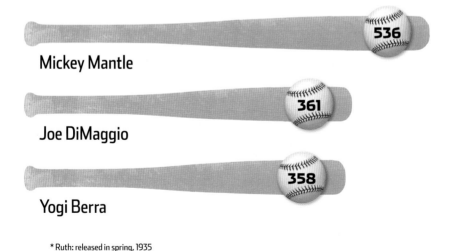

536
Mickey Mantle

361
Joe DiMaggio

358
Yogi Berra

* Ruth: released in spring, 1935

MICKEY MANTLE HITS 18 WORLD SERIES HR

Reggie Jackson is known as Mr. October, but Mickey Mantle is October's standard-setter for home run power.

Mantle hit a record 18 World Series home runs. His first came in 1952. His last came in 1964. His best was the one that both broke Babe Ruth's record of 15 and won the Yankees Game 3 of the 1964 World Series against the Cardinals. The score was tied 1–1 in the bottom of the ninth with Mantle leading off. He crushed the first pitch, a knuckleball from reliever Barney Schultz, for a walk-off shot.

The famous story from that game, shared in newspapers the next day, is that manager Yogi Berra told Mantle to hit a home run. Mantle's quote in responding to that after the game was simple.

"I followed orders."

Mantle's mark isn't going to be caught any time soon. The active leader, Chase Utley, has seven World Series home runs.

When the season ended, Mantle became the first player to win the Triple Crown since Ted Williams in 1947, and the second Yankee to do so, joining Lou Gehrig in 1934. Mantle is the only switch-hitter to have this distinction.

Two of the three races finished close, but were not really so.

Mantle won the batting title, edging out Red Sox legend Ted Williams, .353 to .345, though he had a 20-point lead entering September.

Mantle won the RBI title by two, topping Tigers future Hall of Famer Al Kaline, 130–128, a tight race because of Kaline's September surge.

But even with a slow final month, Mantle blew the field away in the home run race, winning that 52–32 over Indians slugger Vic Wertz.

The latter may explain how Mantle soars high above the rest by every sabermetric measure. Mantle finished with 188 Runs Created, a stat that establishes value based on everything a player does on offense. That's the most in a season by a Yankee not named Ruth or Gehrig.

How rare is Mantle's batting average, home runs, and RBIs combination?

Only three others have hit for that high a batting average, with that many home runs and that many RBIs. Ruth did it for the Yankees in 1920, 1921, and 1927. Hack Wilson did it for the Chicago Cubs in 1930. Jimmie Foxx did it for the Philadelphia Athletics in 1932.

No one has done so since Mantle.

Mantle's Triple Crown chase was one that captured baseball's attention. Mantle wrote a book with Phil Pepe about that season, titled *My Favorite Summer.*

"1956 was the first time I accomplished the things that had been predicted of me and I finally established myself in the major leagues," he wrote. "And that's why, at least from a personal standpoint, 1956 was my favorite summer."

THE FOLLOW-UP

As amazing as Mantle's 1956 season was, he was arguably just as good, if not better, in 1957, though that season gets less fanfare.

	1956	1957
BA	.353	.365
OBP	.464	.512
Slug Pct	.705	.665
WAR	11.2	11.3

Roger Maris Hits 61 Home Runs in 1961

The pursuit of the most famous single-season record in sports began rather innocuously, with a 5-for-31 slump, a demotion to seventh in the lineup, and a 10-game wait before the first blow was delivered.

Roger Maris' 1961 start didn't look promising. He didn't look anything like a guy who would best Babe Ruth's single-season record of 60 home runs. Yes, Maris was the reigning AL MVP and had hit 39 home runs the season before, but there was no reason to think he'd do something so historic.

The beauty of baseball is when the unexpected becomes reality. The story captivated the nation, even if he was not appreciated to the fullest degree.

Maris didn't move to the No. 3 spot regularly until mid-May, but once he did, he took off. Having Mickey Mantle hitting behind him meant Maris would see a lot of good pitches. It was up to him to do something with them.

He crushed them.

After hitting three home runs in his first 28 games, Maris took his power to an incredible level. He hit 24 home runs in his next 38 games. That's a 102-home run pace over a 162-game season!

DID YOU KNOW?

Roger Maris is the only player with 4 hits and 2 HR in his Yankees debut (1960).

* Source: Elias Sports Bureau

The significance of his home runs grew. Maris had one stretch in which he hit five home runs in the seventh inning or later that either tied the game or put the Yankees ahead. Three of those home runs came in Yankees defeats, depriving Maris of some recognition for coming through in the clutch.

Not that Maris minded.

Maris preferred being out of the spotlight, but as the home runs piled up, he and Mantle plowed ahead toward Ruth's mark. Mantle did so as the fan and media favorite, the homegrown hero, while Maris, who was acquired via a trade with the Kansas City Athletics, didn't receive the same fanfare.

In mid-July, as Mantle and Maris stood side-by-side for the league lead, commissioner Ford Frick ruled that to be considered a record, the mark had to be broken within 154 games, and any home runs beyond that would be applied to a separate record for a 162-game schedule.

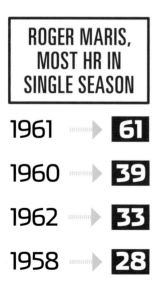

ROGER MARIS, MOST HR IN SINGLE SEASON

Year	HR
1961	61
1960	39
1962	33
1958	28

That didn't deter or unnerve either hitter. Though there was rumored to be friction between the teammates, this was a collaborative rather than competitive situation.

"Boy, I just want [Mantle] to keep hitting em too," Maris said. "The way he's going, they've got to pitch to me first.... I'm going to just keep banging away."

Maris banged away in one August stretch, homering in six consecutive games, including two in a 5–4 win over the White Sox on August 16 (which happened to be Babe Ruth Day!). Maris had 48 home runs with a month and a half left in the season.

The next day was a big day for media coverage of the chase.

UPI's columnist, Oscar Fraley, wrote of how big a deal the rest of the season would be. "If Roger Maris or Mickey Mantle achieves the magic 61 in 1961, that feat of breaking Babe Ruth's home run record will be hailed in America, at least, as the greatest sports accomplishment of the century."

ROGER MARIS outfield

But an Associated Press reporter made it clear that Maris wasn't necessarily the people's choice. "In general, the public would not like to see Ruth's record broken. Most people, however feel that if someone must break it, the fellow most entitled is Mantle, because of his greater stature as a slugger and home run hitter."

Maris had the support of his fellow North Dakotans, who prayed for him in church. In fact, after learning that Maris homered twice, Senator Milton Young interrupted a foreign-aid debate in Washington D.C. to announce the news to his Senate colleagues.

"We expect him to break the world's record by quite a few," Young said.

Easier said than done.

As the pressure mounted, Maris had some good days and some bad ones. He ended August with a 51–48 lead over Mantle, and Ruth still within reach.

Maris started September well. He homered twice in a win over the Tigers on September 2, and his willingness to talk about the pursuit increased a little bit.

"I'm still not home yet by a long shot, but I guess you'd have to say my chances are fairly good now," he said.

After another brief slump, Maris hit three home runs in four games to give him 56. Mantle came down with an illness that slowed down his power production (he finished with 54 home runs) leaving Maris as the lone man pursuing Ruth. But there was another obstacle, a seven-game homerless drought that made catching Ruth before Frick's deadline almost impossible.

Maris snapped out of this funk with a home run in back-to-back games, with the second (his 58th) a game-winner in the 12th inning against the Tigers. In the Yankees' 154th game, Maris hit his 59th home run against the Orioles but could not hit a second one to match Ruth before Frick's deadline.

But the record meant a lot to Maris regardless of whether it came in 154 games or 162. After three homerless games, he got another shot at the Orioles and homered in the third inning against Jack Fisher to tie Ruth.

1961 YANKEES HIT 240 HOME RUNS

It wasn't just Roger Maris and Mickey Mantle bashing baseballs for the Yankees in 1961. The Yankees totaled 240 home runs, setting a major league record (since broken) for most home runs in a season.

Four other Yankees hit at least 20 home runs, and having six players do so was also a record. Moose Skowron had 28. Yogi Berra had 22. Elston Howard hit 21. And perhaps most amazingly, Johnny Blanchard hit 21 in only 243 at-bats. At the time, that was the most home runs by a player in a season that consisted of fewer than 250 at-bats.

Power propelled the team to 109 wins and talk that it ranked among the best teams of all-time. The Yankees hit seven more home runs, though only one came from Maris and none from Mantle (who was injured), in a five-game triumph over the Reds in the World Series.

"I know I'm happy, happier than I've ever been before," Maris said.

Exhausted by the pursuit, Maris sat out the Yankees' next game, giving him three games to break Ruth's record at home against the Boston Red Sox. He didn't homer on September 29 or 30, and Maris' position in history came down to a final regular-season game on October 1.

Maris flied to left in his first at-bat. In the fourth inning he got another turn. This was the one to remember.

MANTLE VS. MARIS 1961 HOME RUN PROGRESSION

End of...	Roger Maris	Mickey Mantle
April	1	7
May	12	14
June	27	25
July	40	39
August	51	48
September	60	54
October	61	54

Maris took a ball away and another low before clubbing Tracy Stallard's next pitch about 10 rows deep into the right-field bleachers.

"Holy cow! He did it!" screamed Yankees radio announcer Phil Rizzuto.

A relieved Maris circled the bases, but had to be coaxed out of the dugout for a curtain call.

Though Maris' record has since been broken, his place in baseball history is secure, even if he was a bit reluctant to be a part of it, as he acknowledged in a famous quote at his post-record-breaking press conference.

"As a ballplayer, I would be delighted to do it again," Maris said. "As an individual, I doubt if I could possibly go through it again."

Derek Jeter's Perfect 3,000th Hit

It doesn't get any better than this.

The setting for the baseball game on July 9, 2011, was ideal—84 degrees and sunny for a Saturday afternoon matchup in the Bronx between the Yankees and Rays, just before baseball's All-Star break.

But this wasn't an ordinary Saturday. A Yankees legend was on the verge of history.

Derek Jeter entered the day with 2,998 career hits. He had done so in a way that was rather un-Jeterian and had some thinking the end of his career was approaching rapidly.

Jeter was hitting .257 entering the day. An injury in mid-June forced him to miss three weeks, and he was 4-for-18 since his return.

"It looked like his career was dwindling to a quiet end," said ESPN.com's Yankees beat writer, Andrew Marchand.

This was not the same Jeter of whom *Sports Illustrated*'s Joe Sheehan said, "[He] displayed just about every skill a player could have at one time or another. He hit home runs, drew walks, hit for a high average, and had a tremendous throwing arm. He did just about everything you could do."

But if Jeter established one thing in his career with the Yankees, it was a sense for the dramatic. From the game-tying home run in the eighth inning of Game 1 of the 1996 ALCS against the Orioles to his

Derek Jeter's 3,000th hit brought cheers from all who knew him.

leadoff homer in Game 4 of the Subway Series against the Mets in 2000 to the "Flip Play" and the "Mr. November" walk-off home run in the 2001 postseason to the amazing fly-into-the-stands catch against the Red Sox in 2004, Jeter thrived in being the man of the moment.

MOST HITS, YANKEES HISTORY

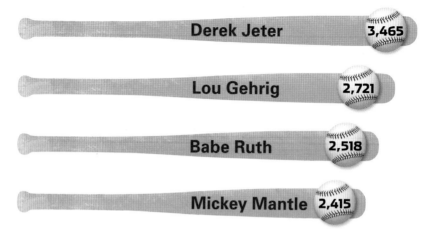

Derek Jeter	3,465
Lou Gehrig	2,721
Babe Ruth	2,518
Mickey Mantle	2,415

The man pitching to him that day posed a challenge. Rays starter David Price had a 95-mph fastball, the pitch that Jeter hadn't been able to catch up to for much of the season.

Jeter was not the type to shy away from a challenge.

"Every at-bat, he was competing his ass off," said former Red Sox pitcher Curt Schilling.

And yet Jeter was hiding something. He was feeling the pressure.

That wasn't supposed to be. Jeter was always the Yankees player who took the pressure off his teammates.

"The night of the first round [in 2005], I'm sitting in the dugout a few minutes before introductions like I'm nervous," said his former teammate, Aaron Small. "He comes by and says 'What's up man? You nervous? This is the big time. We're just playing a little kid's game. Just relax.'"

Jeter saw eight fastballs in his first at-bat and got a hit on the last one, which put him one hit away from 3,000.

When Jeter came up again, it was the third inning and the Yankees trailed 1–0 with one out and no one on base. He worked the count to 2–1 and fouled off a changeup. He took another slider to run the count full.

Price tried another 95-mph fastball and that didn't work. Jeter fouled it off. Price tried a changeup, and Jeter fouled that one away too.

DEREK JETER IN 2011

Here's a look at Jeter's performance entering the day of his 3,000th hit compared to the rest of the season.

	Through 7/8	After 7/8
BA	.257	.338
OPS	.649	.843
Hits	72	90
Games	66	65

Price decided to try something new. He went to his curveball.

This one Jeter timed just right.

"I didn't want to hit a slow roller to third base and have it replayed forever," he said afterward.

Instead, he hit a fly ball into the left-field stands for a home run.

Yankee Stadium erupted. Even the Rays paid tribute. First baseman Casey Kotchman tipped his cap to Jeter as he rounded the bases.

"I felt like it was the right thing to do," Kotchman said.

The game stopped for five minutes as the Yankees players came onto the field to congratulate their captain, who became the first Yankees player to reach the 3,000-hit mark.

Meanwhile, in the stands, the ball was caught by a young fan, Christian Lopez, who decided to return the ball to Jeter. The Yankees rewarded that by allowing Lopez to personally deliver the ball, and gave him tickets to every remaining game that season.

DID YOU KNOW? Derek Jeter won more World Series titles with the Yankees (5) than Babe Ruth did (4).

But that came afterward. There was still a game to play. Jeter got a hit in the fifth as part of a two-run Yankees rally and another in the sixth, but was left stranded at second base.

The Yankees led by a run in the eighth inning, but the Rays tied it when Jeter's former teammate Johnny Damon tripled, and Ben Zobrist singled him in. Yankees reliever David Robertson kept the game tied into the bottom of the eighth.

Jeter was due up third in the Yankees half of the eighth and the Yankees set the table in front of him. Eduardo Nunez doubled and Brett Gardner bunted him to third base.

It would have been easy for Rays manager Joe Maddon to walk Jeter. But with solid-swinging Curtis Granderson on deck, he declined. He also thought about doing something extreme and playing a five-man infield, stationing a man behind second base to cut off that gap in his defense. But since it was the eighth inning

---

11/1/01, 12:04 AM—DEREK JETER BECOMES MR. NOVEMBER

The Yankees made their first foray into November baseball when the clock struck midnight in the bottom of the 10th inning of Game 4 of the 2001 World Series against the Diamondbacks.

The game continued for another four minutes, when in a moment that would be one of the signatures of his illustrious career, Derek Jeter capped an epic nine-pitch at-bat by homering just over the fence in right field. The walk-off shot evened the World Series at two games apiece.

"I don't really know if I can describe how it felt going around the bases," Jeter said in a 2010 interview with ESPN. "But it feels like you're floating. I remember it. I tried to enjoy it and look around but it happened so quickly, it was over with before you know it."

Jeter was asked how he celebrated. He responded in Jeterian fashion.

"How did I celebrate? I didn't do much celebrating because we had to come right back and play Game 5."

DID YOU KNOW?

Jeter's other home run against Price came in 2008 and tied Lou Gehrig's record for most hits at the old Yankee Stadium.

and not the ninth, Maddon didn't have the guts to try that bold a move.

As it turned out, Maddon had the right idea.

On a 1-2 pitch from Joel Peralta, Jeter hit a single right up the middle, scoring Nunez with the go-ahead run in the Yankees' win.

"I'm pretty happy with how things went today," Jeter said in typically modest fashion.

"He went above and beyond," Maddon said of Jeter afterward.

Jeter went above and beyond the rest of the season as well, batting .338 from that game through the end of the season. And then he went beyond that.

In 2012, he led the American League in hits and batted .316. The old Jeter was back, though eventually age caught up to him in the form of a freak injury, suffered in the ALCS, that didn't heal easily.

Still, Jeter had one more amazing moment in him. In his final regular-season game at Yankee Stadium in 2014, his walk-off hit against the Baltimore Orioles plated the winning run. It's as if it was meant to be.

"Everything is perfect for that guy," Marchand said. "He's not perfect, but his career is as close to perfect as you could have."

1996 Yankees Win 4 Straight vs. Braves in World Series

The first moment in the first night of the most recent Yankees dynasty was a case of déjà vu for David Cone.

This was the sixth inning of Game 3 of the World Series in Atlanta, with the Yankees trailing two games to none in the Series and clinging to a 2–1 lead.

The Braves had the bases loaded with two outs and Cone had just walked Ryan Klesko to score a run. A year earlier, in a similar situation against the Mariners in the eighth inning of Game 5 of the ALDS, Cone walked Doug Strange to bring in the tying run in a game and series the Yankees went on to lose.

Cone still had a one-run cushion this time, but the Braves had the perfect opportunity to take the lead, with catcher Javy Lopez at the plate. Lopez, the MVP of that year's NLCS, was hitting .439 in the postseason entering that at-bat and had singled in his previous turn against Cone. Another hit would likely put the Braves ahead.

In 1995, Joe Torre had gone to Mariano Rivera after the walk to Strange. This time, Rivera was again warming in the bullpen, but Torre stuck it out with Cone, who was flustered after a close pitch to Klesko was called ball four.

Cone composed himself and threw a breaking ball that Lopez swung through for strike one. Cone threw another breaking ball, this one was a hanger, but Lopez popped it up in foul territory to the right side. Catcher Joe Girardi raced over by the stands and made the catch, hanging on as he stumbled to avoid running into two security officers.

"It was definitely a mistake but I got away with it," Cone told reporters afterward.

It was one of many times the Yankees would come through in this game and the next three. The Yankees hung on to win Game 3 by a score of 5–2.

"I believe with one win that the whole mood and momentum changes," Torre said.

But that didn't happen at the start of Game 4.

1996 WORLD SERIES, RUNS SCORED

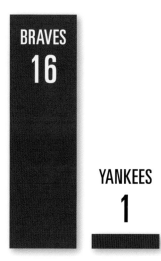

First 2 Games

Last 4 Games

DID YOU KNOW?

The comeback from six runs down is tied for the second-biggest deficit overcome in a World Series win.

This time the Yankees trailed 6–0 after five innings and were on the brink of trailing three games to one. But a three-run rally in the sixth inning cut the lead to 6–3.

The eighth inning against Braves closer Mark Wohlers started innocuously when Charlie Hayes led off with a swinging bunt that appeared to be heading foul but hugged the chalk for about 50 feet before coming to a stop just shy of third base. Hayes' single was followed by a single by Darryl Strawberry.

> *"I believe with one win that the whole mood and momentum changes."*
>
> *—Joe Torre*

Mariano Duncan hit a grounder to short that looked like a double-play ball, but Braves shortstop Rafael Belliard bobbled it and was only able to get a force at second base.

Wohlers entered the day having thrown 7⅓ scoreless innings with 11 strikeouts that postseason, thanks largely to a 99-mile-per-hour fastball. But his air of invincibility disappeared against the next batter. On 2–2, he hung a slider to Jim Leyritz. The Yankees backup catcher took a full, albeit awkward, swing and watched the ball carry until it just eluded the leaping attempt by Andruw Jones at the left-field wall.

Tie game.

"He doesn't get to play a whole lot," Torre said afterward of Leyritz. "And he's struggled this year. But he can hit a ball out of a ballpark."

With the score tied, The Yankees got a rally going with two outs and nobody on in the 10th inning. They put two men on base for red-hot Bernie Williams. Braves manager Bobby Cox gambled, intentionally walking Williams to load the bases for Wade Boggs.

The strategy backfired when Boggs worked his way back from a 1–2 count to draw a walk. The Yankees added another run when Klesko muffed a popup at first base and won 8–6. That tied the Series at two games apiece.

Game 5 wouldn't require a comeback, but it was epic nonetheless. It pitted Andy Pettitte against 24-game winner John Smoltz, who was 4–0 in that postseason.

Again the Yankees capitalized on a Braves mistake, this one being a dropped fly ball by four-time Gold Glove–winning center-fielder Marquis Grissom in the fourth inning, putting Charlie Hayes on second base. He scored on Cecil Fielder's double.

That run held up...barely.

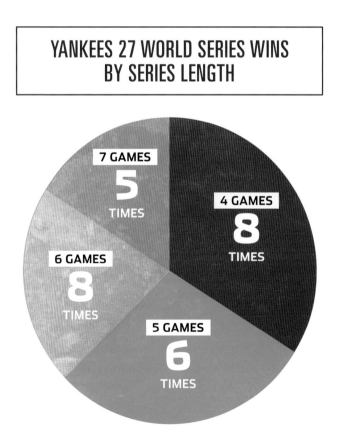

YANKEES 27 WORLD SERIES WINS
BY SERIES LENGTH

7 GAMES
5 TIMES

4 GAMES
8 TIMES

6 GAMES
8 TIMES

5 GAMES
6 TIMES

DID YOU KNOW?

The Yankees are one of three teams to come back to win a World Series after losing the first two games at home (along with the 1985 Royals and 1986 Mets).

The Braves put at least one man on base in eight of the nine innings, but could not bring one around to score. Pettitte stymied them time and time again.

Atlanta's best chance came in the ninth inning, thanks to a leadoff double by Chipper Jones, who advanced to third base on Fred McGriff's groundout.

Whether the Yankees would take a lead back to New York came down to closer John Wetteland's ability to get two outs without letting Jones score.

Lopez got another chance at a potential game-breaking hit, but on Wetteland's first pitch, he grounded to Hayes. After an intentional walk, Cox sent up former Yankee Luis Polonia to pinch hit.

Wetteland came after Polonia with high fastballs, and on the seventh pitch, Polonia whacked one to right-center field. It looked like a game-winning double. But Paul O'Neill, playing on a bad hamstring, made a running catch near the warning track to give the Yankees a one-run win and a 3–2 series lead.

YANKEES VS. BRAVES, 1996 WORLD SERIES

	YANKEES	BRAVES
RUNS	18	26
BATTING AVG	.216	.254
HR	2	4

"My thought process was to try to get to it," O'Neill said. "I thought off the bat I had a good play on it. But it just kept carrying and carrying."

"It's a game of inches," said Cox.

At that point, the 1996 Yankees could not be stopped, even though they were going up against Greg Maddux in Game 6 at Yankee Stadium. They took a 3–0 lead in the third inning with the key hit being a triple to center by Girardi against his former Cubs teammate.

The Braves clawed back with a run in the fourth, but Jimmy Key shut down any further offense by inducing a bases-loaded double play from Terry Pendleton.

The Yankees bullpen took over in the sixth inning and held the score at 3–1 heading into the ninth. Wetteland, going for his fourth save of the Series, ran into trouble as the Braves cut the lead to 3–2 on Grissom's two-out single.

With the tying run on second, Wetteland induced a popup from Mark Lemke near the Braves dugout. But Charlie Hayes ran into a Braves player who stepped out of the dugout and couldn't make the play.

The Braves, however, could not take advantage. On 3–2, Lemke again popped one foul on the third-base side.

This time no one got in Hayes' way. When he made the catch, the Yankees were champions for the first time in 18 years in one of their hardest-fought World Series triumphs.

1998 Yankees Win 125 Games (Most of Any Team)

Oh, to have been a fly on the wall in the clubhouse of the New York Yankees on April 6, 1998.

The Yankees didn't just lose. They got blitzed. They fell to the Mariners 8–0 in Seattle to fall to 1–4 for the season. The Yankees were wounded in more ways than one. They struck out 15 times against soft-tosser Jamie Moyer and reliever Paul Spoljaric.

One of their top starters, Andy Pettitte (who had lost twice in a crushing ALDS defeat against the Indians the year before), was 0–2 with a 5.54 ERA after allowing four runs in seven innings. Closer Mariano Rivera was on the disabled list with a groin injury.

The Yankees had allowed as many runs in their previous two games as they had scored all season (15).

The *New York Daily News* went with a headline on the Yankees game story of "Clueless in Seattle."

"I don't know what's going on," said first baseman Tino Martinez.

This is not the setting from which you'd expect a championship three-peat dynasty to emerge. But this is where it all began.

The Yankees made their statement on how things would be the rest of the season in the first inning of their next game against the Mariners.

It took four pitches for the Yankees to take a 2–0 lead. Chuck Knoblauch homered on Jim Bullinger's first pitch. Derek Jeter and Paul O'Neill followed with back-to-back doubles. Martinez plated O'Neill with a single. Darryl Strawberry followed with a home run. Jorge Posada added another two batters later. The Yankees led 6–0.

This was the setting from which you'd expect a championship three-peat dynasty to emerge. The Yankees won eight in a row, 14 of 15, 22 of 24, and 34 of 40. Before you knew it, they were 35–10.

The Yankees went 20–7 in May, 19–7 in June, 20–7 in July, and 22–10 in August. After a mini-slump in September, they closed the regular season with a seven-game winning streak in which they outscored their opponents 45–16.

This was a team on which Jeter, Posada, Bernie Williams, Pettitte, and Rivera were all in their prime. Mix that with ring-hungry

MOST WINS ALL-TIME, INCLUDING POSTSEASON

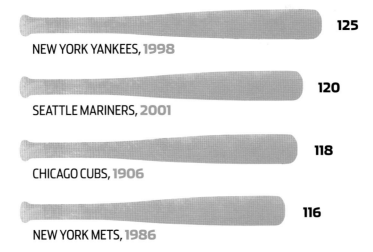

NEW YORK YANKEES, 1998 — 125

SEATTLE MARINERS, 2001 — 120

CHICAGO CUBS, 1906 — 118

NEW YORK METS, 1986 — 116

veterans like Paul O'Neill, Tim Raines, David Wells, and David Cone. That gave you something pretty special.

"This is the best team I've seen in my 35 years covering baseball," said ESPN baseball analyst Tim Kurkjian. "Just look at the seasonal numbers and look at the dominance."

The Yankees were ready for October. They swept the Rangers in the ALDS, winning 2–0, 3–1, and 4–0.

The Indians put up a fight in the ALCS, leading two games to one. Orlando Hernandez set the tone for the rest of the series with a win in Game 4. The Indians didn't win again.

The Yankees were heavily favored in the World Series against the San Diego Padres. And yes, they swept the Padres in four straight. But you wouldn't have guessed who the key player in the Series turned out to be.

30-YEAR-OLD BRIAN CASHMAN NAMED YANKEES GM

Many big companies have a success story of the intern who becomes president. That's true with the Yankees as well. One of their biggest front-office successes is current GM Brian Cashman.

Cashman's career with the team began in 1986 as a security intern. He moved up and up and up and up the corporate ladder quickly, and in February 1998, the 30-year-old was named general manager of the team.

"I think the game of baseball today is a young man's game," Steinbrenner said. "I tell you Cashman is a very bright young man. I could go outside and bring in a figurehead name, a well-known guy, but after 10 years this guy deserved a chance."

The bright young man has done more than alright with his chance. The Yankees won the World Series in each of the first three years of his tenure and won another title in 2009. And he knows the mandate of the position.

As he noted after signing his most recent extension late in 2014: "I've got to find a way to get our fan base back to enjoying October sooner than later."

DID YOU KNOW?

The 1998 Yankees had 10 players with at least 300 plate appearances and an on-base percentage above .350, the most of any team in MLB history.

It wasn't Jeter or Williams or O'Neill. It was third baseman Scott Brosius.

Brosius had gone from potential star with the Athletics in 1996 to an afterthought after his batting average plummeted to .203 in 1997.

"It's kind of a fishbowl atmosphere," Brosius said when news of the trade to the Yankees broke that off-season. "The town expects you to win. But sometimes it's good to play under pressure."

The pressure of the World Series turned out to be just right for Brosius. He played in four World Series in four years with the Yankees and the team was 15–5 in his 20 starts. Brosius hit .314 in the World Series, with his best work coming in his first one.

Brosius hit .471 (8-for-17) with two home runs and six RBIs in that year's Fall Classic.

There were two turning points in the Series. One was in Game 1 when Padres reliever Mark Langston thought he had Tino Martinez struck out, but his pitch was called a ball. Martinez took advantage of a second chance by hitting a grand slam.

The other was in Game 3. The Padres led 3–2 in the eighth inning and brought closer Trevor Hoffman in to try to get a six-out save. Brosius came up with two on and one out. On 2–2, he got a good cut and drilled a fly ball to deep-center field.

Padres center-fielder Steve Finley kept racing back but to no avail. He ran out of room, as the ball landed over the fence for a go-ahead three-run home run.

Brosius did not hold back as he ran around the bases, raising his fist and screaming.

The fist pumping and screaming would continue the next day as the Yankees wrapped up the title with a 3–0 win in Game 4.

Brosius got to field the final ball of the season, a groundout by Mark Sweeney that made the Yankees champions for the second time in three years.

"Following the success of the 1995 season, the 1996 World Series, and the playoff run of the 1997 season, Yankees fans were becoming spoiled," said ESPN *SportsCenter* anchor Kevin Connors, who covered that team while working in New York. "The 1998 team blew all that away. Eighteen players were All-Stars at some point. At least six deserve some consideration for the Hall of Fame. They won the division by 22 games and went 11–2 in the postseason. That's dominant."

It's not hard to make a case that this was the best Yankees team of this era, and among the best baseball teams of all time.

1998 YANKEES

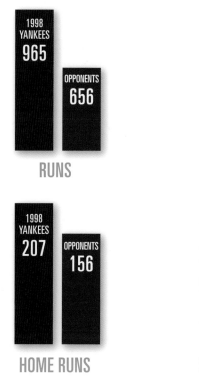

RUNS

OPS

HOME RUNS

STOLEN BASES

Mariano Rivera: 42 Saves in Postseason

Mariano Rivera was made to handle October baseball.

Under the most pressure-packed of circumstances, Rivera thrived. He was 8–1 with a 0.70 postseason ERA, with 42 saves in 47 chances. The 42 saves are appropriate, as they matched the number on the back of his jersey.

Though we're focusing on October baseball, let's not ignore the regular-season work. That consists of the most saves all-time (652) and the lowest ERA of any pitcher who worked at least 1,000 innings in the Live-Ball Era (since 1920).

"He is by far the greatest closer of all-time," said ESPN baseball analyst and historian, Tim Kurkjian.

"As much of a guarantee as anyone who ever played the game," said former Red Sox pitcher Curt Schilling.

"The ultimate safety net," said former teammate Mike Stanton.

The path to greatness began in Panama, where Rivera grew up with thoughts of being a fisherman. In February 1990, he signed with the Yankees, pitched for the Gulf Coast League team in Tampa, and allowed one earned run in 52 innings.

This was the pre-Rivera, Rivera. He didn't have the cutter, but in some ways, it was the same Mariano. Coaches worked with him to slow his delivery, such that it would take him 1.1 seconds to the plate.

Twenty-one years later, I put a stopwatch on his delivery time for three pitches as he approached the all-time saves record. He clocked in at 1.1 seconds.

By 1995, Rivera was in the majors and having his share of ups and downs, primarily as a starting pitcher. But he did enough to earn Buck Showalter's trust. Rivera threw 3⅓ scoreless innings of relief in Game 2 of the ALDS against the Mariners, and got the win when Jim Leyritz hit a walk-off home run in the bottom of the 15th.

Then, Rivera emerged with the bases loaded and two outs in the eighth inning of a tied Game 5 to blow Mike Blowers away on three straight pitches. The Yankees lost that game, but in that moment they discovered a future star that could stand up to the most stressful situations.

The next year, Rivera was the set-up man to John Wetteland in the greatest one-two reliever combination in Yankees history, if not baseball history. The Yankees got back to the postseason and won the title. Rivera pitched 121⅔ innings to a 1.92 ERA between the regular season and postseason.

That off-season, the Yankees did something they would never regret. They let Wetteland go as a free agent and made Rivera the closer.

MOST CAREER POSTSEASON SAVES

Mariano Rivera

42

Brad Lidge

18

Dennis Eckersley

15

Mariano Rivera was always stoic on the mound, until it was time to celebrate a World Series triumph.

MARIANO RIVERA VS. BABE RUTH

	RIVERA	RUTH
REGULAR SEASON ERA	2.21	2.28
POSTSEASON ERA	0.70	0.87

"There were questions that spring as to whether he was going to be able to do it," said his former teammate, Mike Stanton. "I think he answered them pretty well."

Rivera did so with the help of what he called a gift from God, a cut fastball which had a sharp late break against left-handed hitters. It also turned out to work well as a pitch that broke away from right-handed hitters. He first noticed it during an innocent game of catch with Ramiro Mendoza. When he threw it in games, hitters could not make good contact against it.

"His cutter may go down as the greatest weapon in the history of the game," said ESPN *SportsCenter* anchor Kevin Connors.

The key moment in Rivera's closing career was not a win, but a loss. Every closer has to deal with failure, and in Rivera's case, he had to live through that all winter after allowing the key hit in the 1997 ALDS—a game-tying home run to Sandy Alomar Jr. with the Yankees on the verge of clinching.

Again, the Yankees lost the series, but won for the long term.

"It didn't bother him at all [for the next season]," said former teammate Jeff Nelson. "One of the best assets he has is a short memory."

The legend of Rivera emerged in the next three seasons, as the Yankees became a baseball dynasty. Not only was he amazing in the regular season, he was dominant come October. In 41⅓ postseason innings, he allowed three runs. That included a major league record 33⅓ inning scoreless streak. In 1999, he won World Series MVP honors in a sweep of the Braves.

He was on the mound for eight of the nine series-clinching outs, including the final out of three straight World Series.

The Yankees went for a four-peat in the 2001 World Series against the Arizona Diamondbacks. Pitching in the shadows of the September 11 tragedy, they came from behind on multiple occasions to get to Game 7.

Rivera had told his teammates before the game, "Get me the ball and we will win," and it looked like he'd live up to that promise after blowing the Diamondbacks hitters away with a one-run lead in the eighth inning.

But in the ninth inning, he and the Yankees were done in by a hit batsman, an error (the second one of his *career*), and some bad luck (a broken-bat bloop for the Series-winning hit).

It was a crushing defeat, but Rivera was again undaunted. Two years later, he got the ball for a Game 7 and lived up to his promises. With the score tied in Game 7 of the ALCS against the Red Sox, Rivera pitched a scoreless ninth, 10th and 11th inning. A few minutes later, he was kissing the pitcher's mound when Aaron Boone's walk-off home run ended the series. Rivera was named series MVP.

"Those three innings—you're not gonna get that with any other closer," Nelson said. "He could have gone five."

LOWEST ERA IN LIVE-BALL ERA (SINCE 1920)*

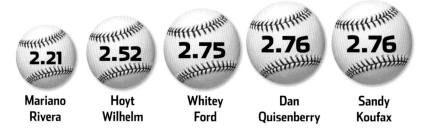

2.21	2.52	2.75	2.76	2.76
Mariano Rivera	Hoyt Wilhelm	Whitey Ford	Dan Quisenberry	Sandy Koufax

*Only retired pitchers

MOST CAREER REGULAR-SEASON SAVES

Mariano Rivera

Trevor Hoffman

Lee Smith

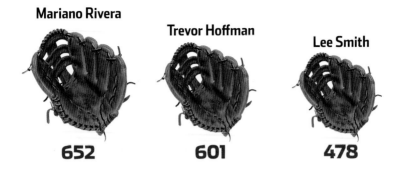

652

601

478

The Yankees transitioned into a different team over the next six years, one that blew a 3–0 ALCS lead to the Red Sox in 2004, then got knocked out in the ALDS in 2005, 2006, and 2007, before failing to make the playoffs in Joe Girardi's first year, 2008.

The 2009 postseason featured Rivera at his very best. He allowed one run in 16 innings as the Yankees beat the Twins, Angels, and Phillies for their 27th World Series title.

There was one more tough moment for Rivera to overcome. While shagging fly balls in Kansas City in May 2012, Rivera tore his ACL, ending his season and potentially his career.

But Rivera would not let his career end that way. Instead, it ended the way it should.

Rivera had a 2.11 ERA and 44 saves at age 43 in 2013. Though he didn't get another crack at October, he pitched like it was October all season. He was dominant to the very end.

There was one last cool moment. In Rivera's final game, Joe Girardi had Derek Jeter and Andy Pettitte go to the mound to pull Rivera. "It's time to go," Jeter said, and Rivera started to cry as he hugged his teammates.

And then he walked off the mound. The crowd cheered. Just as if it were October.

The 66-Pitcher Bridge to Mariano

The bridge to Mariano Rivera spanned 66 pitchers wide but held as steady as the Yankees closer it supported for 17 seasons.

That number, provided by the Elias Sports Bureau, refers to the number of pitchers who got a hold in a game saved by Rivera in either the regular season or postseason.

The two pitchers who originated the role are Jeff Nelson and Mike Stanton. In many cities, they would be easily forgotten, but in New York, there is an appreciation of their value.

The standard was set by that pair in 1997, Rivera's first season as full-time closer. The Yankees were coming off a World Series triumph, but there was trepidation as Rivera was asked to replace John Wetteland at the back of the bullpen after a standout sophomore season. Nelson, who was a member of the 1996 team, and Stanton, a newcomer who had previously excelled for the Braves, were there to ease the transition.

The pair combined to log 145$\frac{1}{3}$ innings, posted a 2.72 ERA, allowed 103 base hits, and tallied 48 holds. They put Rivera in position to succeed as often as possible.

"We told the starters, just go six innings," Nelson said. "We'll piece together the seventh and eighth. We wanted to limit Mariano to just that one inning."

There was talk in spring training that season that Stanton would be given an opportunity to close, but he found a comfort zone in being a setup man. He set the all-time record for holds, with 266 over his 19-season career.

Most Holds Games Saved by Mariano Rivera (Includes Postseason)	
Mike Stanton	83
Tom Gordon	61
Jeff Nelson	58

Source: Elias Sports Bureau

"I must have done the job okay because they kept running me out there," Stanton said.

Stanton and Nelson were more than okay. They were integral parts of the three consecutive Yankees championships.

"One of the things that I thought was so remarkable about them is that they never accumulated gaudy or 'wow' stats because they essentially shared the bridge role," said Katie Sharp, a writer for the well-known fan blog *River Avenue Blues*. "But as a fan watching, you never doubted that they'd get the ball to Mo in the ninth inning with the lead."

The 6'8" Nelson used a funky delivery to put together a streak of 15 straight scoreless outings spanning the 1998 to 2000 postseasons. He was the master of getting the big eighth-inning outs, doing his best Rivera impersonation to retire some of the top hitters in baseball. Nelson has the major league record for postseason holds with 13, 10 of which came for the Yankees.

Stanton, the lefty who said he pitched as if his hair was on fire, was the pitcher who could be stretched out to go longer than an inning if necessary. In the 1999 and 2000 postseasons, he was 3–0 with a pair of holds and a 0.96 ERA. Stanton got the wins in the clinching games of both the 2000 LDS against the Athletics and World Series against the Mets, games eventually saved by Rivera.

"My approach throughout my career was that my job was to get someone else out of trouble," Stanton said. "And I would jokingly say that [with the Yankees] my job and Jeff Nelson's job were to be the offensive linemen. The thing I prided myself on was, one, being available every day, and two, inherited runners—getting other guys out of trouble."

Stanton and Nelson would go elsewhere eventually, though each would find their way to New York again. Nelson returned to the Yankees for their run to the AL pennant in 2003. Stanton came back briefly in 2005.

Their presence was a part of the Yankees even after they left because of the caliber of their work. They paved the way for others, like Tom Gordon, Joba Chamberlain, and David Robertson, to thrive as the game evolved into one in which having multiple high-caliber relievers was a necessity.

"[The most impressive thing] was how they always managed to make a bridge," said YES Network research manager Jeff Quagliata. "It was a bunch of nondescript guys, but they always seemed to get the job done and get the ball to Mo."

The 1990 Reds "Nasty Boys" combination of Norm Charlton, Rob Dibble, and Randy Myers originated that sort of bullpen setup. But the Bridge to Mariano that began a few years later was a longer-lasting symbol of significance.

Most Postseason Appearances by a Pitcher Not Named Mariano Rivera

Jeff Nelson	55
Mike Stanton	53
Mike Timlin	46
Andy Pettitte	44

"It makes you think we may have started something," Nelson said. "The seventh, eighth, and ninth innings are sometimes why teams win the World Series now. [I'd like us] to be remembered as the best bullpen in the game. You look at the list of most playoff appearances and it goes Rivera, Nelson, Stanton. I hope that's how it stays forever."

David Robertson Retires 25 Straight Hitters in Bases-Loaded Situations

David Robertson doesn't know any magic tricks, except for the one he pulled on the mound that was akin to pulling 25 rabbits out of a hat.

Over a three-season stretch, Robertson was like a magician (hence his nickname, Houdini) in his ability to wiggle out of the toughest jam for any pitcher—a bases-loaded situation.

From April 19, 2011, to August 12, 2013, Robertson faced 25 hitters with the bases loaded. He retired all 25 of them, striking out 18.

We can estimate the odds of an average major league pitcher going 25-for-25 in that situation at approximately 7,500-to-1, but Robertson is no average pitcher. He has the highest career strikeout-per-9 rate in Yankees history and three of the six best single-season marks in club history.

Robertson served as both a bridge to Mariano Rivera and as Rivera's successor and excelled at both.

The foundation for his future bases-loaded work and the game that put him on the map came in the first postseason appearance of his major league career. In Game 2 of the 2009 ALDS, the Yankees and Twins were tied 3–3 in the 11th inning with Robertson on the mound. The first batter he faced singled, filling the bases with nobody out.

In one of the pivotal moments of that Yankees' championship run, Robertson needed only five pitches to make his escape. He got Delmon Young to line out, Carlos Gomez to ground into a force out, and Brendan Harris to fly out.

About five minutes after Robertson was done, he was on the field celebrating his first postseason win, on Mark Teixeira's walk-off home run.

"I felt I could do it because I'd gotten myself into jams like that in college [at the University of Alabama] over and over again," said Robertson after the game. "I'd walk the bases loaded, then I'd have to strike my way out of it. I don't know how I did it [this time] without striking anybody out."

MOST K PER 9, SINGLE SEASON WITH YANKEES
(Minimum 50 IP)

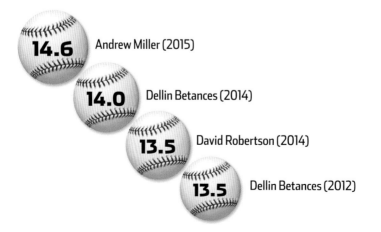

14.6 Andrew Miller (2015)

14.0 Dellin Betances (2014)

13.5 David Robertson (2014)

13.5 Dellin Betances (2012)

Robertson didn't strike anybody out that day, but his knack for whiffing hitters in those encounters was impressive. His tools of choice were a mid-90s fastball and a curveball that could deceive a batter into swinging when the pitch bounced six inches in front of him.

It's a pitch that Robertson picked up in the Cape Cod League just prior to signing with the Yankees.

Robertson also benefited from having one of the longest strides in the game, allowing him to get closer to the hitter than most as he released his pitch.

"He doesn't look like he's throwing that hard," FiveThirtyEight.com baseball writer Ben Lindbergh said. "His called strike rates were high because guys didn't see [his pitches] well. They would be strikes over and over again. His pitches were a trick that helped him get out of binds with regularity."

MOST K PER 9, CAREER WITH YANKEES
(Minimum 250 IP)

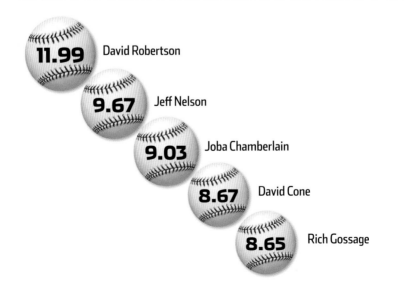

11.99 David Robertson

9.67 Jeff Nelson

9.03 Joba Chamberlain

8.67 David Cone

8.65 Rich Gossage

Robertson takes an old-school approach to pitching in one regard, hiking his stirrup socks up as high as they'll go. Fans took a liking to this, which led to Robertson and his wife Erin calling their charitable endeavor (to raise money for those affected by tornadoes) "High Socks for Hope."

He posted **39** saves and averaged more than **13** strikeouts **per 9** innings.

Among the highlights for Robertson in this stretch:

- On August 28, 2011, he faced a bases-loaded, no-out situation protecting an 8–3 lead in the eighth inning against the Orioles. He struck out Vladimir Guerrero, Mark Reynolds, and Russ Adams in succession to get out of the jam. That season, Robertson struck out 14 batters with the bases loaded, the first pitcher to record that many such whiffs in 33 years.

- On August 12, 2013, Robertson was clinging to a 2–1 lead with the bases loaded and one out in the ninth inning. This time, he struck out Mark Trumbo and Chris Nelson to emerge victorious.

Robertson was given the closer's job in 2014 after Mariano Rivera announced his retirement. He posted 39 saves and averaged more than 13 strikeouts per 9 innings.

After seven seasons with the Yankees, Robertson departed in free agency, signing with the Chicago White Sox.

"I'm glad I don't have to face him anymore," then–White Sox catcher Tyler Flowers said upon hearing of Robertson's signing.

Robertson struck him out in all three of their matchups.

Whitey Ford's 33 Straight Scoreless Innings in the World Series

He is the starting pitcher to whom all great Yankees get compared, fitting since he's known as "Chairman of the Board."

When it comes to pitching, Whitey Ford qualifies as a CEO. His .690 winning percentage ranks second-best among those whose career began in the modern era.

Ford was renowned for rising to the occasion. He is a rarity in that he pitched as well against the good teams as he did against the bad ones. Consider this:

These are his numbers against teams that finished a season with losing records: ERA: 2.68, opponents' BA: .236, opponents' OPS: .639, K to BB rate: 1.9.

These are his numbers against teams that finished .500 or better: ERA: 2.83, opponents' BA: .234, opponents' OPS: .642, K to BB rate: 1.7.

The sum is a 236–106 record and a 2.75 ERA in a career that spanned from 1950 to 1967 (minus military service that cost him two seasons).

But most notable is that Ford was at his best when it counted most. He's still the all-time World Series record-holder with 33 consecutive scoreless innings. Ford and baseball legend Christy Mathewson are the only pitchers to throw three consecutive World Series shutouts.

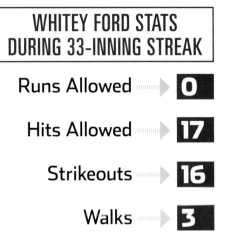

WHITEY FORD STATS DURING 33-INNING STREAK

Runs Allowed ⟩ **0**

Hits Allowed ⟩ **17**

Strikeouts ⟩ **16**

Walks ⟩ **3**

The first of those was a 10–0 drubbing of the Pittsburgh Pirates in Game 3 of the 1960 World Series. The Yankees offense was overpowering that day, but Ford would have been fine with only one run. He allowed only four hits and one walk in cruising to the victory.

Later in the Series, with the Yankees trailing three games to two, Ford came back on three days' rest and won 12–0. This time, he not only excelled on the mound but at the plate, with the game's first

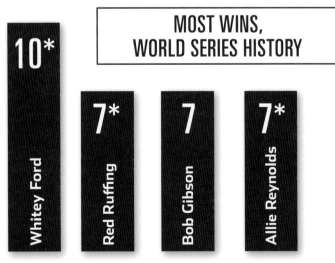

MOST WINS, WORLD SERIES HISTORY

10* Whitey Ford

7* Red Ruffing

7 Bob Gibson

7* Allie Reynolds

*All with Yankees

RBI and a successful squeeze later in the contest. He's the most recent Yankees pitcher to drive in two runs in a World Series game.

The Yankees lost the Series in Game 7 on Bill Mazeroski's walk-off home run, which Ford once referred to in an interview as "one of the worst days of my life."

There were plenty of good days for the Long Island native, who grew up a Yankees fan. The Yankees won 11 pennants and six World Series with Ford at the head of the rotation.

That includes the 1961 season, Ford's winningest, in which he was 25–4 with a 3.21 ERA. In Game 1 of that World Series against the Reds, he pitched his best game, allowing no runs and two hits in a 2–0 win.

The *New York Times* provided arguably the best description of his pitching skill:

"Possessed of an instinctive sense of gamesmanship, evidenced from his first appearance in Yankee pinstripes, Whitey is a cool and calculating operation.... He revels in such challenges [of being the

SPUD CHANDLER'S .717 WINNING PERCENTAGE

The only pitcher to have a higher winning percentage than Whitey Ford is Spud Chandler.

Chandler excelled for the Yankees from 1937 to 1947 and had a won-loss record of 109–43. No pitcher in baseball's modern era has bettered his .717 winning percentage. Chandler's best season was his AL MVP-winning year, 1943, when he went 20–4 with a 1.64 ERA. He also went 2–0 in that year's World Series.

In retirement, Chandler was saluted as a pitcher whose career came together as the product of learning from others.

"To the fastball he owned when he came up through the Yankees, he added through hours of hard work, Atley Donald's slider, Hank Borowy's screwball, and Ernie Bonham's fork ball, and what he learned by studying the rest of the league would have made fine reference reading for any pitching staff in the circuit," wrote W.C. Heinz.

Pitchers could probably learn a thing or two from Chandler as well.

BEST REGULAR-SEASON WINNING PERCENTAGE, MLB HISTORY*

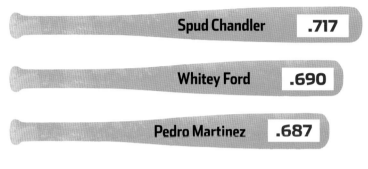

Spud Chandler **.717**

Whitey Ford **.690**

Pedro Martinez **.687**

*Career began since 1900

ace or the losing-streak stopper] because to his way of thinking, they are what make pitching fun."

Said Ford that day: "Control is the key to pitching. I have a lot of confidence in my stuff and am not afraid to lean on it in a pinch. But with good control, you can get batters out, even without good stuff, just by moving the ball around and keeping balance."

Ford probably would have thrown his fourth straight shutout in Game 4 of the World Series, were it not for a couple of maladies (a sprained ankle and a bruised toe) that forced him out of the game after five scoreless innings. Instead, he settled for extending his scoreless mark to 32 frames, which broke Babe Ruth's all-time mark of $29^2/_3$, set when Ruth was with the Boston Red Sox.

All good things must come to an end, and in Ford's case the streak concluded in the 1962 World Series against the San Francisco Giants on a squeeze bunt.

Undaunted by the streak's conclusion, Ford pitched a complete game, scattering 10 hits in a 6–2 win. This was Ford's 10th and last World Series win. To that point in his career, his Fall Classic record stood at 10–4 with a 1.98 ERA. Though that mark would come down with losses in his final three World Series decisions, Ford's efforts are a combination of longevity and effectiveness that has never been matched.

Reggie Jackson's
3 HR on 3 Pitches
in Game 6 of
1977 World Series

You could make a legitimate case that Reggie Jackson is the greatest hitter in World Series history.

Jackson ranks among the all-time leaders in both World Series on-base percentage and slugging percentage. The bulk of those numbers were put up in three World Series appearances with the Yankees, in 1977, 1978, and 1981.

In 27 career World Series games, Jackson hit .357 with a .457 on-base percentage and a .755 slugging percentage, with 10 home runs and 24 RBIs.

Though "Mr. October" was originally a sarcasm-tinged nickname given to Jackson by Yankees captain Thurman Munson, the moniker was befitting of its recipient. And Munson knew of Jackson's value.

When Jackson was a free agent, Munson reportedly told Yankees management to "Go get that SOB. He's the slugger we need."

Jackson signed a five-year deal with the Yankees after the team got swept in the World Series by the Cincinnati Reds in 1976. He joined a team that became known as the "Bronx Zoo" because of the many issues between the players, manager Billy Martin, and owner George Steinbrenner.

It didn't help matters that before he even played a game with the Yankees, an article quoted him as saying, "I'm the straw that stirs the drink. Munson thinks he can be the straw that stirs the drink, but he can only stir it bad." Those words hurt his relationship with his teammates, particularly Munson, though to this day, Jackson denies saying them.

But despite disagreements off the field, this was a team that could play ball with the best of them. Jackson hit .286 with 32 home runs and 110 RBIs in 1977.

REGGIE JACKSON
Champion Base Ball Batter

The biggest of Jackson's big hits in the 1977 regular season came on September 14, against the Red Sox. Jackson helped keep the game scoreless with a leaping catch and a diving catch. Then, after taking two pitches in which he tried to bunt, Jackson hit a two-run walk-off home run in the ninth inning. The win put the Yankees 3½ games up on Boston with 16 to play.

"I prayed when I was on-deck that I would hit one out," Jackson told the media afterward. "This is my most satisfying game."

That last sentence held true for just over a month because it was in that year's World Series that Jackson had one of the legendary games in baseball history.

DID YOU KNOW? Jackson had two three-HR games during the regular season—they came as a 23-year-old in 1969 and a 40-year-old in 1986.

To get there, the Yankees had to hang on to hold off the Orioles and Red Sox in the AL East. Then they barely survived a second consecutive five-game ALCS with the Royals, rallying in the ninth inning to win Game 5.

The World Series was a *little* easier. The Yankees won three of the first four games, with Jackson hitting a key home run in Game 4. He also homered in his final at-bat in Game 5, a game the Dodgers won to cut the Series deficit to 3–2. The Series headed back to New York for Game 6 with the Yankees trying to clinch their first championship since 1962.

"I should have known in batting practice," wrote Jackson in his autobiography, *Reggie*, of Game 6. "I hit maybe 40 balls during my time in the cage. I must have hit 20 into the seats ... The baseball looked like a volleyball to me."

The Dodgers scored twice in the first inning and once in the third inning, but their hopes of forcing a seventh game didn't last long. Jackson, who walked on four pitches his first time up, came up in the bottom of the fourth with Thurman Munson on base and no one out.

On the first pitch, Jackson extended his arms, took a huge swing, and crushed a home run over the right-field fence to put the Yankees ahead 4–3.

"It didn't have a lot of lift, but ooh did it have a lot of velocity," said TV play-by-play man Keith Jackson.

MOST HR IN SINGLE WORLD SERIES BY YANKEES

Player	Year	HRs
Reggie Jackson	1977	5*
Hank Bauer	1958	4
Babe Ruth	1926	4
Lou Gehrig	1928	4

* Ties all-time record

An inning later, Jackson got another turn, this time against Elias Sosa. Again Jackson took a huge cut, and this time the ball left the playing field on a line over the right-field fence in about two seconds. Jackson was all smiles in the Yankees dugout, reveling in the moment.

"Victory can bring harmony," said ABC's Howard Cosell.

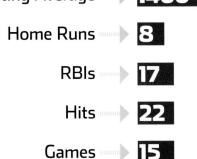

REGGIE JACKSON IN WORLD SERIES WITH YANKEES

Batting Average ⟶ **.400**

Home Runs ⟶ **8**

RBIs ⟶ **17**

Hits ⟶ **22**

Games ⟶ **15**

By the bottom of the eighth inning, the outcome of the game was not in doubt. The Yankees led 7–3 and the Dodgers went to knuckleballer Charlie Hough. Jackson saved his best blow for last. Hough's first pitch was a knuckleball that his catcher Steve Yeager intended to scoop. The ball never reached his mitt. Instead Jackson hit it 475 feet to center field.

"A colossal blow!" yelled Cosell.

It was Jackson's third home run of the game and record-setting fifth home run of the Series.

"I was looking for a ball in," Jackson said in a 2013 interview with *CBS This Morning*. "We had great scouts. Birdie Tebbetts, Jerry Walker, and Gene Michael had given me the tendencies on pitchers. I had great insights. I knew what they were gonna do."

Thirty-six years earlier, Jackson was a little brasher about it.

"You can pitch me in, but don't knock on the door and announce it," he said. "Even a dummy will adjust, and I adjusted."

This was a case where Jackson could back up any sort of cocky talk. He became the second player to hit three home runs in a World Series game, joining Babe Ruth.

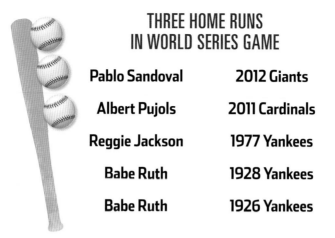

THREE HOME RUNS
IN WORLD SERIES GAME

Pablo Sandoval	2012 Giants
Albert Pujols	2011 Cardinals
Reggie Jackson	1977 Yankees
Babe Ruth	1928 Yankees
Babe Ruth	1926 Yankees

After the game, Steinbrenner put the pressure on by stating, "Now we're on top and we're gonna stay there."

Doing so wasn't easy.

Jackson and Martin again clashed the following season. Eventually Martin was replaced as manager by Bob Lemon and talent overcame discontent. After the Yankees came back to overtake the Red Sox for the AL East, Jackson carried them in the postseason, with 14 RBIs in 10 games, homering again in Game 6 of the World Series against the Dodgers. The Yankees won the title for the second straight year.

It would be the last of the five championships (including three with the Athletics) that Jackson celebrated.

"Whether you thought he was a hot dog or a loudmouth or anything else," said his biography co-author, sportswriter Mike Lupica, "if you were a Yankee fan, go back and see how many World Series you had won in all those years before he got to town, and how long it took you to win the World Series again after he left town."

Jackson, who went into the Hall of Fame as a Yankee in 1993, knows his value and how he'll be remembered in Yankees history.

"I would say I was the final ingredient that helped this team get over the top and become a champion," Jackson said.

Ron Guidry's
25 Wins in 1978

The 1978 Yankees' remarkable run to a division title would not have been possible if not for arguably the greatest season ever by a Yankees starting pitcher.

Ron Guidry came from Lafayette, Louisiana, and his birthplace netted him two nicknames—Louisiana Lightning and Gator. His big-league success was sudden, like the former, and he attacked with ferocity, like the latter.

Guidry got brief big-league looks in 1975 and 1976, two seasons in which he was exclusively used as a relief pitcher in the minor leagues, and he grew frustrated, tempted even to quit baseball because he wanted to be a starter.

Thankfully for the Yankees, Guidry's wife talked him out of retirement.

After making the Yankees and pitching out of the bullpen for the first couple of weeks of the 1977 season, Billy Martin gave Guidry a chance to start on a day when no one else was available to pitch.

In that April 29 start, Guidry pitched 8$\frac{1}{3}$ scoreless innings in a win over the Mariners. He didn't pitch again for two weeks, but after one relief appearance, he returned to the rotation to stay on May 17.

Guidry was fantastic down the stretch that season as the Yankees held off the Red Sox and Orioles to win the American League

East. He went 7–1 with five complete games and a 1.58 ERA to end the season. He followed that up with complete-game wins in the ALCS and the World Series—a three-hitter against the Kansas City Royals and a four-hitter in Los Angeles against the Dodgers—as the Yankees won their first championship since 1962.

That set the tone for a remarkable 1978, one in which Guidry evolved into the best pitcher in the game. Guidry began that season 13–0. His fastball was effective in combination with a nasty slider (taught by teammates Sparky Lyle and Dick Tidrow) that ranked fourth-best (behind Hall of Famers Bob Gibson, Steve Carlton, and Don Drysdale) in a survey of players by authors Eugene and Roger McCaffrey, conducted in the mid-1980s.

Guidry began racking up strikeouts with his wins. He whiffed 11 Athletics on June 2, 10 Mariners on June 7, and 11 more Athletics on June 12. But that was nothing compared to what happened in his next start.

MOST STRIKEOUTS IN GAME, YANKEES HISTORY

Ron Guidry (1978)	18
Michael Pineda (2015)	16
David Wells (1997)	16
David Cone (1997)	16

MOST STRIKEOUTS IN SEASON, YANKEES HISTORY

Ron Guidry (1978)	248
Jack Chesbro (1904)	239
CC Sabathia (2011)	230
David Cone (1997)	222

On June 17, Guidry overpowered the California Angels at Yankee Stadium in a 4–0 win that was arguably as good as any ever pitched by a Yankees starter. It is one that is believed to have started the baseball custom of the "strikeout clap"—crowds clapping in unison when a pitcher reaches a two-strike count.

"The thing that I remember most about the game was that I wasn't trying to strike anybody out," Guidry said. "It was just something that wound up happening."

Bobby Grich led off the game with a double,

The best hitter (Reggie Jackson) and best pitcher (Ron Guidry) on the 1970s Yankees teams got to celebrate two Yankees' titles.

but after that, Guidry went through the rest of the night almost untouched. He struck out six hitters in the first three innings, then blew the side away in the fourth to give him nine whiffs. He added two more in the fifth and three in the sixth, putting him at 14 with three innings to go. His 16th strikeout was Ike Hampton in the eighth inning, breaking the team record for strikeouts in a game.

Guidry entered the ninth inning with those 16 whiffs. He changed his approach, for good reason.

MOST WINS BY YANKEES PITCHER, SINGLE SEASON (SINCE END OF WWII)

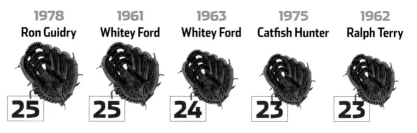

1978	1961	1963	1975	1962
Ron Guidry	Whitey Ford	Whitey Ford	Catfish Hunter	Ralph Terry
25	25	24	23	23

"Munson told me if I didn't try for the record [the MLB mark was 19 at the time], he'd break my left shoulder," Guidry said with a laugh. "The guys in the ninth were the only ones I was trying to strike out."

Guidry struck out two of three, to come up one shy. His 18 strikeouts remain the team record.

The Angels started Joe Rudi in the cleanup spot that day. Rudi, who went 3-for-25 in his career against Guidry, struck out four times in four turns.

Guidry struck out *only* eight in his next start, but he kept winning. Back to-back starts allowing five and six runs and his first loss of the season didn't daunt him. Guidry followed up with consecutive shutouts to improve to 15–1.

As the Yankees charged back from a double-digit deficit toward the Red Sox, Guidry rose to the challenge. He pitched a two-hit shutout on September 9 at Fenway Park in the famous four-game sweep of the Red Sox and threw another two-hit shutout against them six days later. Guidry made seven starts in September and October and went 6–1 with a 1.19 ERA.

The most notable of those came in the one-game playoff in Boston on October 2. Pitching on three days' rest against former teammate Mike Torrez, Guidry fell behind 2–0, but escaped jams in the third and sixth innings to keep the Yankees in the game.

His teammates rewarded Guidry for his efforts. Bucky Dent's three-run homer in the seventh put the Yankees ahead and put Guidry in position for the win. He got one more out in the bottom of the seventh, and turned the game over to the bullpen. The Yankees won 5–4, and went on to win their second straight World Series, with Guidry winning twice more in the postseason.

His *.893* winning percentage is the best in major league history by a **20-game winner.**

The last of those wins came with the Yankees down 2–0 in the World Series to the Dodgers—another complete-game victory. It was the first of four straight wins by the Yankees that clinched the World Series.

Guidry went 25–3 with a 1.74 ERA, won the Cy Young Award, and finished second in the AL MVP voting. His .893 winning percentage is the best in major league history by a 20-game winner.

PETE SHEEHY WORKS FOR YANKEES IN PARTS OF 7 DECADES

Pete Sheehy was much more than the Yankees' clubhouse attendant from 1927 to 1985. He was an educator, well versed in the lives of his players and their roles as part of the Yankee legacy. He was both a storyteller and a keeper of secrets.

"I would talk with Pete for 30 to 40 minutes every time I pitched," said Ron Guidry, who wasn't the only one to have such frequent conversations. "That's how I got to learn about the Yankees greats before me. I'd always ask him to tell me about a player—Babe Ruth, Joe DiMaggio, Yogi Berra, Mickey Mantle. He would tell you about them and their character."

Sheehy was someone of unimpeachable character. As Don Mattingly said simply after Sheehy died: "He was a great man."

25 WINS, SUB-2.00 ERA, YANKEES HISTORY

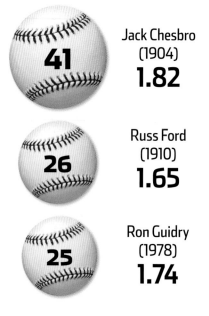

41 Jack Chesbro (1904)
1.82

26 Russ Ford (1910)
1.65

25 Ron Guidry (1978)
1.74

Guidry was the Yankees' staff ace for the next seven seasons and was highly respected by his teammates, sharing the team captaincy with Willie Randolph in the final years of his career. He led the league in ERA in 1979 and won 20 games twice more, including a league-best 22 in 1985. He also won five consecutive Gold Gloves from 1982 to 1986.

"Guidry was like an older brother type," said former teammate Dave Righetti, "somebody who looked out for you. He didn't tell me a lot of things, but he'd give me a little look or a whisper here or there."

Guidry retired after the 1988 season, finishing with a career record of 170–91 and going on to work for the team in multiple capacities, including two seasons as a pitching coach.

He ranks among the top five pitchers in Yankees history in career wins, starts, and wins above replacement. That was good enough to earn him a retired number (49), a Monument Park plaque, and a place in the hearts of a generation of Yankees fans.

1978 Yankees Overcome 14-Game Deficit to Win AL East

Rock bottom for the 1978 Yankees came on July 17. That day, the Kansas City Royals finished a three-game sweep with an extra-inning win. They rallied from two runs down in the ninth inning against Yankees closer Rich Gossage, and scored four runs in the 11th inning for the victory.

Gossage allowed six runs, but only one was earned due to a couple of ill-timed errors.

The loss put the Yankees 14 games behind the first-place Red Sox.

The next day was an off-day, but the Yankees made big news, with an announcement that made the front page of the *New York Times*. They suspended star slugger Reggie Jackson for five days (four games) for "deliberately disregarding the managers' instructions." Jackson repeatedly tried to bunt in the 10th inning of that Royals loss even after manager Billy Martin took the bunt sign off.

Martin and owner George Steinbrenner acted decisively.

AL EAST W-L RECORDS AFTER JULY 17, 1978

Yankees	53–21
Orioles	41–29
Tigers	41–32
Brewers	41–33
Red Sox	38–36
Indians	27–42
Blue Jays	27–44

"It'll pull the team together," Martin told reporters. He was trying to offer positivity, as general manager Cedric Tallis had a couple of weeks earlier when he said, "The situation is not too pleasant. But it's not impossible. Maybe we'll make a miraculous recovery."

Both were proven right, though Martin wasn't around to steer the team to its final result.

So began arguably the greatest comeback in baseball history, as the Yankees rallied to win the division, the AL pennant, and the World Series.

The Yankees won five straight from the Twins and White Sox, but upon Jackson's return, Martin was still angry, both at Jackson and Steinbrenner.

The quote that did Martin in came at the airport after completing a three-game sweep of the White Sox, when Martin said, "Jackson and Steinbrenner deserve each other. One's a born liar, the other is convicted."

The next day, Martin resigned. His replacement was Bob Lemon, who had been fired as White Sox manager a month earlier.

The move paid immediate dividends in that it got Jackson on the right track. In Jackson's first eight games with Lemon as manager, he had 16 hits and batted .571 with seven RBIs. The Yankees, who had cut the lead to 10 games at the time Martin resigned, trimmed 3½ more off the deficit in Lemon's first nine days as manager.

"As we started to get healthy, we put a little bit of a streak together," said former Yankees shortstop Bucky Dent in an interview for *Yankees Magazine* on the YES Network.

But the Red Sox AL East lead was still secure. Boston came to New York and swept a pair of games, rallying from 5–0 down to win in

17 innings in the first game, then winning 8–1 in the finale to push the lead back to 8½.

The Yankees were 59–49 after a loss to the Orioles. They went 41–14 the rest of the way. That's a 120-win pace! And that was only good enough to win the division by one game.

How did they do it?

Jackson led the team in RBIs with 39 in his last 51 games, but Graig Nettles and Lou Piniella were unsung heroes. Nettles had 22 extra-base hits and only 19 strikeouts in that span, batting .292. Piniella hit .322 with 31 RBIs, and he and Willie Randolph each repeatedly came through with runners in scoring position (Piniella hit .365, Randolph .341 in those situations from August 5 on).

The Yankees' starting pitching was amazing, with Ron Guidry, Ed Figueroa, and Catfish Hunter combining to go 27–5 down the stretch. Guidry had a 1.29 ERA in his last 12 starts.

The most famous series in the comeback was a four-game sweep of the Red Sox in Fenway Park, in which the Yankees outscored the Red Sox 42–9 and left town tied for first place. In what proved to be foreshadowing, the Yankees leader in RBIs in that series was light-hitting shortstop Bucky Dent, with seven.

The Yankees took the lead in the division by as much as 3½ games before the Red Sox rallied back to tie on the final day. The division

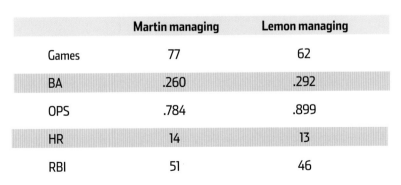

REGGIE JACKSON IN 1978

	Martin managing	Lemon managing
Games	77	62
BA	.260	.292
OPS	.784	.899
HR	14	13
RBI	51	46

title came down to a one-game playoff at Fenway Park, with Guidry facing former Yankee Mike Torrez.

Carl Yastrzemski's second-inning home run put Torrez and the Red Sox up 1–0. The Yankees did nothing against Torrez for six innings and the Red Sox added to their lead on Jim Rice's RBI single.

The Yankees finally put more than one man on base in the seventh, but it looked like any hopes of a rally fizzled when Jim Spencer flied out. That brought up Dent with two on and two out. Dent entered the at-bat 0-for-his-last-13, but his luck was about to change.

On 1–0, Dent fouled a pitch off his left foot and the pain was enough to necessitate a visit from Yankees trainer Gene Monahan. The batboy brought Dent a new bat.

What happened next was so improbable that it fit perfectly into the narrative of the comeback.

Dent turned on Torrez's next pitch and hit it over the Green Monster for a three-run home run. It was the only home run Dent hit in the last 44 games of the season.

CATFISH HUNTER'S $1 MILLION SIGNING BONUS

The first big fish that Yankees owner George Steinbrenner reeled in was a Catfish—as in free agent pitcher Catfish Hunter, who signed a five-year deal with the Yankees worth more than $3 million on December 31, 1974. The eye-popping figure was the signing bonus: $1 million.

Hunter was the sport's first big-money free agent, a mark he earned by averaging 22 wins and 286 innings over the previous four seasons, the last three of which resulted in championships for the Oakland Athletics. Steinbrenner wanted big winners and Hunter was the best he could get. He came with a 7–2 record and a 2.55 ERA in postseason play.

Injuries caught up to Hunter by the third year of his deal, but he still finished second in the Cy Young voting in 1975 and helped the Yankees to World Series titles in 1977 and 1978. He was inducted into the Baseball Hall of Fame in 1987.

Tragically, Hunter battled ALS in the latter stages of his life. He died in 1999 at age 53.

"The last guy on the ball club you would expect to hit a home run just hit one into the net!" yelled Yankees television announcer Bill White.

The Yankees pushed their lead to 5–2 before the Red Sox battled back, scoring twice in the eighth inning against Gossage, who got out of a jam to keep the lead 5–4.

In the ninth, the Red Sox took another shot, but an alert play by Piniella saved the game. With one on and one out, Jerry Remy singled to right, but Piniella deked

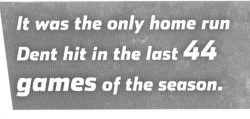

*It was the only home run Dent hit in the last **44** games of the season.*

the base runner, Rick Burleson, into thinking he was going to catch the ball. As a result, the Red Sox had first and second instead of first and third.

That was huge because Jim Rice followed with a fly ball that would have been far enough for a sacrifice fly. Burleson ended up on third instead of scoring.

The next hitter was Yastrzemski, the guy Red Sox fans wanted up in that spot. And a guy Gossage probably didn't want to face. But Gossage had a mental edge in situations like this one.

"I said, 'This is silly, this is a game and you play games for the fun of it, so what's the worst thing that could happen to you—that you have to go home to Colorado?'" Gossage told the *New York Times* 20 years ago. "There are worse fates. And it was like the weight of the world lifted off of me. I just relaxed and threw the ball."

On a 1–0 pitch, Yastrzemski swung and hit a high pop to third. Nettles backtracked nine steps and squeezed the ball with his glove. Gossage sprinted over and Nettles leapt into his arms.

The struggle was real, but the comeback was spectacular. The Yankees were AL East champions.

Graig Nettles Makes 4 Great Plays in a World Series Game

If you were to create a list of the best *games* by a hitter in Yankees history, there are many to choose from.

But if we're talking the best defensive display by a Yankee, there should be only one game that comes to mind.

We're referring to Game 3 of the 1978 World Series in which third baseman Graig Nettles had a game that put him on par with some of the all-time greats.

"That's a pretty cool way to put it," Nettles said in a 2015 interview.

The Yankees trailed the Dodgers in the Series 2–0 at the time, so the importance of Nettles' performance was greatly magnified.

With the Dodgers trailing 2–0 and threatening in the second inning, Nettles speared a line drive hit right at him by Davey Lopes.

"Billy Martin [who managed Nettles at the start of his career with the Twins and in New York] taught me how to position myself," Nettles said. "He taught me a lot of little things."

It would take more than great positioning for Nettles to thwart the Dodgers' hopes that inning, as his lightning-fast reflexes allowed him to make a diving stab of Reggie Smith's bid for an extra-base hit to end that inning.

"When he'd dive, he'd never miss a ball," said Nettles' teammate Bucky Dent.

Even when the Dodgers hit one that Nettles couldn't handle, like Smith's smash down the third-base line with two on and two outs in the fifth, he did enough to keep the ball in the infield and prevent a run from scoring.

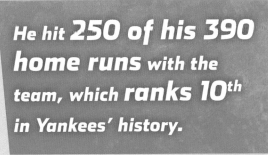

He hit **250 of his 390 home runs** with the team, which **ranks 10th** in Yankees' history.

That was huge because of what happened next. With the bases loaded and two outs and the Yankees leading by one run, Steve Garvey hit another rocket down the third-base line. This time Nettles ranged to his right, reached and corralled the ball, then pivoted, settled, and threw just in time to get a force play at second base.

"That play was just magnificent," said NBC's Tony Kubek.

"Any play down the line at Yankee Stadium was a tricky play," Nettles said. "Starting at third base down to the outfield, the field was sloped down for drainage purposes. Any time a ball was hit down the line, it seemed to bounce a little higher. I was able to judge it a little better than most."

The Dodgers got another bases-loaded, two-out opportunity the next inning, this time with Lopes, who hit what looked to be a go-ahead shot down the line.

But Nettles, who used to have E-5 noted both on his gloves and his license plate as a reminder to concentrate hard, went to a knee, picked off the hop, spun, and secured the force out at second base to end the inning.

MOST HR BY A YANKEES PLAYER DURING THE 1970s

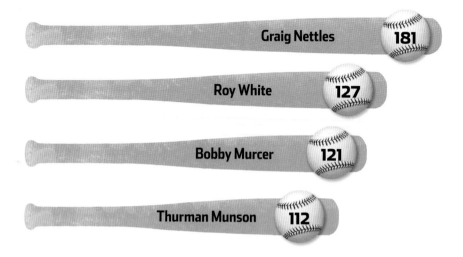

Graig Nettles **181**

Roy White **127**

Bobby Murcer **121**

Thurman Munson **112**

"You have to concentrate on every pitch," Nettles once said on an episode of *The Baseball Bunch*, a kids' instructional TV show. "You have to expect every ball to be hit at you."

The Yankees won 5–1, the first of four straight wins by the Yankees on the way to repeating as baseball's champions.

"It was the greatest exhibition by a third baseman I have seen in my career," said Dodgers manager Tommy Lasorda after the game.

Nettles saved at least four runs, which made the difference in the game.

"I'd rather save four runs with my glove than score four runs with a bases-loaded home run," said Nettles.

Nettles did his share of hitting too. He hit 250 of his 390 home runs with the team, which ranks 10th in Yankees' history. Nettles still holds the AL record for career home runs as a third baseman.

Nettles had some clutch postseason moments with his bat. He won 1981 ALCS MVP honors by becoming the first player to drive in at least three runs in three straight postseason games.

But it is defense by which Nettles is best known. Nettles won Gold Gloves in 1977 and 1978 and finished in the top six in the AL MVP voting in each of those seasons. Nettles and Wade Boggs are the only third basemen in Yankees history to win multiple Gold Gloves.

Nettles won Gold Gloves in 1977 and 1978 and finished in the top six in the AL MVP voting.

Nettles' overall numbers in a 22-year career are borderline Hall of Fame worthy. If there was a Hall of Fame just for defense, Nettles would likely be a member.

"I'm proud that people know me for my defense now," Nettles said. "When I first started playing, I was told I'd better hit a lot or I wouldn't make it to the major leagues. I'm proud of the hard work I put in and the recognition I got for it."

The recognition is still there. Just ask anyone who he robbed on that October day 38 years ago.

Sparky Lyle's 57 Saves of 6-Plus Outs

There was a time in baseball history in which it wasn't unusual for a closer to pitch more than one inning.

The Yankees had one of the best when it came to that in outstanding lefty Sparky Lyle, whose nasty slider left opponents befuddled when they returned to the dugout.

"When Sparky is pitching, you don't have to ask what the pitch was," said Royals star George Brett in 1977. "Slider, slider, slider."

Lyle excelled with the Red Sox for five seasons, but was then traded to the Yankees in spring training of 1972 for infielders Danny Cater and Mario Guerrero.

"We've been trying to get him for two years," said Yankees GM Lee MacPhail of a pitcher the *New York Times* described as having "long hair and a short earned-run average."

The trade ranks among the biggest steals in Yankees history.

In his first season with the Yankees, Lyle finished with an AL-best 35 saves. No other pitcher in the league even reached 30. Lyle was a workhorse. In 18 of those saves, he pitched at least two innings. That still stands as the most in a season in Yankees history. His total of 57 such saves with the Yankees is also a team record.

Lyle was so good in 1972 that he finished third in the AL's MVP voting.

Lyle recorded 27 saves in making the All-Star team in 1973, but then his totals dipped under new manager Bill Virdon in 1974 and 1975. Billy Martin's hire late in the 1975 season paid off for Lyle the next two seasons, as Martin put Lyle to work often.

In 1976, Lyle led the American League with 23 saves and helped the team win its first pennant in 12 years.

The 1977 season was Lyle's hallmark. He saved 26 games, won 13 more, and had a 2.17 ERA in 137 innings.

Lyle also became known as the guy who sat bare butted on team birthday cakes. But on the field, he put all the jokes aside.

That season, Lyle pitched in 45 games in which he was working either for the second time in a doubleheader, on no days' rest, or on one day rest. In those, he went 9–1 with 18 saves and a 1.23 ERA.

Lyle won without overpowering stuff. He struck out only 4.5 batters per nine innings, but made up for that by inducing 18 ground-ball double plays, at a rate that ranked among the 10 best for major league pitchers that season.

Lyle put his signature on this season in the LCS and World Series. He pitched 12⅔ innings in four games in a five-day span, in which he won three.

"I pitch better when my arm is a little tired," Lyle said at one point in that run.

MOST SAVES, 1972 TO 1977

Rollie Fingers 140

Sparky Lyle 132

Mike Marshall 98

Tug McGraw 89

With the Yankees trailing the Royals two games to one and on the brink of elimination, Martin pulled out every stop to keep the season alive. He went to Lyle in the fourth inning of Game 4, with the Yankees leading 5–4. Lyle got a vital out, retiring George Brett on a liner to left, to squash a Royals rally.

Since Lyle was the closer, he stayed in the game. And he never gave Martin a reason to take him out. Lyle's 5⅓ scoreless innings closed out a 6–4 win and forced a Game 5 the next day.

He **struck out only 4.5 batters per nine innings,** but made up for that by inducing 18 ground-ball double plays, at a rate that **ranked among the 10 best** for major league pitchers that season.

"Sparky Lyle was amazing," said Royals manager Whitey Herzog afterward.

Lyle had a hand in Game 5 too. He entered in the eighth inning with the Yankees trailing 3–2 and struck out Cookie Rojas with two men on base. After the Yankees rallied to take the lead, Lyle came back out for the bottom of the ninth and closed the game out, putting the Yankees in the World Series.

The team and its closer had one day of rest and then it was back to work in Game 1 of the World Series against the Los Angeles Dodgers. This time Lyle wasn't pristine. He entered with a one-run lead and two men on base and allowed a game-tying single to the first batter he faced.

But he retired the next 11 after that and he earned the win after Paul Blair knocked in the winning run in the 12th inning.

Lyle was doubly rewarded, as the Yankees won the World Series and Lyle won the AL Cy Young Award.

That off-season, the Yankees signed free agent Rich Gossage, ushering in an era of Yankees relief pitching marked by power rather than finesse.

Lyle was fully understanding of the Yankees taking the opportunity to get a younger, elite closer in Gossage. But Lyle made it clear he still wanted to close. The Yankees won another World Series in 1978, but Lyle had a tougher time in his supporting role. A book Lyle co-authored titled *The Bronx Zoo* told some behind-the-scenes stories that some did not like and Lyle was traded to the Rangers that off-season.

He pitched four more seasons in the major leagues with the Rangers, Phillies, and White Sox and became a highly successful manager of the Somerset Patriots, an independent league team, for 15 seasons.

Looking back, he's highly appreciative about his time with the Yankees, even though there were plenty of issues.

As Lyle often points out when he speaks to groups about those 1970s teams: "Come game time, when we got on the field, we fought for each other."

Rich Gossage's
100 MPH Fastball

Rich Gossage was both the Goose and the golden egg, the former his nickname, the latter another way of describing the prize that Yankees owner George Steinbrenner bestowed upon his team in November 1977, when he signed Gossage to a six-year, $2.5 million contract.

"Our scouts never graded a player higher for tenacity, aggressiveness, and overall ability," Steinbrenner said of the then-26-year-old, who was coming off a season in which he saved 26 games, posted a 1.62 ERA, and struck out 151 batters in relief for the Pirates.

The Yankees were ahead of their time, trying to create the equivalent of a Rivera-Wetteland or Betances-Miller combination in Gossage and incumbent closer Sparky Lyle. All Lyle had done in 1977 was win the Cy Young Award and play a huge role in the team's postseason success.

The closer job became Gossage's because he was younger and because he threw harder—a lot harder. Earl Weaver claimed Gossage's fastball peaked at 104 mph.

That may not actually have been true, but just about anyone you speak to or read acknowledges that Gossage was capable of hitting triple digits with his heat. And at a burly 6'3" with a big, thick mustache, Gossage was an intimidator.

However, things didn't go well at the start for Gossage. He lost three of his first four appearances in 1978, the last defeat coming as the result of his throwing error in the bottom of the ninth inning.

"I'm almost ready to cry," he said after the game.

But things got better after that, as Gossage was fine handling the pressure that came with pitching in New York.

What made Gossage so good was that (similar to Lyle) he could pitch great lengths and maintain the same level of stuff. In one May relief appearance, he entered in the seventh inning and pitched until Willie Randolph beat the Blue Jays with a hit in the 13th. The next month, Gossage pitched 2⅔ innings against the Red Sox, then came back the next day to throw five scoreless innings of relief.

What also made him good was that he was overpowering.

"I think the way I throw makes the ball tougher to see than for 80 to 90 percent of the other pitchers," Gossage once told the *New York Times*. "I rear back and they see a lot of butt, arms, and legs coming at them. It's tough."

As the Yankees made their run to catch Boston in the summer of 1978, Gossage got even better. In one stretch of 17 appearances, he saved nine games, won four others, and had a 1.15 ERA.

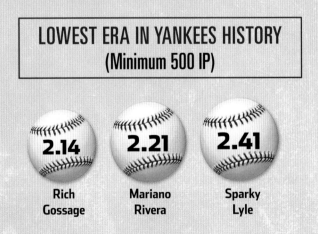

LOWEST ERA IN YANKEES HISTORY
(Minimum 500 IP)

2.14 — Rich Gossage
2.21 — Mariano Rivera
2.41 — Sparky Lyle

GOSSAGE'S 151 SAVES WITH THE YANKEES

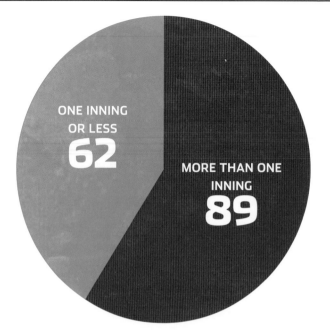

ONE INNING
OR LESS
62

MORE THAN ONE
INNING
89

In the one-game playoff against the Red Sox, he survived a rough ninth inning, getting Carl Yastrzemski to pop out with the tying run on third base to clinch the division.

Gossage also got the ball to close out both the ALCS against the Royals and the World Series against the Dodgers. He pitched six scoreless innings in the Fall Classic, including the last two of a 7–2 win in Game 6.

Two years later, the Yankees were back in the postseason, only this time the Royals got revenge for the times the Yankees had previously beaten them. Gossage entered Game 3 with the Yankees down two games to none but leading in the seventh inning and AL MVP-to-be George Brett at the plate with two men on base. The season was on the line in this at-bat.

Gossage brought the heat and Brett turned on it, for a three-run home run that put the Royals ahead and eventually put them in the World Series.

If there was any question as to whether Gossage would recover from such a tough defeat, he answered that the following season.

In the strike-shortened 1981 season, Gossage put together one of the best years ever by a relief pitcher.

In 46²/₃ innings, he had a 0.77 ERA and allowed 22 hits. In fact, if you combine his regular season with his 14¹/₃ scoreless postseason innings, his ERA drops to 0.59, the lowest ever by anyone whose regular season and playoff workload exceeded 50 innings.

Gossage was impeccable in the postseason, saving six games in the three rounds, but the Yankees blew a two-games-to-none lead and lost to the Dodgers in a six-game World Series.

Gossage played out the final two seasons of his contract as the Yankees began a downward slide. He left angry after the 1983 season, though he eventually made amends with Steinbrenner over perceived slights. Gossage did get another chance at the

GEORGE BRETT: 220 GAMES AGAINST YANKEES, EVERY ONE A BATTLE

The face of the Kansas City Royals at the height of the Yankees-Royals rivalry was George Brett.

Brett was Kansas City's version of Derek Jeter, a one-team, classy superstar who was a winner on and off the field.

Brett came through against the Yankees time after time. In the 1980 regular season, he had 22 RBIs in 10 regular-season games, then hit the ALCS-clinching home run versus Rich Gossage. He hit .358 with 14 RBIs in 17 postseason games against the Yankees.

The most famous moment in the Brett-Yankees rivalry was his Pine Tar Game home run in 1983, when he stormed out of the dugout in a rage after he was ruled out (the call would later be overturned).

When asked to sum up the rivalry in 2014, Brett did so succinctly.

"I hated the [expletive] Yankees and the Yankees hated the [expletive] Royals," he said.

World Series, helping his new team, the Padres, reach it in 1984. He pitched 10 more years in the majors after his initial departure from the Yankees, returning briefly for an 11-appearance stint in 1989. He retired after the 1994 season after becoming the second pitcher to reach 300 career saves.

Gossage was a pioneer at his position and this was eventually recognized by Cooperstown. He was elected to the Baseball Hall of Fame in 2008, his ninth year on the ballot.

In 2014, the Yankees provided him with one more glory day, as he was given a plaque in Monument Park on Old-Timer's Day. Gossage was overwhelmed by the honor.

"Outside of the day my kids were born and going into Cooperstown, it doesn't get any better than this," Gossage said.

Dave Righetti Sets MLB Record with 46 Saves in 1986

A new era in the Yankees bullpen began on January 7, 1984, six months removed from the finest moment of Dave Righetti's major league career, when he no-hit the Red Sox on July 4 at Yankee Stadium.

When Rich Gossage departed to sign a five-year deal with the Padres, he left behind huge shoes to fill.

Rather than attempt to fill that role externally, the Yankees turned to Righetti as their new closer.

"I'm willing to take the heat of pitching in that spot," Righetti told reporters in spring training.

Righetti was the predecessor who paved the way for extraordinary closers such as Dennis Eckersley and John Smoltz in the future.

Righetti had previously been a fine starting pitcher for three seasons after being obtained in a trade from the Texas Rangers as a minor leaguer. In 1981, he pitched to a 2.05 ERA in 15 starts, was the first Yankee to win Rookie of the Year honors since Thurman Munson in 1970, and helped the Yankees reach the World Series.

Righetti excelled because he kept the ball in the ballpark, allowing only one home run in 105$\frac{1}{3}$ innings in that 1981 season. It was 15 years before another pitcher would throw that many innings and allow so few home runs. That pitcher was Mariano Rivera in 1996.

Righetti wasn't Gossage and he wasn't Rivera, but he was very successful in making a name for himself. Righetti's 223 saves from 1984 to 1990 are the second-most by a reliever in that time, one behind Jeff Reardon, and his 224 saves rank second in Yankees history to Rivera.

Righetti's experience as a starter came in handy with regard to multi-inning saves. He was a rarity as a lefty in a time when most closers were right-handed.

In 1986, Righetti was greater than any reliever who preceded him. He broke the single-season record for saves by recording 46.

The Yankees got off to a hot start that season, winning 19 of their first 28 games. They spent most of the season chasing the eventual division champion Red Sox.

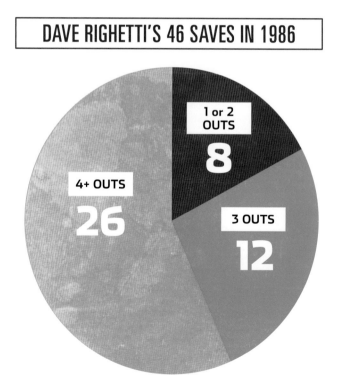

DAVE RIGHETTI'S 46 SAVES IN 1986

1 or 2 OUTS
8

4+ OUTS
26

3 OUTS
12

There were a few bumps. In mid-June, Righetti struggled in three straight games of a series against the Blue Jays, allowing five runs in 2⅓ innings. Yankees owner George Steinbrenner had been critical of Righetti's performance. The closer was in need of a confidence boost and his manager provided one.

"I remember Lou [Piniella] stepping up and saying, 'He's my guy and as long as he's here, he's going to be my closer,'" Righetti said. "I guess it relaxed me. I knew this guy was in my corner, so what else did I need? I didn't want to let him down."

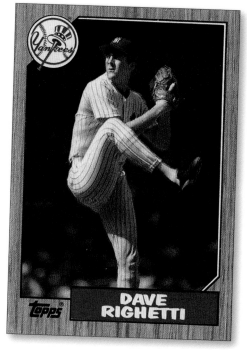

DAVE RIGHETTI

Once the Yankees dropped a little bit further back, Piniella realized the importance of every victory and began to use Righetti even more often.

After that Blue Jays series, Righetti pitched in 42 games, converted 30 of 32 save chances, and posted a 1.36 ERA.

Once the Red Sox clinched the division title, getting Righetti the saves record became a Piniella priority. Righetti recorded six saves in the final two weeks of the season, including four in a five-day stretch. Righetti tied the mark by saving the opening game of a doubleheader in Boston, then broke the record by notching the final out in a 3–1 win in the nightcap.

"He deserves it," Piniella told reporters after the game.

There was a postgame champagne celebration at Righetti's locker, but he remembers the moment as bittersweet.

DAVE RIGHETTI, YANKEES RANK

Saves	224	2nd
Games Pitched	522	2nd
K per 9	7.4	9th

"The tough part was that we finished [a little bit] back," Righetti said. "Even when I broke the record, I was kind of low-key about it. Because one more day [of baseball remained] and then we were packing to go home."

Righetti lasted four more years with the Yankees. His saves record was broken in 1990 by Bobby Thigpen, who had 57 for the White Sox.

Righetti's Yankees record for saves lasted until Rivera broke his single-season mark in 2001 and his franchise-high total a year later.

"I was really good, but I don't think I ever got to that 'great' level," Righetti said.

We would beg to differ. Especially in 1986.

Don Mattingly Hits .343 to Win Batting Title

Talk to Yankees fans in their thirties or forties and they'll tell you the player they most revere is Donnie Baseball.

"I would put my Don Mattingly fandom against any other person on the planet," said *Sports Illustrated* baseball writer Joe Sheehan. "I would go to Strat-O-Matic Tournaments, draft him, and shout out 'Don Mattingly is God!'"

For so many Yankees fans, he was the iconic figure of a difficult time in Yankees history. Mattingly played 14 seasons with the team and the Yankees did not make the postseason until 1995, the final year of his career.

But in that time, Mattingly was so important to so many people.

In the six-year period from 1984 to 1989, he was one of the best players in baseball. His .327 batting average was bettered only by Hall of Famers Wade Boggs and Tony Gwynn. His 428 extra-base hits and 684 RBIs were easily the most in the majors in that span. He also won five Gold Glove Awards.

"His numbers were Stan Musial-like," said former Yankees coach Roy White.

Mattingly's offense and defense were held in the highest regard. His swing is often described as among the prettiest in baseball history.

"I never looked at it as being a pretty swing," Mattingly said. "I think a lot of guys have pretty swings. Mine was short and compact. There was not a lot of swing-and-miss there."

That crouch and swing, often emulated, produced so many great numbers and so many great memories.

"Statistics to me are the pile that's there at the end of the season," Mattingly said. "That's what happens when you stay focused every day and help your team do whatever it can to win. The pile that's there is the accomplishments, the whole of all the little preparations."

The first big part of his statistical pile came in 1984, when Mattingly edged out teammate Dave Winfield for the batting title on the final day of the regular season. Mattingly hit .343 that season, with an AL-best 207 hits and 44 doubles, along with 23 home runs and 110 RBIs.

It was the first batting title for a Yankees player since Mickey Mantle won one in his Triple Crown season of 1956.

"The batting title was huge for my career," Mattingly said, referring to the confidence boost he got from being so good for a full season.

Mattingly's 1985 was a signature season. Mattingly helped keep the Yankees in the hunt for the AL East title down to the season's final weekend when the Yankees were finally knocked out by the Blue Jays. Mattingly won AL MVP honors by hitting .324 with 35 home runs, 145 RBIs, and 48 doubles.

In 1986, Mattingly was an established star. But he found a motivation that enabled him to set Yankees *franchise* records with 238 hits and 53 doubles.

DON MATTINGLY'S YANKEES SINGLE-SEASON RECORDS

Hits: 238 in 1986 (Previous record: Earle Combs, 231 in 1927)

Doubles: 53 in 1986 (Previous record: Lou Gehrig, 52 in 1927)

"You want to continue to prove that you're not going to stop and they're not going to figure you out," Mattingly said.

No one could quite figure out what went so right for Mattingly in 1987, a year in which he made home run history. He tied the major league record for most consecutive games with a home run by hitting one in eight straight.

"I look at it as a hot streak," said Mattingly. "What I remember about that streak is Bobby Murcer. I was struggling before I hit that first home run [note: We should all "struggle" like this—he was hitting .370 in 13 games since returning from a DL stint!]. We were getting close to the All-Star Break. Bobby Murcer came in to see me. George [Steinbrenner] would send someone in to talk to you [if you were struggling]. Bobby showed me a little something. It just clicked and then I went on that tear."

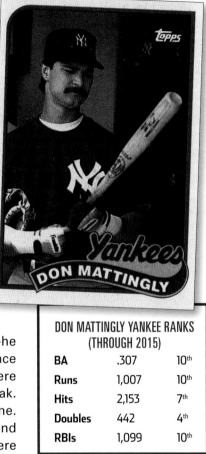

DON MATTINGLY YANKEE RANKS (THROUGH 2015)		
BA	.307	10th
Runs	1,007	10th
Hits	2,153	7th
Doubles	442	4th
RBIs	1,099	10th

But that wasn't all. Mattingly, who never had a home run streak longer than two games after that eight-game run, also hit six grand slams to set the mark for the most such home runs in a single season. He came up clutch to set that mark by hitting two of those grand slams in late September.

Coming through in important situations was a Mattingly trademark. He hit .318 in his career in what Baseball-Reference.com defined as "high-leverage situations" (those in a game that are most important to determining victory or defeat).

Mattingly recalled one favorite clutch hit from a game in late 1993. The Yankees trailed the Red Sox with two outs and nobody on, and the game appeared to be over when Mike Stanley flied out. But the umpires ruled that time was called when a fan ran onto the field. Given a second life, the Yankees staged a rally, one that concluded when Mattingly's bases-loaded hit brought home the tying and winning runs.

But the one that fans will always remember is a bittersweet one.

The last several years of Mattingly's career were ravaged by a back injury, preventing the superstar in him from carrying on. Mattingly gutted it out through the 1995 season, when the Yankees finally made the playoffs.

Mattingly closed out his career with 10 hits and six RBIs in five games against the Mariners in the ALDS, including a home run at Yankee Stadium in Game 2, after which the stadium shook from the cheering.

In the winner-take-all Game 5, it looked like Mattingly was going to be the hero, as his two-run double in the sixth inning put the Yankees ahead 4–2. But the Yankees could not hold on, as the Mariners rallied to tie, and then rallied again to win in the 11th inning.

Mattingly's playing career ended with that loss. But his legend did not.

MOST CONSECUTIVE GAMES WITH A HR, YANKEES HISTORY

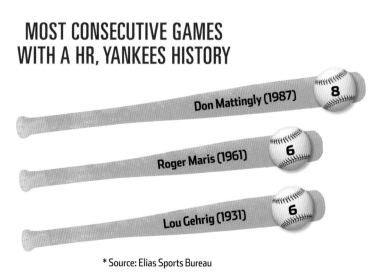

Don Mattingly (1987) 8

Roger Maris (1961) 6

Lou Gehrig (1931) 6

* Source: Elias Sports Bureau

Rickey Henderson's 1985 Season Was Worth 9.9 WAR

He is among the greatest players to wear a Yankees uniform, though he may not be remembered that way. His time with the team was controversial, though there is little mystery to "The Man of Steal" as he is so dubbed.

Rickey Henderson spent five glorious and tumultuous seasons in the Bronx from 1985 to 1989.

Henderson was unique in so many ways. He was often imitable but never duplicable.

Henderson was obtained in a trade with the Oakland Athletics in December 1984 and the price wasn't cheap (five prospects, including a noteworthy young pitcher, Jose Rijo) but was worth it.

"He is the No. 1 disruptive force in the American League," new teammate Dave Righetti told the *New York Times* shortly after the trade.

Henderson demonstrated that and then some in his first season with the Yankees, which is among the most amazing seasons in franchise history. Not only did he hit .314 with a .419 on-base percentage and a .516 slugging percentage, with 24 home runs out of the leadoff spot and great defense as well, but...

- His 80 stolen bases broke Fritz Maisel's club record of 74 that was set in 1914. Henderson became the first player to have 20 homers and 80 steals in a single season.

- He scored 146 runs, the most by a Yankees player since Joe DiMaggio scored 151 in 1937.

- He finished with 9.9 wins above replacement (as measured by Baseball-Reference.com), making it the most valuable season by a Yankees player since Mickey Mantle tallied 10.5 WAR in 1961. Only four position players have netted at least 9.9 WAR in a season for the Yankees—Babe Ruth, Lou Gehrig, Mickey Mantle, and Henderson.

"I don't ever remember watching a more electrifying player than Rickey Henderson," said *SportsCenter* anchor Kevin Connors, who grew up a Yankees fan in the 1980s. "When people talk about five-tool players, he is the model."

Had Henderson's season happened in a year in which the Yankees won the World Series, it probably would be as well remembered as Ruth's 60 home runs in 1927 or Mantle's Triple Crown in 1956.

"That [1985] team is the best team the Yankees had between 1981 and 1994," said *Sports Illustrated* writer Joe Sheehan, an avid Yankees fan at that time. "Everything was set up for that team to win."

The Yankees didn't. They finished with 97 wins, which would have been more than enough in a wild-card playoff system, but was only good for second place, two games behind the Blue Jays at that time. The Yankees finished second again in 1986 and fourth in 1987.

MOST STOLEN BASES IN SEASON, YANKEES HISTORY

93 Rickey Henderson (1988)

87 Rickey Henderson (1986)

80 Rickey Henderson (1985)

74 Fritz Maisel (1914)

George Steinbrenner and Yogi Berra were pleased to bring in one of the game's best all-around players in Rickey Henderson.

Henderson couldn't quite replicate what he did in 1985, but still found ways to amaze. He stole 87 bases and scored 130 runs in 1986 (despite hitting only .263), and had 93 more steals in 1988.

This was at a time when the Yankees were led by Don Mattingly, so Henderson's play was overshadowed a little bit.

"I don't think Yankees fans [of the time] understood just how great he was," Sheehan said.

Henderson was hard to understand from an off-the-field perspective too. But he was certainly entertaining. You've probably heard the stories about how he spoke about himself in the third person ("This is Rickey calling on behalf of Rickey. Rickey wants

DID YOU KNOW?

Rickey Henderson's 146 runs scored in 1985 would be a single-season record for 19 franchises. On the Yankees, it ranks 12th.

to play baseball.") or how he struggled with names and faces (he referred to teammate Lee Guetterman as "Guzman"). But he took his craft seriously.

"Rickey had a good time, but Rickey took care of himself, unlike a lot of players," said his teammate, Dave Winfield. "He didn't drink, didn't smoke, didn't do drugs."

Henderson's departure was an eventful one. During his Yankees career, Henderson dealt with injuries and the frustrations of owner George Steinbrenner, who publicly criticized Henderson for not returning quickly from a hamstring issue in 1987.

Henderson hit only .247 (albeit with a .392 on-base percentage) in 65 games in 1989 before the Yankees traded him back to the Athletics. The Yankees got back two middle relievers and outfielder Luis Polonia, not anywhere close to Henderson's true value.

GUY ZINN STEALS HOME TWO TIMES IN ONE GAME

Guy Zinn is a baseball rarity.

We say that with multiple meanings in mind with regards to the five-year major leaguer who played 115 games with the New York Highlanders (as the Yankees were then known) in 1911 and 1912. His picture appears on a one-of-a-kind baseball card for which one auction posted an asking price of $250,000 because of its unique status.

But in baseball terms, Zinn did something that has never been bettered. He's the only player in franchise history to steal home twice in a game. Both executions came on double steals, but that didn't lessen the impressiveness.

"Guy Zinn was the king pin base stealer," wrote the *New York Times*, the next day.

Zinn was unable to consistently replicate that success. He finished with 17 steals that season but only 28 in his career.

Henderson hit .294 with 52 steals in 85 games, won ALCS MVP honors, and hit .474 in a World Series sweep. Yankees fans could only watch with envy.

"I remember being so appalled at how little we got back for him," Sheehan said.

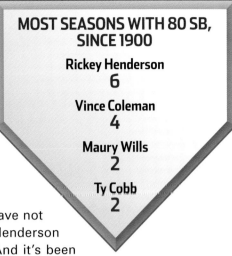

MOST SEASONS WITH 80 SB, SINCE 1900

Rickey Henderson
6

Vince Coleman
4

Maury Wills
2

Ty Cobb
2

In many ways, the Yankees have not been able to match what Henderson brought since he departed. And it's been more than 25 years since he left.

Since Henderson's steals barrage, no Yankees player has even reached 50 stolen bases in a season. Only one position player has come close to that 9.9 wins above replacement season, Alex Rodriguez (9.4 in 2005 and 2007). As good as Derek Jeter was, he never had more than 8.0 WAR in a season. Robinson Cano maxed out at 8.4.

Like him or hate him for how his career in New York went, you have to admit that Henderson was a one-of-a-kind player. Those who remember him well will tell you that.

"Never before and maybe never again will there be a leadoff hitter like Rickey Henderson," Connors said.

Yankees Sign Dave Winfield to 10-Year Contract

The contract was big, appropriate given the gigantic stature of the player who signed it. The result of it was not what the player or team hoped for, and the long-term effects stemming from Dave Winfield's tumultuous time with the Yankees still linger.

But the contract should not detract from Winfield the ballplayer and we should remember that his time with the Yankees was a significant part in the career of one of baseball's all-time greats.

The shame of Winfield's Yankees tenure is that it didn't have a great start or a great finish, with the back injury that caused him to miss a full season and the subsequent scandal in which Howie Spira tried to blackmail both Winfield and George Steinbrenner.

But there was a lot of good in-between that gets overshadowed.

Winfield signed a 10-year contract with the Yankees on December 15, 1981, after starring for the San Diego Padres.

"We'll see how good I am now," Winfield said at his press conference.

The deal was one of grandness, one even larger than Steinbrenner initially thought, thanks to a clause that Winfield's agent inserted that made the agreement potentially worth $25 million.

Steinbrenner's resentment over this contract was both well-documented and long-lasting. And his anger simmered.

How good was Winfield?

Maybe he wasn't as good as the Yankees hoped, but in retrospect, he was very, very good. He was an All-Star every full season that he played with the Yankees and received MVP votes in six seasons.

During the strike-shortened 1981 season, Winfield hit .294 with 13 home runs in 105 games, good enough to finish seventh in the MVP voting. But what's most remembered is how Winfield fared in the games that counted most. He went 1-for-22 in a six-game World Series loss to the Dodgers.

Years later, Steinbrenner, known for having a low tolerance for losing, referred to Winfield as "Mr. May," a criticism that stung Winfield for a long time. That characterization was an unfair one.

From 1982 to 1988, the 6'6" Winfield hit .291, slugged .500, averaged 27 home runs and 106 RBIs, and won five Gold Gloves. And he gave everything he had every day.

"I don't recall any player, great, good, mediocre, or whatever, hustling as much from day one through the end of his career," said former *New York Times* Yankees beat writer Claire Smith. "I loved watching Dave run out a ground ball as much as I loved watching him run out a triple. For a man that size, he ran the bases with such grace. He was a heck of an athlete and a privilege to watch."

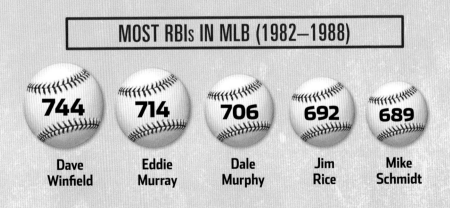

MOST RBIs IN MLB (1982–1988)

744	714	706	692	689
Dave Winfield	Eddie Murray	Dale Murphy	Jim Rice	Mike Schmidt

After a below-.500 season in 1982, the Yankees averaged 90 wins a season over the next six years. They were the winningest team of the 1980s.

But in the Bronx, success is measured by championships, and the Yankees won none, the first decade in which they failed to do so since the pre–Babe Ruth 1910s.

> He hit **better than .300** with runners in scoring position with the Yankees five times.

There were lots of disappointments and just-misses. It wasn't Winfield's fault that the Yankees had pitching issues. He did all he could and did it well.

"My memories of Winfield will always be his frequently scaling the right-field wall in pursuit of all of Ed Whitson's, Rick Rhoden's, and Charlie Hudson's home runs allowed," said ESPN.com fantasy baseball writer Tristan Cockcroft.

"I was going to do everything they asked me to do and more," Winfield said. "I always felt like we had a chance and I was going to prepare myself to do the best I could."

In 1984, Winfield and Don Mattingly battled for the batting title all the way to the final day. Winfield finished at a career-best .340, good for runner-up status three points behind Mattingly.

Winfield was upset at the time that there seemed to be more support for Mattingly than there was for him, and at times has suggested that racism was a factor.

Regardless, Winfield carried on the rest of his career with his best efforts. He hit better than .300 with runners in scoring position with the Yankees five times. He had plenty of big hits.

On September 28, 1985, with the Yankees trying to hang in the race with the Blue Jays, Winfield came up in the bottom of the ninth inning of a tie game with runners on first and third after an intentional walk to Mattingly. The Orioles should have known to walk Winfield too. Instead, they pitched to him, and his RBI single gave the Yankees a 6–5 win.

Another big hit came on June 29, 1987. The Yankees and Blue Jays entered the day tied for first place and played a bizarre high-scoring game in Toronto. The Yankees led 11–4, but the Blue Jays totaled 10 runs in the sixth and seventh innings to take the lead. In the top of the eighth, Winfield faced one of the game's top closers, Tom Henke, with the bases loaded, two outs, and the Yankees down by three runs. His grand slam put the Yankees ahead in the game and the standings.

Winfield took a measure of satisfaction in this moment in particular, given the times he'd been criticized in the past.

"It's not an aberration," he said.

Winfield enjoyed another six seasons after his time with the Yankees concluded, and got that elusive World Series ring with the Blue Jays in 1992, shedding the Mr. May moniker with the go-ahead hit in the clinching game.

He was a first-ballot inductee into the Baseball Hall of Fame in 2001.

George Steinbrenner Turns a $10 Million Investment into Billions

"We plan absentee ownership.... We're not going to pretend we're something that we aren't. I'll stick to building ships."

That's what George Steinbrenner said at the press conference introducing the Yankees' new ownership group, which purchased the team from CBS for $10 million in January 1973.

The Yankees had not made the postseason since 1964 and were coming off back-to-back fourth-place finishes, so Steinbrenner made another point clear: "We don't plan to move anywhere except up in the standings."

Steinbrenner lived up to the latter, but not the former. As the Yankees rose to prominence in the 1970s, so did the man known as "The Boss." When the Yankees needed to spend, he was there, with his most prominent early free-agent signings being Catfish Hunter and Reggie Jackson.

The moves worked because the team met the goal—winning a championship—in 1977 and 1978.

"He was committed to putting the best players on the field," said big-money signee Rich Gossage. "He has made everybody in baseball better, because to compete with George Steinbrenner, everybody had to up the ante and their level of play."

Steinbrenner could control a lot of things, but one he couldn't was how well a player played. The Yankees made several ill-advised signings and trades in the 1980s, swapping out prospects like Willie McGee, Fred McGriff, and Jay Buhner for little or no return.

Steinbrenner also had a short fuse. Struggles frustrated him, and when frustrated he'd vent to the media. He famously referred to future Hall of Famer Dave Winfield as "Mr. May" in reference to Winfield going 1-for-22 in a loss to the Dodgers in the 1981 World Series.

> **He famously referred to future Hall of Famer Dave Winfield as "Mr. May."**

When Steinbrenner got ticked off, you had to be ready. There were no holidays when you worked for his Yankees and there was no time off. One famous story is that of how Steinbrenner wanted to dictate a press release and could not wait. The team's PR director, about to shower, took dictation writing the release with his finger on a bathroom mirror.

Steinbrenner took out most of his frustrations on his managers, most of whom didn't last very long. Steinbrenner employed 15 different managers, with some serving multiple stints. Billy Martin had five turns, but after the first one, none lasted more than a season. In nine of Steinbrenner's first 18 seasons as owner, the Yankees made at least one in-season managerial move, including four out of five years from 1978 to 1982 and three years in a row from 1988 to 1990.

Steinbrenner's tenure was controversial. In 1974, he was suspended for two years for pleading guilty to making an illegal campaign contribution to Richard Nixon's presidential campaign (the suspension was shortened to 15 months and Steinbrenner was later pardoned). In 1990, Steinbrenner was suspended again, after being caught trying to pay a gambler named Howie Spira for negative information on Winfield. The resulting suspension was initially a lifetime ban, though Steinbrenner was reinstated in 1993.

"It's important to remember that when he was suspended the second time, he wasn't beloved," said ESPN.com Yankees beat reporter Andrew Marchand. "But his suspension allowed the team to tank for a couple of years and build up the farm system. George wasn't around to trade the Core Four [Derek Jeter, Andy Pettitte, Mariano Rivera, and Jorge Posada] or Bernie Williams. By the time he came back, they were on the verge of winning. He came back to give the final push to put them over the top."

STEINBRENNER EFFECT: YANKEES' YEARLY OPENING DAY PAYROLL*

2000	$107.6M
2001	$112.3M
2002	$125.9M
2003	$152.7M
2004	$184.1M
2005	$208.3M

* Source: Cot's Baseball Contracts (baseballprospectus.com)

This time Steinbrenner spent, but did so carefully, listening to his advisors, such as Gene Michael, Bob Watson, and Brian Cashman. The Yankees weren't perfect in their splurging, but they were right more often than they were wrong. The team added Jimmy Key, David Cone, Tim Raines, Wade Boggs, Darryl Strawberry, and Cecil Fielder, who became integral to the Yankees' championship run.

And after the Yankees let Buck Showalter go, they hired Joe Torre as manager. Steinbrenner could have fired Torre on many occasions, but didn't.

The reward for this was a run of four championships in five years and attendance that surpassed 4 million fans in the last four years the team played at old Yankee Stadium.

The Yankees are by far the most valuable franchise in the sport, with *Forbes* estimating their value at more than $3 billion. They also made a significant amount by creating their own TV network, YES.

Steinbrenner took the money he made and put it back into the franchise. The Yankees had baseball's highest Opening Day payroll every year from 1999 to 2013.

Steinbrenner mellowed a bit as well. He hosted *Saturday Night Live* and enjoyed being lampooned on *Seinfeld.* He could dish it out as well as take it.

"I was in Tampa in 2004 [rehabbing an injury], and he was checking in on everybody," said former Yankees reliever Steve Karsay. "My locker was in the coaches' room. I was watching the Yankees on TV, getting dressed, he came over and said 'Hey Steve, how's it going?' I thought, *Wow, he knows my name.* He asked me, 'You ever play hockey? [Response: Yes], basketball [Yes], football [Yes]. Well you sure don't play baseball!'"

There was also a positive side to Steinbrenner. When the going was good, he treated you well. Bottles of champagne as birthday gifts weren't unusual. Steinbrenner was also known to be charitable for those dealing with illnesses or family tragedy, taking care of the necessary expenses for those in need, and giving pep talks to ill friends.

It was hard to know when you were going to see that Steinbrenner and when you would see the one that caused others to fear him.

"He's about as complex a person as I've ever covered," said former *New York Times* Yankees beat writer Claire Smith. "The George Steinbrenner that Bernie Williams called a second father to him will never be confused with the Steinbrenner who was so difficult to play for."

The Yankees won one last championship for Steinbrenner in 2009. He died in 2010, suffering a heart attack just after his 80th birthday.

The discussion on whether Steinbrenner is a Hall of Famer is a polarizing one. On one hand, the two suspensions and the sometimes tyrannical reign provide a strong case to deny him a vote when his name appears on the ballot. But then there's the argument from the perspective of the Yankees fan, such as this simplistic one offered by longtime fan Gregg Savarese.

"He made baseball better than what it was."

Yogi Berra Won 12 World Series as a Yankees Player and Coach

It can be difficult to pick a favorite Yogi Berra quote; there are just so many to choose from. You may love the Zen surrealism of "If you come to a fork in the road, take it," or the head-scratching humor of "It's déjà vu all over again."

As Jayson Stark wrote in his book *The Stark Truth*, "About 98 percent of [Berra's] raging stardom has to do with Yogi's reputation as some kind of crazy, quote-machinist combo of Benjamin Franklin, Will Rogers, Mark Twain, Steven Wright, and Gandhi."

If I ask you to name a noteworthy moment in which Yogi Berra *appeared,* that's also fairly easy. There's his jump into Don Larsen's arms to celebrate the first perfect game in World Series history, the tag on Jackie Robinson on a steal-of-home attempt in the 1955 World Series (though Berra insists Robinson was out), the amazing catch Sandy Amoros made on his deep fly ball that turned into a double play in that same Series, or the backtracking to the fence to watch Bill Mazeroski's home run clear the left-field wall to end Game 7 of the 1960 World Series.

MOST WORLD SERIES TITLES WON AS PLAYER, YANKEES HISTORY

10	**9**	**8**	**7**	**7**	**7**	**7**
Yogi Berra	Joe DiMaggio	Bill Dickey	Hank Bauer	Frankie Crosetti	Mickey Mantle	Phil Rizzuto

But it's a lot harder to find a moment in which the *focus* is on Yogi. And that's unfortunate because Berra was a remarkable Yankee. He won 10 World Series rings as a player, the most of anyone, from 1946 to 1963, and two more with them as a coach in 1977 and 1978. (He also won one as a coach for the 1969 Mets, giving him 13 rings in total.)

Berra was lucky to be a Yankee in the first place, as *New York Times* writer Arthur Daley detailed. Not long after the Yankees signed Berra, Mel Ott offered to purchase him for the Giants for $50,000. General manager Larry MacPhail declined the offer.

"When I first set eyes on the kid in a tight blue suit, my heart sank," MacPhail said of Berra, who stood a small but stout, 5'7", 185 pounds. "But once I saw him with a bat in his hands, I lost all my regrets. He's a comer."

Berra was very much a comer. By spring training 1949, he impressed enough such that Casey Stengel said, "That kid could make me look like the greatest manager since John McGraw. I never saw a more natural hitter."

Berra won three AL MVPs and finished in the top four in balloting in seven consecutive seasons. In that span, he caught more than 90 percent of the Yankees' games.

He excelled both at hitting for power (358 home runs) and getting double plays (he ranks third all-time in double plays as a catcher). He rarely struck out (from 1955 to 1957: 81 home runs, 73 strikeouts) and rarely had a bad at-bat with men on base.

The website Baseball-Almanac.com has a thorough collection of quotes about Berra. Two stand out—one about his hitting, one about his fielding.

"Yogi Berra had the fastest bat I ever saw. He could hit a ball late that was already past him and take it out of the park."—12-year-major-leaguer Hector Lopez.

"Why has our pitching been so great? Our catcher, that's why. He looks cumbersome, but he's quick as a cat."—Stengel.

Stark named him both the most underrated catcher of all-time and the second-most underrated Yankees player of all-time.

Tops among Berra's best moments is Game 7 of the 1956 World Series, a hard-fought rematch of a Series won by the Dodgers

MOST WORLD SERIES HITS

Yogi Berra	71
Mickey Mantle	59
Frankie Frisch	58

MOST WORLD SERIES GAMES PLAYED

75	65	54	53	53	52	51
Yogi Berra	Mickey Mantle	Elston Howard	Gil McDougald	Hank Bauer	Phil Rizzuto	Joe DiMaggio

the year before. The Dodgers led two games to none before the Yankees took the next three (the third of which was Larsen's perfect game). The Dodgers stayed alive by winning Game 6 by a score of 1–0.

The year before, Johnny Podres shut out the Yankees 2–0 in Game 7 (with Amoros' catch robbing Berra of a potential game-tying hit). Berra ensured that would not happen again. In the first inning, he came up with a man on second, after Billy Martin and Mickey Mantle both struck out, and hit a two-run home run against Dodgers 27-game winner Don Newcombe.

In the third inning, again with two out, Berra hit another two-run home run. The Yankees (or you could say the Berras) were up 4–0 and never looked back on the way to a 9–0 win. Berra finished the Series with 10 RBIs, which at the time was the most ever by a Yankees player in a World Series (Bobby Richardson and Mantle surpassed him with 12 and 11, respectively, in 1960).

Berra was inspired by a conversation he had with his mother, who was in the hospital in St. Louis.

"I talked to mom Monday night [after Larsen's perfect game]," he told reporters after the game. "She asked me to hit a home run [in Game 6]. I tried my darndest, but I couldn't do it. So I got two today."

Berra had a penchant for hitting big home runs. He hit seven walk-off homers in his career.

The best of those came on September 16, 1955, when his game-winning home run against the Red Sox capped a ninth-inning rally

MOST CAREER WALK-OFF HR, YANKEES HISTORY (ENTERING 2016)

Mickey Mantle 12

Babe Ruth 11

Yogi Berra 7

and moved the Yankees into a tie for first place with nine games left in their season. The Yankees turned what was a three-game winning streak into an eight-gamer and topped the Indians by three games for the pennant.

AP's Ed Wilks wrote, "The patent for the big home run still belongs to the New York Yankees."

Another story that day tells of a fan asking the person sitting next to him, "Where are these money guys I keep reading about on the Yankees?" when the ninth inning started. After the Yankees tied the game, the seatmate noted, "It's all over. Berra's up."

What made that man so prescient?

Consider this stat: Berra hit five game-tying or go-ahead home runs in the ninth inning that season. That likely had a lot to do with why he won his third MVP.

It also may have had something to do with another Berra-ism of which many are fond:

"It ain't over till it's over."

Don Larsen Throws a 97-Pitch Perfect Game in the World Series

Don Larsen's World Series perfect game against the Brooklyn Dodgers on October 8, 1956, was as impressive as it was unlikely.

And though Larsen gets a lot of credit for being the pitcher (as he should), his accomplishment was truly a team effort.

The first person to merit mention for his help is pitching coach Jim Turner who worked with Larsen to change his delivery to one with no windup (and instead just a rock back, step forward, and throw).

The move, implemented in the season's final month, made Larsen a harder pitcher to hit. In $34\frac{2}{3}$ innings in September, Larsen allowed only 15 hits and two runs.

It also made him a little wilder. The Larsen that showed up for his start in Game 2 of the 1956 World Series was the wild one. In $1\frac{2}{3}$ innings, he walked four and was charged with four runs.

Catcher Yogi Berra worked with Larsen and seemed to know exactly the right pitch for every situation of Game 5. Against a Dodgers lineup that featured four Hall of Famers (the most to ever be on the losing end of a perfect game), Berra had Larsen establish his curveball in the first inning and the pitch was a nasty one. It made Larsen's fastball even better, as evidenced by the wild hacks some hitters (most notably Gil Hodges) took against it in the second inning.

"Don Larsen has what they call in the trade a sneaky fastball," said Yankees announcer Mel Allen, who was broadcasting the game on TV that day with Vin Scully. "It is not the fastest ball... but he'll play around with you, suddenly sneak it in, and it jumps on you."

In **34²/₃ innings** in September, Larsen allowed only 15 hits and two runs.

The Yankees defense did quite a bit for Larsen. In the second inning, Jackie Robinson led off by smashing a line drive that caromed off third baseman Andy Carey. Had the ball bounced off his hand and along the third-base line, it would have been a sure hit. But this one caromed right to shortstop Gil McDougald, who threw Robinson out at first on a very close play.

As the game went along it was evident that the weather was helping both Larsen and Dodgers pitcher Sal Maglie. Shadows over the field in the early afternoon made it hard for hitters to see, as did the fact that the batter's eye (the black canvas backdrop designed to provide a good hitting background) was removed to

DON LARSEN IN 1956

	April–August	September
ERA	3.91	0.52
K per 9	4.7	7.0
Opp BA	.219	.130

"I think about it maybe 10 to 15 times a day."

—Don Larsen on his perfect game (2012)

accommodate more fans. Each pitcher set the side down in order in the first three innings.

Each team's best hitter got one great swing in the fourth inning. The difference was that though Duke Snider jumped on a Larsen pitch and pummeled it foul, Mickey Mantle timed a slow Maglie curve and hit it into the bleachers to put the Yankees ahead 1–0. The Dodgers employed a defensive shift, the kind you typically see nowadays, to stop Mantle, but to no avail.

Mantle made another contribution in the top of the fifth. Hodges got a much better swing, hitting a fly into the left-center gap, but Mantle raced over and after about a dozen steps reached out to make the backhand catch.

The batter after Hodges, Sandy Amoros, brought the crowd to its feet with a powerful drive down the right-field line, but the ball landed in the seats as a harmless foul.

"This has been a game that has been just spectacular," Allen said. "Hearts have been jumping into throats and mouths all the way."

Larsen helped on the offensive end, by getting down a sixth-inning bunt with two strikes, advancing Carey to second. Carey scored on Hank Bauer's RBI hit.

McDougald made a second really good play in the seventh inning, with a nice pick of a short hop on Gilliam's grounder to short.

In the eighth, it seemed as if the Dodgers were trying to break Larsen's concentration. With an 0–2 count, Robinson stepped out of the batter's box to get something out of his eye, then took a few extra seconds before returning. Undaunted, Larsen got Robinson to ground back to the mound.

Carey, who couldn't corral a line drive earlier, got a second chance and made the most of it. He snagged Hodges' ankle-high line drive for the next out.

Coincidentally, two years earlier, Carey had broken up a Larsen no-hitter with two outs in the eighth. Now he was extending one through two outs in the eighth in the World Series.

Amoros followed with a harmless fly to center.

Larsen was three outs away.

When the time came, Scully began by referring to it as "the most dramatic ninth inning in the history of baseball."

Larsen was not fazed by the moment. Carl Furillo tried to throw off Larsen's timing by stepping back out of the box prior to a 1–2 pitch. That didn't work. Furillo flied to right.

Dodgers catcher Roy Campanella, a future Hall of Famer, hit a line drive off the facade of the upper deck that was foul, then followed that with a weak four-hop grounder that second baseman Billy Martin handled easily.

A 300-TO-1 SHOT COMES THROUGH

It is early afternoon on the campus of Vanderbilt University and a baseball fan named Jim Bowers of Helena, Arkansas, is hanging out with a Mississippian, Jack Williams, who happens to be a Brooklyn Dodgers fan. They are watching or perhaps listening to Game 5 of the 1956 World Series between the Yankees and the Brooklyn Dodgers.

The first batter of the game was Jim Gilliam, and after Gilliam struck out looking on a curve with some nasty spin, Bowers felt rather bold.

He turns to his friend and says something to the effect of: "I'll wager you 300-to-1 odds that Larsen pitches a perfect game. I'll put up a quarter."

We're guessing that Williams laughed. But being a loyal Dodgers fan, he wanted to show some loyalty, so he agreed to the friendly wager.

As the Associated Press reported, Williams sheepishly paid off the bet nine innings later.

"The million-to-one shot came in. Hell froze over..."

—Shirley Povich's lead in his game story, *Washington Post*

The final man for Larsen was left-handed pinch-hitter Dale Mitchell, a six-time .300 hitter who was in his final major league season.

"Yankee Stadium is shivering in its concrete foundation right now," Scully said.

Larsen was shivering too. He told reporters afterward: "I was so weak in the knees out there in the ninth inning, I thought I was going to faint."

Larsen fell behind 1–0, then got a called strike on the outside corner. On 1–1, Mitchell took a huge cut and missed by a mile, moving Larsen to within one strike of perfection.

Mitchell's timing was a little better, but not much, on the next pitch, which he fouled off to the left.

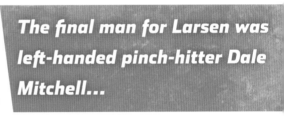

The final man for Larsen was left-handed pinch-hitter Dale Mitchell...

The final pitch of Larsen's perfect game is often considered a controversial one. But a viewing of the entire game (about eight innings exist on video) puts it into proper context.

Home-plate umpire Babe Pinelli had given both pitchers the outside corner-and-then-some the entire game. There were a couple of instances in which hitters appeared to say something to Pinelli, but the 22-year veteran was consistent in his call from start to finish.

Pinelli had also made it known that this was his final season as an umpire and this was his final game behind the plate.

On 1–2 Mitchell checked his swing on a pitch near the outside corner. Was that pitch much worse than the others that Pinelli had rung up for both pitchers throughout the day? Maybe, but not by much.

And was Mitchell able to hold his swing? Perhaps, but it's a very close call.

> *On 1–2 Mitchell checked his swing on a pitch near the outside corner.*

Pinelli immediately put his arm up for strike three. Perfection.

Berra sprinted to the mound and leapt into Larsen's arms. Pinelli walked away back to his locker room, taking one quick look at the Yankees' celebration.

"Boy, what a way to go out," Pinelli said.

Pinelli had the best view of Larsen that day.

But another person played a small part in Larsen's perfection by having no view at all.

Larsen's mother, Charlotte, followed through on a family superstition while home in La Jolla, California.

"I make it a rule never to watch Don when he pitches," she said. "Seems like every time I watch him, he loses. So I just don't do it.

"I didn't today and see what happened."

2 Perfect Games in 14 months

David Cone couldn't watch.

His teammate David Wells was pitching the game of his life and as outs continued being recorded in the last two innings without a baserunner reaching, he couldn't watch. He covered his face with his jacket and his eyes with his sunglasses.

Little did he know.

The Yankees are the only franchise to have its pitchers throw a perfect game in back-to-back seasons. The first was by Wells against the Minnesota Twins on May 17, 1998. The second was by Cone versus the Montreal Expos 14 months and one day later on July 18, 1999.

Wells' perfecto came on a day in which he said he was hungover. He looked very sharp in the bullpen, as pitching coach Mel Stottlemyre watched closely over a pitcher who entered with a 5.23 ERA.

"He had excellent, excellent stuff," Stottlemyre said afterward.

Wells had two pitches working *really* well from the start. He could hit the exact spot he wanted with his fastball (a hair off the outside corner), a pitch home-plate umpire Tim McClelland was calling a strike almost every time. Wells also had a nasty curveball.

David Wells entered his start with a 5.23 ERA, the highest season ERA for anyone entering his perfect-game start.

"It's almost as if the ball pauses in mid-air and then uh-oh, if you haven't reacted correctly, you're going to have a problem," Yankees announcer Ken Singleton said, describing the pitch.

There was one pitch in the first three innings that was a little dicey, a 3–2 fastball to catcher Javier Valentin in the top of the third that might have been high and inside, had Jorge Posada not framed it closer to the middle of the plate. McClelland called it strike three.

Wells got better as the game went on. In one stretch, he struck out six of eight hitters. Meanwhile, Bernie Williams provided the necessary offense, doubling in the second and scoring on a wild pitch, and then homering in the fourth inning.

A 2–0 lead was more than enough for Wells, who got through the middle three innings with ease.

There were a couple of stressful moments in the seventh. Wells fell behind Matt Lawton 2–0 before coaxing a harmless fly-out.

Wells then went 3–2 on Brent Gates, who hit a smash to first, right at Tino Martinez for the second out. Then, facing future Hall of Famer Paul Molitor, Wells fell behind 3–1. He threw a fastball that dinged the outside corner for strike two. He hit nearly the same spot with his next pitch, but maybe an inch or two farther away, and Molitor swung through it to end the inning.

"Once he got that one, he was gonna pitch the no-hitter," said Yankees manager Joe Torre.

It may have been a foregone conclusion to Torre, but not quite to the Yankees fielders, who had a four-run lead after the team scored twice in the seventh.

The first two outs of the eighth were a little antsy. Shortstop Derek Jeter nearly bobbled Marty Cordova's grounder, but was still able to get the out. Then, Ron Coomer, who entered the day with the highest batting average of anyone in baseball against Wells, hit a rocket to second that overpowered Chuck Knoblauch.

But since Coomer was slow, Knoblauch had time to knock the ball down, recover, and make the play. Alex Ochoa's pop to first ended that inning.

The ninth inning was one of the easiest ones of the game. Wells got Jon Shave to pop to right, struck out Valentin on a nasty curveball in the dirt, and got Pat Meares to fly out to right.

Wells became the second Yankees pitcher to throw a perfect game, joining Don Larsen. Amazingly, Larsen and Wells graduated from the same high school (Point Loma in San Diego).

On this afternoon, David Wells carried the Yankees to victory, and then they carried him off the field on their shoulders.

"Right now, I'm the happiest man on earth," said Wells.

Cone enjoyed the moment as well. When Wells came into the dugout, Cone, no longer obscured by jacket and glasses, told him to take a curtain call.

Cone longed for a game of his own like this. In 1996, he missed four months due to surgery to remove an aneurysm in his arm. In his first game back, he pitched seven no-hit innings, but was hooked due to a pitch limit.

It was nearly three years before Cone got another such chance. He'd make the most of it against the Expos. Larsen was in the ballpark for this one, there to honor Yogi Berra, who was being welcomed back to Yankee Stadium for the first time since being fired as manager in 1985.

There was plenty to celebrate on a Sunday in which the game-time temperature was 95 degrees, though the second batter of the game nearly rendered what followed moot.

Expos center-fielder Terry Jones hit a fly to right center that required Paul O'Neill to take four full strides and make a full extension with his gloved right hand to make the catch as he tumbled to the grass.

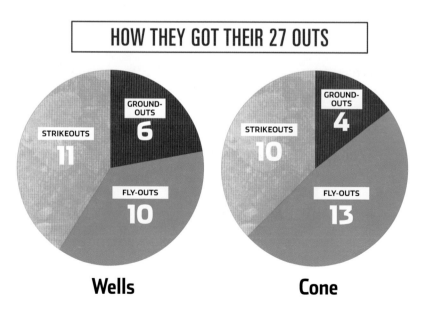

HOW THEY GOT THEIR 27 OUTS

Wells
- GROUND-OUTS 6
- STRIKEOUTS 11
- FLY-OUTS 10

Cone
- GROUND-OUTS 4
- STRIKEOUTS 10
- FLY-OUTS 13

COMPARING THE PERFECT GAMES

	Wells	Cone
Game-time temperature	59 degrees	95 degrees
Pitches	120	88
Strikeouts	11	10
Attendance	49,820	41,930

From there, Cone dominated, and the innings were quick. He averaged fewer than 10 pitches per inning for the game. Cone had a good fastball, but more importantly, his breaking pitches were perfect.

Cone repeatedly got Expos hitters to chase pitches that were in the opposite batter's box. He survived waiting through a five-run Yankees' second inning and a 33-minute rain delay in the third.

"When he went three up and three down in the fourth inning, I was thinking no-hitter," Torre said afterward.

By the fifth inning, Cone's perfection was the talk of the broadcast booth. "He pitches a perfect game on Yogi Berra and Don Larsen Day? That can't happen. No way!" said Yankees broadcaster Tim McCarver.

As Cone took the mound for the sixth, McCarver also noted, "I can see it in his body language. He's going to be very disappointed if the Expos get a hit."

There was no disappointment for any Yankee that day. Cone mowed through the Expos lineup in the seventh and eighth.

"Going into the latter innings, I thought, *This is it. This might be my last chance to do something like this*," Cone said afterward. "Believe me, my heart was pumping. I could feel it through my uniform."

David Cone's perfect game was the last of his 22 career shutouts.

In the ninth, Cone got Expos catcher Chris Widger to strike out on three straight breaking balls. Pinch-hitter Ryan McGuire hit a fly to left on another curve. Ricky Ledee, perhaps a little nervous, had to change his route after a couple of steps in, but recovered to make a basket catch.

That left Orlando Cabrera, who popped to third on a 1–1 pitch. Cone went to his knees, put his hands on his head, and flopped on top of catcher Joe Girardi.

This time it was Cone being carried off on his teammates' shoulders and getting the standing ovation. He also took a congratulatory phone call from Wells, who now was with the Blue Jays.

There was one person in the ballpark who knew how both Davids were feeling at the time of their perfection. He repeated what he said a year earlier.

"I'm sure David is going to think about this every day of his life," Larsen said.

ALLIE REYNOLDS PITCHES TWO NO-HITTERS IN 1951

Allie Reynolds was a good pitcher and a clutch pitcher and has the distinction of being the only Yankees pitcher to throw multiple no-hitters, both coming in 1951.

Reynolds' first came in a matchup with future Hall of Famer Bob Feller and the Indians. The second was against the Red Sox and had a little drama at the end.

With two outs in the ninth, Reynolds coaxed a popup from Ted Williams, but Yogi Berra dropped it in foul territory, giving Williams another chance.

Undaunted, Reynolds induced another popup from Williams and this one Berra hung on to for the final out

Reynolds didn't throw any postseason no-hitters, but he was a great postseason pitcher. He was 7–2 with four saves in the World Series and was a member of six championship teams.

"You can make a case for Reynolds as a Hall of Famer," said baseball historian Lyle Spatz. "There's a fine line between Hall of Very Good and Hall of Famer and Reynolds is right on that cusp."

Mike Mussina's 8 $^2/_3$ Perfect Innings

Mike Stanton was fascinated with teammate Mike Mussina's control in bullpen sessions in between starts.

"You could watch him throw and you'd be amazed at his command," Stanton said. "And at the end of it, he's ticked off because he missed his spot on two of his pitches. He was the epitome of a perfectionist."

It is a moment of imperfection for which Mussina is probably best remembered as a Yankee.

That refers to September 2, 2001, in which Mussina and former-Yankee-turned–Red Sox pitcher David Cone participated in one of the greatest pitchers duels in Yankees history.

The teams entered the game at Fenway Park in vastly different states. The Yankees were in first place and at the beginning of a stretch in which they won 11 of 12 games. The Red Sox had lost seven in a row.

The nationally televised *Sunday Night Baseball* game was the perfect stage for the 32-year-old Mussina, who was in the first year of a six-year contract with the Yankees after 10 great seasons with the Baltimore Orioles and a highly successful college career at Stanford.

"Mussina is arguably the greatest free-agent signing the Yankees have ever had," said YES Network head researcher Jeff Quagliata.

Mussina entered the day in a groove, with a 1.55 ERA in his previous four starts.

Mussina's strength was that he got a lot of strikeouts and rarely walked anyone. He currently has the second-best strikeout-to-walk rate in Yankees history, just behind Mariano Rivera.

"Facing Mike Mussina was like battling seasickness," said former major leaguer Doug Glanville, who went 4-for-15 against him. "He would go up in the zone then down in the zone and repeat. High fastball, nasty curve, time-warp change-up. It was a battle in four dimensions. Up-down. In-out. Fast-slow. Nausea-headache. The best strategy was Alka-Seltzer."

Cone, formerly a Yankees star, was a formidable opponent. He knew the hitters in the Yankees lineup well, having played with them from 1995 to 2000. Cone had also thrown a perfect game for the Yankees two years earlier.

Mussina was throwing hard, often hitting 95 mph with his fastball, and with a great changeup and nasty knuckle-curve that dropped dirt-bound to elude hitters' bats. After Cone pitched a scoreless first inning, stranding Derek Jeter on second base, Mussina got the Red Sox on a pair of strikeouts and a lineout to short.

Thus began a pattern that lasted through eight

MOST WINS IN FINAL MLB SEASON POST–BLACK SOX SCANDAL (SINCE 1921)

Sandy Koufax (1966)	27
Mike Mussina (2008)	20
Britt Burns (1985)	18

MOST K PER BB, YANKEES HISTORY

Mariano Rivera	4.10
Mike Mussina	4.02
David Wells	4.01

MOST CONSECUTIVE SEASONS WITH AT LEAST 10 WINS

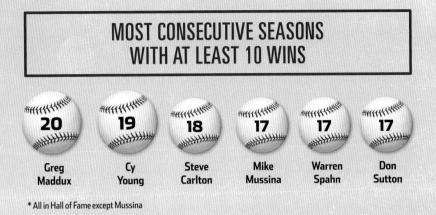

20	19	18	17	17	17
Greg Maddux	Cy Young	Steve Carlton	Mike Mussina	Warren Spahn	Don Sutton

* All in Hall of Fame except Mussina

innings. Cone allowed a base runner in seven of them, but none crossed the plate.

Mussina allowed nothing. No runs, no hits, no walks, and no errors.

In the top of the ninth inning, the Yankees broke through, thanks to an error by Red Sox second baseman Lou Merloni and Enrique Wilson's subsequent RBI double. The Yankees went to the bottom of the ninth up 1–0.

The first two hitters in the home ninth went down, albeit with a little stress. Troy O'Leary grounded to first, where Yankees reserve Clay Bellinger preserved the bid with a diving stop. Merloni struck out.

Then Red Sox manager Joe Kerrigan did something odd. He sent up Carl Everett to pinch hit for his catcher, Joe Oliver.

Everett was picked 10 spots ahead of Mussina, by the Yankees, in the 1990 MLB Amateur Draft. He was great in 1999, when he hit .325 with the Astros, and 2000, when he hit .300 with 34 home runs in his first year in Boston.

But in the 20 games prior to this pinch-hitting appearance, Everett was hitting .187. Not only that, he was 1-for-9 with seven strikeouts in his career against Mussina (all of which occurred that season).

It looked like Mussina was going to get Everett again. He went ahead 1–2 then went with a high fastball. Everett got his quick bat around on it and lined a single to left-center field.

"I'm going to think about that pitch until I retire," Mussina said. "It's probably just not meant to be."

Mussina said that for good reason. Close but not quite was an important part of who he was as a pitcher.

"That game sums up his career and his Hall of Fame candidacy," said Patrick Bohn, a Yankees fan from Ithaca, New York, who along with his friend Ryan Vooris, has started a website promoting Mussina's greatness (musinahof.com). "It was so close to being there...and then it wasn't."

Mussina came close...many times. He took a perfect game into the ninth inning against the Indians in 1997, a no-hit bid into the eighth inning against the Brewers that same season, and a perfect game into the eighth inning against the Tigers in 1998.

He couldn't quite close them out. Mussina threw 10 regular-season complete games in which he allowed two hits or fewer, the second-most of anyone since the start of the 1990 season.

Mussina was also an integral part of two of the Yankees' best wins of the 21st century. He threw seven scoreless innings in Game 3 of the 2001 ALDS against the Athletics, a 1–0 win best remembered for "The Flip" by Derek Jeter that saved the tying run from scoring.

MOST COMPLETE GAMES, TWO HITS OR FEWER, SINCE 1990*

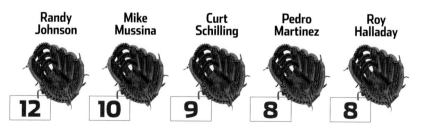

Randy Johnson	Mike Mussina	Curt Schilling	Pedro Martinez	Roy Halladay
12	10	9	8	8

* CG of 9 IP or more

He got a no-decision in the other one, which required pitching three scoreless innings and escaping a first-and-third no-out jam in Game 7 of the 2003 ALCS against the Red Sox in the first relief appearance of his career. The Yankees overcame a four-run deficit to win that game on Aaron Boone's walk-off home run. They lost the World Series in six games to the Marlins, though Mussina won his only start in that Fall Classic.

"I'm going to think about that pitch until I retire," Mussina said.

Mussina never achieved the perfection he was seeking, but he had about as perfect an ending to a career as a pitcher could have.

On the final day of the 2008 season, he pitched six scoreless innings against the Red Sox in Fenway Park to earn his 20th victory. He became the oldest pitcher to reach 20 wins for the first time (age 39).

There was a near-miss aspect to this as well, as the Yankees won the World Series the year after Mussina retired.

Mussina finished his career with a 270–153 record, with 123 of those wins coming for the Yankees. He also won seven Gold Glove Awards. He was able to retire that off-season with the satisfaction of knowing he'd achieved just about everything he could.

"His career has been overlooked and underappreciated," Bohn said. "I hope he gets into the Hall of Fame. And I hope that people realize how great he was."

Orlando Hernandez Wins His First 8 Postseason Decisions

Lots of pitchers with great skills falter under the stress and tension of the postseason. Orlando Hernandez, also known as "El Duque," never had that issue with the Yankees. He thrived like no one else who came before him.

Hernandez set a major league record by winning his first eight postseason decisions.

His was a remarkable story. El Duque was a historically successful pitcher in Cuba who won Olympic gold and set national records for winning percentage, but he was banned from the sport in his homeland not long after his half-brother, Livan, defected to the United States.

Orlando Hernandez eventually left behind his family as well, fleeing the island on a boat on Christmas Day, 1997. Though his boat was eventually stopped by the U.S. Coast Guard and Hernandez appeared headed back to Cuba, he was eventually able to gain asylum in Costa Rica, after which he signed with the Yankees.

Joe Torre was very thankful for the presence of Orlando Hernandez in the Yankees' postseason rotation.

Orlando Hernandez During Postseason Winning Streak

Games	10
W–L	8–0
ERA	1.90
Opp BA	.180
IP	66 1/3
Hits Allowed	42
Strikeouts	59

Hernandez won with a high leg kick, multiple arm angles, and great off-speed stuff. He became an immediate fan favorite, going 12–4 with a 3.13 ERA in 1998 after only a couple of months pitching in the minor leagues.

El Duque showed an ability to bounce back from tough days. After Hernandez allowed 10 runs to the Angels in a July start, he allowed three runs over 33 innings in his next four starts combined.

The game for which Hernandez is most heralded is Game 4 of the 1998 ALCS. The Yankees may have been a dominant team that season, recording 114 victories, but they trailed the Indians, the team that knocked them out of the playoffs the previous season, two games to one.

Hernandez, who had only 21 major league starts to his credit, was tasked with evening the series against a pitcher whose windup was influential on Hernandez's approach to pitching, Dwight Gooden.

The Indians never had a chance.

Hernandez held Cleveland to three hits and two walks in seven scoreless innings as the Yankees knotted the series with a 4–0 win. They took the next two contests to advance to the World Series.

"I knew we had pretty much a must-win situation," Hernandez said after the game. "I had pressure, but I had no fear. I've been through many difficult times in my life on the field and off of the field and I knew that I would be able to handle it."

Hernandez's next start came in the World Series against the Padres, and the Yankees gave him plenty of support. The Padres didn't score until the Yankees had seven runs, and Hernandez limited the damage to one run in seven innings.

The next year, Hernandez won a team-high 17 games and was rewarded by Joe Torre as the choice to start Game 1 of each of the three postseason series. He made that choice pay off. In the ALDS, he beat the Rangers 8–0, allowing only two hits in eight innings.

Hernandez won ALCS MVP honors with two more solid starts in a five-game series win against the Red Sox, but it was in Game 1 of the World Series in Atlanta in which he was at his best.

He struck out seven of the first 10 hitters he faced and allowed only one hit over seven innings, earning a 4–1 win when the Yankees rallied for four runs in the eighth inning.

Hernandez finished that game with 10 strikeouts, one of two times he struck out at least 10 in a World Series game. The only other Yankee with multiple such games is Bob Turley.

Hernandez earned three more wins in the 2000 postseason against the Athletics and Mariners before the streak (and a 14-game Yankees World Series winning streak) came to an end with a loss to the Mets in Game 3 of the World Series. Even in that game, he pitched well, striking out 12 in 7⅓ innings.

MOST STRIKOUTS PER 9—WORLD SERIES HISTORY*

Orlando Hernandez	Josh Beckett	Tim Lincecum	Bob Gibson
11.3	10.8	10.4	10.2

* Minimum 20 IP

MOST CONSECUTIVE POSTSEASON DECISIONS WON, YANKEES HISTORY

Orlando Hernandez	Mariano Rivera	Red Ruffing	Lefty Gomez
8	6	6	6

The Yankees won that Fall Classic, giving El Duque three World Series titles in three major league seasons.

But he wasn't quite done yet.

In Game 4 of the 2001 ALDS, with the Yankees trailing the Athletics two games to one, Hernandez was called upon to keep the season alive. Hernandez struggled most of that regular season, finishing with a 4.85 ERA in 17 appearances.

But he was in top form in the first inning, when the Athletics had first and third with nobody out. He escaped and gutted out $5\frac{2}{3}$ innings of two-run ball to get a win.

Then, in Game 4 of the 2001 World Series, he matched Curt Schilling pitch for pitch for $6\frac{1}{3}$ innings, allowing only one run. He got a no-decision, but the Yankees won on Derek Jeter's home run.

The pitcher who won that game was Mariano Rivera, who years later put it quite simply when telling the story of El Duque's greatness.

"When you needed to win a big game," Rivera said in a documentary about Hernandez and his brother, "that's the guy you go to."

Roger Clemens Gets Win No. 300 with Yankees

There are some who might prefer to forget that Roger Clemens was ever a Yankee.

But his presence in pinstripes was unforgettable. Clemens was a part of some memorable teams and moments in the six seasons he pitched for the Yankees.

Clemens was a great pitcher early in his career with the Red Sox. One of the most satisfying Yankees victories of the 1980s was the day in 1987 when they rallied from 9–0 down against him to win. Toppling a defending Cy Young Award winner at his peak *and* beating the Red Sox as well was highly satisfying.

The second act of Clemens' career came after he went 10–13 for the Red Sox in 1996 and he subsequently signed with the Toronto Blue Jays. The next two seasons, at ages 34 and 35, Clemens returned to the form he showed as a 23-year-old. He went 41–13 with a 2.33 ERA and won two Cy Youngs.

Then in a stunning move in spring 1999, the Yankees, coming off a 114-win season the year before, obtained Clemens for David Wells, Graeme Lloyd, and Homer Bush.

ROGER CLEMENS IN THE WORLD SERIES WITH THE YANKEES

W-L ⟶ **3-0**

ERA ⟶ **1.50**

Starts ⟶ **5**

K-BB ⟶ **37-6**

IP ⟶ **36**

"We're acquiring the Michael Jordan of pitchers," general manager Brian Cashman said.

Much of what Clemens did in New York is asterisked, tainted by the allegations in the Mitchell Report that he used performance-enhancing drugs (which Clemens has repeatedly denied). Thus, every one of his 175 appearances with the Yankees receives a different level of scrutiny.

The first year's worth weren't so great. It took Clemens a little while to warm up to New York. He pitched to a 4.60 ERA in his first season, though he redeemed himself in the eyes of fans with a win over the Atlanta Braves that clinched the 1999 World Series.

Clemens was better the following season, going 13–8 with a 3.70 ERA, but nearly cost the Yankees a trip to the LCS. He pitched poorly in a Game 1 loss to the Oakland Athletics in the LDS and got pummeled for six runs in five innings in an 11–1 loss in Game 4. But he put his stamp on that season in Game 4 of the 2000 ALCS against the Seattle Mariners.

His make-good came in the form of arguably the greatest start in postseason history—a 15-strikeout, one-hit shutout, a 5–0 victory.

Baseball historian/sabermetrician Bill James devised a formula for Game Score, which rates a pitcher's starts, usually on a 0–100 scale. Clemens ranks first in postseason history with a 98. Yankees manager Joe Torre described it in two words: "total dominance."

"Tonight was special," Clemens said. "The ball was jumping out of my hands. I had three pitches working today and that makes a big difference."

When Clemens pitched, he owned the mound, owned the plate, and tried to own the opposing hitter. He won with intimidation.

"He was like a ferocious bull," said ESPN.com Yankees beat writer Andrew Marchand. "He was so tenacious about how he went about his business. He treated it like he was in a bullring and he wanted to take out the matador."

Clemens was that good and that intimidating in his next start, Game 2 of the 2000 World Series against the Mets, pitching eight scoreless innings, allowing two hits and striking out nine.

That and much of Clemens' Yankees career is overshadowed by Clemens' own doing—the bizarre sequence in which Mike Piazza broke his bat on a foul ball, and Clemens picked up a shard that bounced to him and threw it at Piazza, later claiming, "I thought it was the ball."

"It was so over the top absurd, complete with the most ridiculous excuse ever," said Jason Rosenberg, a writer for the Yankees blog, It's About the Money, Stupid. "Why would you throw the ball toward the player and the dugout?"

PHIL NIEKRO ALSO GOT WIN NO. 300 WITH YANKEES

Phil Niekro is the *other* pitcher to reach 300 wins with the Yankees. And he couldn't be more different than Roger Clemens.

Niekro won by softly throwing a knuckleball that danced and dove. Niekro was 45 when he joined the Yankees, but was still effective with his signature pitch. He won 16 games in each of his two seasons with the team.

His final start for them came against the Blue Jays on the final day of the 1985 season, a day after the Blue Jays eliminated the Yankees from playoff contention.

Niekro failed in four previous attempts to record his 300th win, but he put together something special. He went the distance in an 8–0 win.

What made this game distinct was that Niekro didn't throw a knuckleball until there were two outs in the ninth inning. Niekro dropped three knucklers in for strikes and pounded his fist into his glove to celebrate.

"I don't think the 1927 Yankees would have hit him today," said Blue Jays manager Bobby Cox.

MOST STRIKEOUTS ALL-TIME

Nolan Ryan	5,714
Randy Johnson	4,875
Roger Clemens	4,672
Steve Carlton	4,136
Bert Blyleven	3,701

Clemens did everything possible to help the Yankees to a fourth straight title in 2001, when he went 20–3, won a club-record 16 straight decisions and his sixth Cy Young, and started Game 7 of the World Series against the Diamondbacks. But the Yankees lost to the Diamondbacks.

In 2003, Clemens chased the historic 300-win plateau. He got off to a great start that season, winning six of his first eight decisions, which put him at 299 wins going into a start against the Red Sox.

Clemens couldn't get 300 against his former team, which clubbed him for eight runs. It looked like he'd get there his next time out against the Tigers, but after being given a 7–1 lead, he got rocked for five runs in the fifth and the bullpen couldn't protect the advantage.

There was another near-miss against the Cubs, as Clemens fought through 6⅓ innings, before leaving with two men on and a 1–0 lead. Cubs first baseman Eric Karros hit the first pitch from Yankees reliever Juan Acevedo for a three-run homer, giving Clemens a loss instead of a win.

Clemens finally reached his goal on June 13 against the Cardinals. He struck out 10 in 6⅔ innings and left with a 3–2 lead that the bullpen held up. He not only got his 300th win in that game, but also his 4,000th career strikeout. There were a few good moments with the Yankees after that, but this was as good as it could get for him.

"It couldn't have been better," Clemens said.

Aaron Small's
10–0 Miracle

In 1929, veteran left-hander Tom Zachary went 12–0 for the Yankees, setting the major league record for most wins in a season without a loss.

This was a surprise, given that Zachary posted that season a year after putting up a 4.98 ERA.

But Zachary's surprise season has nothing on Aaron Small's 2005.

Small has the second-best perfect season in Yankees history, a memorable and miraculous 10–0 record. It is the only time a pitcher has recorded double-digit wins with no losses in the last 30 years.

Small's story is one of perseverance, belief, and belief.

"I look back and sometimes I have to ask myself if that really happened to me," he said.

That season was Small's 17th in professional baseball, but his major-league success was limited. He pitched for four major league teams in five seasons from 1994 to 1998 as an average middle reliever. From 1999 to 2004, his time in the big leagues totaled eight games, in which he allowed 16 runs in 16⅔ innings.

"I always felt like I could get big league hitters out," he said. "That's why I continued to bounce around Triple-A."

In 2005, at age 33 (coincidentally the same age as Zachary in 1929), Small went to big-league camp with the Yankees. When he walked into the spring training facility in Tampa, he felt like he was walking into Cooperstown.

"Jeter, A-Rod, Bernie, Mariano, Posada," he said. "I thought, *What am I doing here?*"

Small was assigned to Triple-A. At midseason, he was pitching for the Columbus Clippers and recovering from a groin injury. He was 1–4 with a 4.96 ERA when he went to work in mid-July and saw his name was crossed off the lineup card.

Small was summoned to Clippers manager Bucky Dent's office and figured that he was going to be released. Small is very religious and he thinks that what happened was a moment of divine intervention.

"I was ready to walk away from baseball that day, but God had other plans," Small said.

Dent had good news. With multiple starting pitchers injured, the Yankees needed a fill-in starter for a game against the Rangers and Small was their choice. Small hadn't started a major league game since 1996.

> *Small was a little shaky in his next three starts, **allowing 13 runs in 18 innings,** but was helped by an offense that totaled 29 runs to help him get to 9-0.*

Small's former high school teammate Jason Giambi was among those who welcomed him back to the big leagues. Giambi hit two homers and Small pitched alright—5$\frac{1}{3}$ innings of three-run ball.

Small was still with the team three days later when Joe Torre used him to eat an inning out of the bullpen against the Angels.

The Yankees gave him another shot against the Twins five days after that. He pitched better, going seven innings, allowing three runs, and retiring the last 12 hitters he faced. The Yankees won 6–3 and Small was now 2–0.

AARON SMALL

	1994–2004	2005
W–L	15–10	10–0
ERA	5.49	3.20
WHIP	1.69	1.25

Those 12 outs got the attention of Joe Torre and Mel Stottlemyre, who liked what they saw.

"I definitely was not a power pitcher," Small said. "That year in New York, I learned how to pitch with what I had. I had a fastball around 86 mph, that I could get to 90 occasionally. I moved the ball around and changed speeds. I got the eye levels [of the hitters] to be different. I learned how to be a pitcher and not just a thrower."

Now Small was in a groove. He allowed one run in 6⅔ innings in a win over the Blue Jays, then pitched seven innings of one-run ball against the White Sox.

Jaret Wright's return from injury put Small in the bullpen and he picked up two more wins there; the first came via a walk-off home run by Bernie Williams (with whom Small often talked guitar playing), the second with four scoreless innings against the Mariners.

The Yankees shuttled Small back into the rotation after that one and were rewarded. On September 3, Small shut out the Athletics in front of a crowd that included his wife and two children. Small was demonstrative on the mound that day, psyched to have that kind of moment.

"Something I had to learn over the years was to be a little more fiery," he said. "I teach kids that now [Small runs a baseball academy in Tennessee]. You want your mechanics to be good, don't get me wrong. But you want to have some fire and some passion about what you're doing."

When you're going as well as Small was, sometimes you catch a few breaks, too. Small was a little shaky in his next three starts, allowing 13 runs in 18 innings, but was helped by an offense that totaled 29 runs to help him get to 9–0. He got a well-deserved standing ovation from a Yankee Stadium crowd of more than 55,000 after getting through 6$\frac{1}{3}$ innings against the division-leading Red Sox.

"Your knees start shaking when you take that in," Small said.

Small got put back in the bullpen near the end of the regular season, but after throwing 6$\frac{2}{3}$ scoreless innings in relief of Wright against the Blue Jays, the Yankees gave him a shot to start and get his 10th win, which he did, beating the Orioles at Camden Yards.

Small's magic ran out with a loss in relief in Game 3 of the ALDS against the Angels, but he got to have one more moment to remember.

With the Yankees losing 5–0 early in the game, an unhappy crowd started chanting "Aaron Small" when Randy Johnson was faltering.

Joe Torre made the move and Small responded by escaping a first-and-third no-out jam, much to the delight of the fans. Though he didn't know it at the time, that would be his last great highlight. His career ended the following season due to injuries and age.

"It was an incredible three months," he said. "I couldn't have scripted it any better. People use the word magical, if you want to use that. I say it was orchestrated by God for sure."

Joe Torre Manages Yankees to 4 Titles in 5 Years

They greeted him with "Clueless Joe."

That was the back page of the *New York Daily News* on November 3, 1995, the day after Joe Torre was introduced as the Yankees' newest manager.

The paper was harsh, largely because Torre seemed undaunted by the idea of dealing with George Steinbrenner. One headline inside the paper read "Crowning of a Puppet." Another said his taking the job was a "Torre-ble Mistake."

GM Bob Watson spoke highly of Torre's past, noting that he was well respected by his players in previous stops with the Mets, Braves, and Cardinals (where he made one playoff appearance in 14 seasons).

It's worth noting that in the upper-right corner of the back page, in a small box, was the headline "Go Nellie"—a reference to New York Knicks head coach Don Nelson and the start of the NBA season. Nelson's eventual fate was what everyone expected Torre's fate to be. Nellie didn't even make it through a full season in New York.

Torre lasted a dozen years with the Yankees, tied for the second-longest tenure in franchise history and by far the longest under

JOE TORRE AS MANAGER

Winning Percentage by Team

Yankees	.605
Dodgers	.533
Braves	.529
Cardinals	.498
Mets	.405

Steinbrenner's ownership. In that time he won 10 division titles, six pennants, and four World Series titles. His teams won at least 90 games 11 times and never won fewer than 87. The two years the Yankees didn't win the AL East, they finished second.

The difference between this job and the others that Torre had was in the talent on his roster. The Yankees were coming off a crushing defeat to the Mariners in the 1995 ALDS. But they had a strong combination of established stars and rising youngsters.

Torre's job was to let the players do theirs, stay out of the way, and serve as a buffer against harsh headlines.

"Players have always shown him respect," wrote Bill Madden in a scouting report of Torre, the day he was hired. Madden also noted: "He's a great communicator."

He earned that respect through both his actions and his words. Tino Martinez's go-to story about the 1996 season is of how he was facing the pressure of replacing Don Mattingly at first base and was slumping. Torre called Martinez into his office and gave his struggling first baseman the names of an Italian restaurant and a bottle of wine to order, and sent him away.

Martinez broke out of the slump, went on to drive in 117 runs that season, and played an integral role in helping the Yankees win the World Series that year and then three in a row from 1998 to 2000.

"Joe had a way of casually and cordially defusing things, both with the media and in his own clubhouse," said Andrew Marchand, who covered the Yankees for the *New York Post*. "I think his demeanor was perfect for New York."

DID YOU KNOW?

Joe Torre played in 2,209 games, the sixth-most of anyone who never reached the postseason.

Joe Torre got to celebrate his fourth title in five years against the first team that made him a major-league manager, the New York Mets.

Torre was great at dealing with both the stars and the role players.

He had a rule that if there was news about a player's status, he would not talk about it until the player had been informed. Torre inadvertently broke that rule when he let it slip that Aaron Small would be moving to the bullpen when Jaret Wright came off the disabled list. Torre sought Small out and apologized profusely.

"I respected him for that," said Small, who to this day refers to Torre as "The King of New York."

It was good to be king, because as Torre won, he won the fans and the media over. And that was great leverage to have in dealing with Steinbrenner, who had a long-standing history of giving his managers a hard time when things weren't going well, and then eventually dismissing them.

"Mr. Steinbrenner wanted to win every game," said former Yankees reliever Jeff Nelson. "Joe Torre took Mr. Steinbrenner's pressure away from us. He let us go out on the field and play to the best of our abilities."

Torre handled the stresses of managing in combination with the stresses of life. He managed through the 1996 World Series while his brother Frank was about to get a heart transplant. Joe Torre also survived prostate cancer while managing the team.

No one stays in the same position forever, and after the 2007 season, Torre moved on to take a job with the Dodgers, where he managed for three seasons. He moved on from managing to a job with Major League Baseball, where as an executive vice-president he's led the instituting of developments such as instant replay.

MOST POSTSEASON WINS

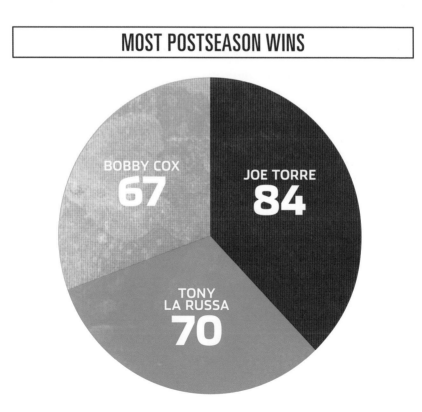

BOBBY COX
67

JOE TORRE
84

TONY
LA RUSSA
70

MOST WINS, AMERICAN LEAGUE TEAMS, FROM 1996 TO 2007*

1,173 Yankees

1,079 Red Sox

1,044 Athletics

*1996–2007: Joe Torre's tenure as Yankees manager

He is also an advocate against domestic violence with his Safe at Home Foundation.

In 2014, at age 74, Torre was inducted into the Baseball Hall of Fame.

"I'm here because of the New York Yankees," Torre said.

He closed his speech with this eloquent thought.

"There is a power to both patience and persistence. Baseball is a game of life. It's not perfect, but it feels like it is. That's the magic of it. We are responsible for giving it the respect it deserves. Our sport is part of the American soul and it's ours to borrow, just for a while. To take care of it for a time and then pass it on to the next generation; when I say 'us,' I mean us as managers, as players. If all of us who love baseball are doing our jobs, then those who get the game from us will be as proud to be a part of it as we were and we are. The game is a gift and I am humbled, very humbled to accept its greatest honor."

It takes us back to something that a fan said when interviewed by the *Daily News* the day of Torre's hiring. It looks pretty smart today.

"If you give someone a chance, you never know what might happen."

Mel Stottlemyre Wins 9 Games to Help 1964 Yankees Win Pennant

The Yankees have had their share of noteworthy phenoms. But they haven't had anyone who carried them quite like Mel Stottlemyre did in the final two months of the 1964 season.

Stottlemyre is best known to younger fans as the pitching coach by Joe Torre's side on the Yankees World Series–winning teams. But there was a time when he was a star pitcher. It's not unusual to talk to a Yankees fan of the mid-1960s who says that when they were a schoolyard ballplayer, they wanted to be the next Mel Stottlemyre.

"Why do certain players become our favorites?" wrote baseball historian Bill Ryczek on The National Pastime website. "They usually have to have ability, but that is only one criterion. Fans care about their team, and their heroes have to care just as much. Mel was very good and cared very much."

The 22-year-old Stottlemyre, who came up for the Yankees in August of 1964, was one whose talents were needed as the team dealt with injuries.

Stottlemyre was 13–3 with a 1.42 ERA at Triple-A Richmond; dominating with a sinkerball, he allowed only two home runs in 152 innings.

Stottlemyre was in the majors for a month when then-manager Yogi Berra said, "Any pitcher who keeps the ball low the way he does, can't miss sticking in the majors. He's a wonderful prospect."

Stottlemyre was just what the Yankees needed. The Yankees were in third place, 3½ games out of first at the time of Stottlemyre's debut, and in his first two starts he pitched a complete-game win against the second-place White Sox and 8⅔ innings on three days' rest in a victory over the first-place Orioles. He followed that up with a six-hit shutout of the Red Sox, in which he induced three double plays.

The Stottlemyre sinker played at the big-league level as well as it did in Triple-A. He allowed only three home runs in 96 innings with the Yankees and coaxed 16 ground-ball double plays. Berra trusted Stottlemyre, using him for an average of nearly eight innings per start.

"When he was on the mound, he was all business," said Stottlemyre's former teammate, second baseman Bobby Richardson. "We had much shorter games when he pitched. It was fun to play behind him."

The capper to Stottlemyre's regular season was a game against the Washington Senators. Stottlemyre allowed two hits in a 7–0

LOWEST ERA BY YANKEES PITCHER, CAREER BEGAN AFTER WWII
(Minimum 100 Starts)

Whitey Ford	Mel Stottlemyre	Fritz Peterson	Stan Bahnsen	Rudy May
2.75	2.97	3.10	3.10	3.12

MEL STOTTLEMYRE, YANKEES RANKS (THROUGH 2015)

Wins	164	7th
Losses	139	1st
Strikeouts	1,257	7th
Innings Pitched	2,661⅓	4th
Shutouts	40	T–2nd

win. The win was the Yankees 11th straight and by that time, they were four games ahead of the Orioles and White Sox.

But the shutout wasn't the only thing noteworthy about this win. Stottlemyre also went 5-for-5 with two RBIs at the plate. He is the most recent pitcher to record five hits in a game.

Berra made Stottlemyre the Yankees' No. 2 starter behind Whitey Ford in the World Series against the Cardinals. Ford injured his shoulder in Game 1 and lost 9–5, but Stottlemyre's run continued in Game 2 of the Fall Classic. He went the distance in an 8–3 win over Bob Gibson.

The two met again in Game 5 and this time Gibson had the edge. Stottlemyre left after seven innings trailing 2–0, and though the Yankees rallied to tie, they lost in 10 innings to fall behind in the Series 3–2.

The Yankees won Game 6, and each team went back to its hot hand for Game 7, setting up the third Gibson versus Stottlemyre matchup of the Series.

The Yankees had the first scoring chance of the game, but Gibson struck Stottlemyre out with the bases loaded to end the second inning.

Stottlemyre got through three scoreless innings, but had some issues in the fourth that were only partly of his own doing. With two on and nobody out, a potential 3-6-1 double play failed when shortstop Phil Linz's throw went past Stottlemyre, allowing the first run of the game to score.

With first and third and one out, the Cardinals executed a successful double steal with catcher Tim McCarver, who stole only two bases that season, and Mike Shannon, who nabbed only four. Each was safe due to poor throws, and McCarver's run made it 2–0.

Stottlemyre's day ended with the Yankees down 3–0 after four innings. The Cardinals won 7–5 behind Gibson to take the Series, four games to three.

"I'm satisfied with this year, but the ending could have been better," Stottlemyre said after the game.

It turned out that this was just the beginning for Stottlemyre, who won 20 games the next season, the first of three times in his career that he hit that benchmark.

He won 164 games and ranks in the top 10 in Yankees history in just about every notable pitching category. He was a capable fielder, whose 88 assists in 1969 are the most by a pitcher in a season since the end of World War II.

He added another notable hitting accomplishment to his ledger with an inside-the-park grand slam against the Red Sox in 1965, the only inside-the-park slam by a pitcher since 1922.

Stottlemyre became a mentor to many young pitchers during his time as pitching coach and helped them get through tough moments in pennant races and postseason play. He got through tough times on his own, battling cancer since 2000. He still influences fans and Yankees players across generations, as evidenced by the reception he got when he was honored by the team with a Monument Park plaque in 2015.

"He gives those pitchers that confidence that they can accomplish something, with a little bit of a rough edge, letting them know how tough it is and not to take anything for granted," Torre once told reporters. "He's a special guy."

Willie Randolph:
1,000 Walks, 1,000 Double Plays

It could be argued that the Yankees have never had a player better versed in the fundamentals and the little things than Willie Randolph.

Randolph made the most of an 18-year major league career, and nearly 40 years as a player and coach. He is in the discussion with Tony Lazzeri and Robinson Cano when considering the team's best second basemen of all-time.

Randolph is one of the most successful hometown-kid-makes-good stories in New York baseball history.

He learned the game playing youth league baseball in his hometown, Brooklyn. Randolph grew up a shortstop but converted to second base a year after being drafted by the Pirates in 1972. It was the best possible thing that could have happened.

"I went over [to second base] and it's like I'd been there all my life," Randolph said.

Randolph impressed very quickly at the minor league level, drawing 110 walks in his third pro season and hitting .339 as a 20-year-old in Triple-A. That earned him a brief major league look in 1975.

That off-season, with the Yankees in need of a roster makeover, general manager Gabe Paul went to the winter meetings intent on procuring the necessary speed, defense, and pitching to give manager Billy Martin the best chance at a pennant in his first full season as Yankees manager.

On December 11, Paul made two blockbuster trades, one netting speedy outfielder Mickey Rivers and starting pitcher Ed Figueroa from the Angels for Bobby Bonds and another plucking Randolph and pitchers Dock Ellis and Ken Brett from the Pirates for Doc Medich. Martin immediately made Randolph the Yankees everyday second baseman.

Randolph lived up to expectations in most areas and exceeded them in others. At the plate, he worked pitchers to deep counts and drew walks in abundance. On the bases, he used his speed to net the Yankees extra runs. In the field, he was terrific. And in the clubhouse, he wasn't afraid to speak up.

It took only two months before *New York Times* writer Dave Anderson noticed Randolph in the locker room consoling a teammate and wrote, "He has established himself as the Yankees' second baseman, perhaps for the next 15 years."

Randolph was their everyday second baseman for the next 13 seasons and made five All-Star teams.

"I was taught from my young coaches and mentors on the importance of team and everyone's role on the team," Randolph said. "I was of an era where that stuff was defined to me at an early age."

Randolph's role, as he knew it, was "to get on base, steal bases, bunt, run, and make solid plays behind your pitching staff, which gives them confidence."

Randolph's peers recognized his value.

DID YOU KNOW?

Randolph is one of three Yankees to draw 1,000 walks and turn 1,000 double plays. The others are Lou Gehrig and Derek Jeter.

WILLIE RANDOLPH, YANKEES CAREER

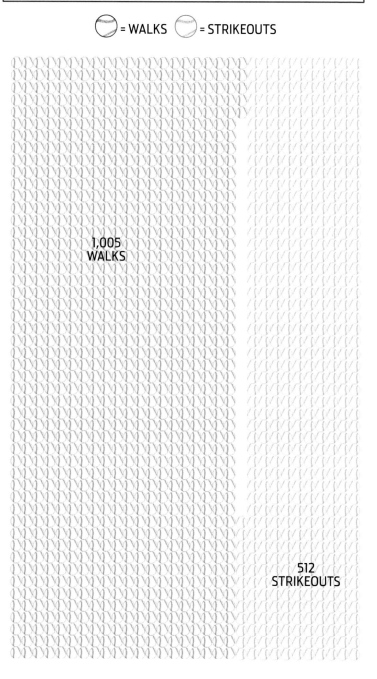

= WALKS   = STRIKEOUTS

1,005
WALKS

512
STRIKEOUTS

"I knew we had something special when we got Willie," said his former Yankees teammate Roy White.

The two plays that epitomized Randolph's Yankees career came in Game 5 of the 1977 ALCS against the Kansas City Royals. The Yankees entered the ninth inning trailing by a run and three outs from postseason elimination. Rivers tied the game with a single and then Randolph hit a go-ahead sacrifice fly.

The Yankees went up by two runs, but the Royals gave themselves a chance to draw even, putting a man on first with one out for Fred Patek.

Patek hit a ground ball to third base, which Graig Nettles snagged. He made a perfect throw to Randolph at second base for the second out, but the play wasn't done.

Patek was one of the fastest men in baseball. Randolph had been barreled into earlier in the series by Hal McRae, who nearly knocked Randolph into the outfield with a hard slide more resembling a football tackle.

Randolph braced himself for contact from the baserunner, fellow second baseman Frank White, and made an on-the-money throw to first base to beat Patek by an eyelash.

1,200 WALKS AND FEWER THAN 700 STRIKEOUTS

	Walks	Strikeouts
Stan Musial	1,599	696
Eddie Collins	1,499	468
Tris Speaker	1,381	394
Luke Appling	1,302	528
Ty Cobb	1,249	681
Willie Randolph	1,243	675

* All in Baseball Hall of Fame except Randolph

"I hung in and took my lumps," Randolph said. "I was fearless. I played a lot of football in high school, so I didn't mind getting knocked around second base."

Two days later, Randolph homered and scored the winning run on Paul Blair's 12th-inning hit in Game 1 of the World Series against the Los Angeles Dodgers. The Yankees won the World Series in six games, their first title in 15 years. Randolph earned another ring in 1978, though he was injured and didn't play in the World Series.

Randolph eventually became captain of the Yankees, continuing the legacy of those who came before him. In those 13 seasons, he regularly ranked in the top 10 in the AL in on-base percentage, stolen bases, toughest to strike out, and almost every defensive stat for second basemen.

"The thing that made me appreciate Willie Randolph more was his on-base percentage," said Kevin Hines, a statistician for the Elias Sports Bureau. "A lot of people might have looked at his batting average and home runs and said he wouldn't have been productive in this era. His on-base percentage would make you say otherwise."

BRIAN DOYLE HITS .438 IN 1978 WORLD SERIES

With Willie Randolph hurt at the end of the 1978 season, the Yankees were forced to play an untested rookie, Brian Doyle, whose career spanned 52 regular-season at-bats, at second base in the World Series.

Boy, did he come through.

Doyle went 7-for-16 (.438 batting average) with four runs scored and two RBIs in the six-game Series win. That included back-to-back three-hit games in Game 5 and Game 6, both of which the Yankees won.

"[That success] couldn't happen to a nicer guy," said Randolph. "When I think about '78, it's funny. Brian Doyle comes to mind even more than the comeback, because of the job he did. Bucky Dent did a great job as [World Series] MVP, but I think Brian could have been co-MVP because he did such a phenomenal job for us."

Randolph had an on-base percentage of .374 for the Yankees, and walked twice as often as he struck out. When Randolph's Yankees career ended, he ranked fourth in club history in walks. The three players ahead of him were Babe Ruth, Mickey Mantle, and Lou Gehrig.

"I understood the art of hitting," Randolph said. "You have to match wits with the pitcher. It's about hitting your pitch and not hitting the ones he wants you to hit."

Randolph still holds the Yankees record for double plays by a second baseman with 1,233. He ranks third all-time for double plays at the position, trailing only Hall of Famers Bill Mazeroski and Nellie Fox.

In those 13 seasons, he regularly ranked in the top 10 in the AL in on-base percentage, stolen bases, toughest to strike out, and almost every defensive stat.

"You know who is underappreciated?" said Don Mattingly. "Willie Randolph. He wasn't flashy, but he was a guy who did his thing every day and got better as he went on."

Advanced baseball metrics have illuminated Randolph's value. He ranks among the 10 best position players in Yankees history in wins above replacement.

"I'm kind of blown away by that," said Randolph. "It's nice to hear that. I just know that I was a really good player. I know we won. I cared about winning. I was about winning."

In his time with the team, Randolph was as responsible for helping the Yankees win as anyone.

Billy Martin Is Hired and Fired 5 Times

George Steinbrenner was a believer in second chances. And as it turned out, he was a believer in third chances, fourth chances, and fifth chances, too. The Yankees managerial merry-go-round of the 1970s and '80s featured five stints for Billy Martin.

Martin played for the Yankees from 1950 to '57 and played in four World Series the Yankees won, primarily as a second baseman. He was known for a key catch in Game 7 of the 1952 World Series and a walk-off hit in Game 6 of the '53 Series that clinched the Yankees' fifth straight title.

The 5'11", 165-pound Martin was known as being scrappy and intense to the point of combative. His drive helped make him a good manager in terms of wins and losses, though he didn't last particularly long anywhere.

Martin won 97 games with the Twins in his only season there, then had a .549 winning percentage in three seasons with the Tigers. He also turned a 57-win Rangers team into an 84-game winner in 1974.

But a year later, he was let go, as the Rangers went 44–51 in their first 95 games.

"He may think he knows more about baseball than anybody else, but it wouldn't surprise me if he was right," said his former manager Casey Stengel, shortly after Martin was fired. "He knows the slickest way of making plays you ever saw and he's an outstanding man from his shoulders up."

Others felt that way as well. Within two weeks of his firing, Martin was hired to replace Bill Virdon as Yankees manager.

"Every time I get fired they say it's my last chance," Martin told the media that day.

Yankees GM Gabe Paul acknowledged Martin's availability was the reason Virdon was let go. Martin's style was a winning style, even if it was an irritating one.

"I'm unorthodox," Martin said. "I do the basics. But aside from that, I like to do what the other teams don't expect."

If nothing else, the move immediately impacted the Yankees offense. The Yankees' batting average the rest of the season was .278, 21 points higher than under Virdon, and their OPS jumped 51 points.

What really mattered was the Yankees' win total, and that jumped dramatically in 1976, as the Yankees won 97 games and their first AL pennant since 1964. But they got swept in the World Series by the Reds.

Owner George Steinbrenner made a bold move that off-season, bringing in the big bat (and big ego) of Reggie Jackson. The presence of both Jackson and Martin, as well as some other strong

WINNING PCT. AS YANKEES MANAGER, 1975 TO 1988

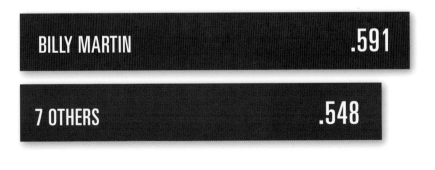

| BILLY MARTIN | .591 |
| 7 OTHERS | .548 |

Billy Martin, George Steinbrenner, and Lou Piniella had their share of good times and bad times in the Bronx.

personalities, made for a volatile clubhouse ("The Bronx Zoo") and resulted in one on-field confrontation between the two in which Martin yanked Jackson from a game for a perceived lack of hustle. Martin was nearly fired as a result.

In late July, with the Yankees in third place, Martin was again nearly fired, only to be saved by third-base coach Dick Howser's insistence that Martin was a better choice to manage out the season than he was.

Sometimes the best move is no move at all.

The Yankees went 49–18 in their last 67 games to win the AL East, beat the Royals for the pennant, and defeated the Dodgers to win the World Series, with Jackson hitting three home runs in the clinching game.

But asking Martin, Steinbrenner, and Jackson to coexist for another season was asking for too much. In 1978, when Martin said of Jackson and Steinbrenner, "They deserve each other. One's a born liar and the other's convicted," not long after suspending Jackson for detrimental conduct, the Yankees forced Martin to resign.

And amazingly a week later, Martin was back, receiving a five-minute standing ovation at Old-Timer's Day where it was announced he'd be Yankees manager again, in 1980, with his replacement from a week ago, Bob Lemon, told he was moving to the general manager's role.

> **The timetable sped up for Martin's return when the Yankees started 34–31 in 1979.**

What made Martin so beloved?

"He is the hero of every poor slob who would like to talk back to his boss," Will Grimsley wrote.

And there were players who appreciated him.

"He taught me how to win," said Graig Nettles.

The timetable sped up for Martin's return when the Yankees started 34–31 in 1979. Martin replaced Lemon and promised a kinder, gentler approach when it came to dealing with Jackson. But this Yankees team had to deal with the tragic death of captain Thurman Munson and multiple significant injuries (including one to Jackson) and could not catch the Orioles.

The Yankees' record wasn't what did Martin in, but rather an altercation a few weeks after the season ended in which he punched out a marshmallow salesman. The Yankees dismissed Martin, who landed with the Oakland Athletics, and did a quick fix there, guiding the team to the ALCS in 1981 (in which it lost to the Yankees) before being fired after the team fell apart in 1982.

Martin had many faults, but he was loyal and he was always there to pick up the phone when George Steinbrenner called. He got three more chances as Yankees manager, in 1983, 1985, and 1988.

"You've got to go with a winner to get a winner," Steinbrenner said at that 1983 hiring.

Martin always won games. The 1983 Yankees won 91 games, the 1985 team went 91–54 after Martin replaced Yogi Berra, and the 1988 squad was 40–28 before Martin was let go. There are some players, such as Dave Winfield, Willie Randolph, and Ron Guidry, whose relationships with Martin were successful and respectful.

"Billy was the best," Winfield said. "He was a heck of a manager. If you were a good player, he'd put you out there and you knew what you were doing."

But Martin's style annoyed other players, which in one case led to a memorable brawl at the end of the 1985 season between Martin and pitcher Ed Whitson, resulting in a broken arm for Martin. Martin also had his share of off-the-field issues, most involving alcohol, including one altercation in a topless bar that was not well received by management and ownership.

Martin was also stubborn. At the press conference announcing his hiring prior to the 1988 season, he said, "I'm not gonna change. My job is not to win a popularity contest. It's to win ballgames for the New York Yankees."

Martin might have had a chance to win more games were it not for his untimely death from injuries suffered in a car accident on Christmas Day 1989.

More than 3,000 people attended his funeral at St. Patrick's Cathedral in Manhattan. Reverend Edwin Broderick, one of the speakers, summed Martin up succinctly.

"Billy gave us thrills and spills, ups and downs, but his was an interesting show with exciting and different endings."

Casey Stengel Wins 5 World Series Titles in First 5 Years as Yankees Manager

When Casey and Edna Stengel's family gathered at Christmas, one thing was inevitable. Perhaps it came after the latest session of Casey teaching his nieces and nephews the proper technique for signing a baseball, or after his latest attempt to dance the waltz.

At some point, someone would ask Casey a question about a baseball player.

If you're familiar with the man known as "The Old Perfessor," you can probably guess what happened.

"You would get him going and he would just keep talking," said Stengel's grand-niece, Toni Harsh, laughing at the memory. "He would go all over the place and he would never identify [the subject]. He would always say 'that fellow.' Half an hour later, we're all asking each other, 'Who is he talking about?' Some of us would go into the kitchen and ask each other, 'Do you even remember the question?'"

Stengel was memorable for many reasons. His legacy endures more than 125 years after his birth.

CASEY STENGEL AS YANKEES MANAGER

World Series won: **7**

World Series lost: **3**

Seasons with 90 wins: **11**

Seasons with fewer than 90 wins: **1**

That he won a record-tying seven World Series titles with the Yankees, including five straight from 1949 to 1953, is a significant part of his story.

It's one that dates back to his days as a New York Giant and a friendship with Giants manager John McGraw, who saw something he liked in his goofy but fundamentally sound outfielder.

"He spent a lot of time on the bench with John," Harsh said. "And they spent a lot of time talking [baseball] late into the night."

Stengel got multiple managerial opportunities in the 1930s, first with the Dodgers and then with the Boston Braves, but in nine seasons, his team only finished with a winning record once.

Stengel was still confident that he could be a successful manager, and in the minor leagues he was one. From 1944 to 1948, Stengel managed teams in Milwaukee, Kansas City, and Oakland, winning nearly 57 percent of his games.

In 1948, George Weiss became the Yankees' general manager and fired the Yankees' then-manager, Bucky Harris. Weiss had known Stengel a long time and believed Stengel was ready for major league success.

Harsh noted that Weiss once saw Stengel teaching baseball fundamentals to little kids at a field in Oakland and was impressed with how passionate Stengel was. That made Weiss think Stengel would be the right fit.

"I think he will do a good job for us," Weiss said at Stengel's press conference. "He is a proven man."

Stengel realized it as well.

"Casey believed in himself," Harsh said. "He wouldn't have taken the position [otherwise]."

With Weiss as general manager and Stengel as manager, the Yankees began an incredible run of success. The 1949 pennant race was dramatic and the Yankees pulled out wins over the Red Sox in the final two games of the season to win the AL title.

In the World Series against the Dodgers, Yankees stars Joe DiMaggio and Yogi Berra went a combined 3-for-34, but Stengel found a hot hand among his pitchers in reliever Joe Page and a hot hitter in infielder Bobby Brown. He rode them to his first World Series title.

CASEY STENGEL AS MANAGER

WINNING PCT. WITH OTHER TEAMS
.397

WINNING PCT. WITH YANKEES
.623

"Stengel's work with the 1949 Yankees is among the best that any manager has done," said Craig Wright, publisher of the newsletter *Pages from Baseball's Past*. "There are managers in the Hall of Fame today who would have taken that team and struggled to just make the first division. At the end of play on October 9th, Casey's Yankees were the last team standing. A heck of a job."

"Not even the Lord could have done a better job with the Yankees than old Casey," Dodgers manager Burt Shotton said.

Four more titles in four years followed as Stengel and Weiss turned the Yankees into a dynasty, with the help of future Hall of Famers like Berra and Mickey Mantle.

Stengel employed a number of tactics to get the most out of his players. The one he's best known for is that he was one of the first managers to regularly platoon players, getting his best left-handed hitters into the lineup against right-handed pitching and his best right-handed hitters into the lineup against left-handed pitching.

Stengel also developed a calisthenics program that helped get players into game shape during spring training. He encouraged them to take dancing lessons to make them more nimble.

"Dancing taught shifting weight, turning, and stretching," Harsh said. "It was about staying light on your feet."

Stengel took the pressure off his players by entertaining the press with what became known as "Stengelese"—a language and means of description only known to Casey. There was a method to Stengel's madness.

"Baseball was a profession," Harsh said. "He knew when to turn [the silliness] on and when to turn it off."

Though the Yankees' run of five straight championships ended when the Indians won the AL pennant in 1954, Stengel plowed on. The Yankees appeared in the World Series in five of the next six seasons, winning in 1956 and 1958.

Former Yankees second baseman Jerry Coleman told Harsh that winning the 1958 World Series was Stengel's greatest achievement.

In that Series, the Yankees trailed the defending champion Braves 3–1, but won the next three games, including the last two in Milwaukee to take the title.

Two years later, Stengel's time with the Yankees ended after a loss to the Pirates in the 1960 World Series, which ended on Bill Mazeroski's Game 7 home run. It wasn't a pleasant parting of ways, as Stengel felt he was forced out of the job due to his age (70 years old).

Stengel got to manage four more years with the expansion Mets before a broken hip forced him into retirement. He died 10 years later at age 85 in 1975. His memory has endured from generation to generation of baseball fans.

"Major League Baseball has honored him as the greatest character of the game," Harsh said. "His *character* was of perseverance, continuing to believe there was always something better out there. He was an incredible man, amazing through good times and bad. He still speaks to us 125 years after his birth. He transcends time."

YANKEES SCORE 55 RUNS IN 1960 WORLD SERIES... AND LOSE!

What kind of baseball world were we living in that a team that entered the World Series with a 15-game winning streak and then averaged almost eight runs a game in the Series could end up as the losing team?

The 1960 Yankees hold the record for most runs scored in a World Series with 55.

Yet despite outscoring the Pirates 55–27 over seven games (the widest margin separating two teams in World Series history), it was the Pirates who were crowned champions. They won when Bill Mazeroski homered in the bottom of the ninth inning to take Game 7 by a score of 10–9.

Yogi Berra, who became widely known for his unique eloquence, was limited to few words when asked afterward what happened.

"I can't believe it," he told reporters.

It made the Yankees as improbable a World Series loser as there has ever been.

Joe McCarthy's
1,460 Wins
in 16 Seasons

At Joe McCarthy's inaugural press conference as Yankees manager in October 1930, he proclaimed his first goal was to beat his previous employer, the Cubs, in that following year's World Series.

"I will give all that is in me to produce a winning team," McCarthy said. "I ask nothing of my players except hard, conscientious work on the field.... The Yankees need a little of the fighting spirit and that is what I am going to try to give them."

It took McCarthy two years to accomplish that first goal, the first of many grand accomplishments in his tenure. The 1932 team won 107 games and trounced the Cubs in four straight games in the World Series, setting a record for most runs scored in a sweep (37).

Cubs manager Charlie Grimm made it clear that McCarthy was a leader who deserved utmost respect.

"We couldn't have lost to a better fellow than McCarthy," Grimm told the media after Game 4.

McCarthy guided the Yankees to second-place finishes in each of the next three seasons during a transitional time for the Yankees.

Babe Ruth was growing older and Lou Gehrig was now the team's best player.

In 1936, rookie center-fielder Joe DiMaggio added a new touch of star power to the lineup and this marked a turning point in the team's success.

It was the birth of a new Yankees dynasty, with McCarthy at the helm. The Yankees won four consecutive World Series titles.

In total, McCarthy won 1,460 games (most by a Yankees manager), eight pennants, and seven World Series titles. Over the eight-year period from 1936 to 1943, the Yankees came within one victory of averaging 100 wins per season and won six championships.

McCarthy was quiet in his approach, but brilliant by outcome. He introduced a strong sense of discipline to the organization, the kind on which many legacies have been built.

"Never a day went by when you didn't learn something from Joe McCarthy," said DiMaggio.

An understanding of the fundamentals of the game was paramount for McCarthy. He wasn't quite Yogi Berra with a turn of phrase, but he had a unique way of getting his

MOST WINS AS YANKEES MANAGER

Joe McCarthy	1,460
Joe Torre	1,173
Casey Stengel	1,149
Miller Huggins	1,067

MOST WORLD SERIES TITLES AS MANAGER

Joe McCarthy	7
Casey Stengel	7
Connie Mack	5

MOST GAMES OVER .500 AS MANAGER

John McGraw	815
Joe McCarthy	792
Bobby Cox	503

message across. If you've ever heard the phrase, "Nobody ever became a ballplayer by walking after a ball," you should know the origin of that aphorism is an article titled "10 Commandments for Success in Baseball," a list compiled by McCarthy.

> *In total, McCarthy won 1,460 games (most by a Yankees manager), eight pennants, and seven World Series titles.*

McCarthy's .627 winning percentage with the Yankees is the best of anyone who managed the team for multiple seasons. His .615 *career* winning percentage is the best for anyone who managed at least 1,000 games in major league history. He never managed a team with a losing record or that finished worse than fourth place in his 22 full seasons. His World Series managerial record is 26–13.

McCarthy would have fit in well with the modern game in one regard. Baseball historian Bill James wrote in *The Bill James Guide to Baseball Managers* that McCarthy favored hitters who would "wear the pitcher down by taking pitches, taking pitches, taking pitches, until the pitcher started to crack."

"I believe that Joe McCarthy was the greatest manager in baseball history," James wrote. "He had a tenacious memory, never forgot

MOST WINS, 1936 TO 1943

799	723	660	658	657
Yankees	Cardinals	Reds	Red Sox	Indians

any little thing that an opposing player might do, for example. He was well organized."

The *Berkshire Eagle* (a newspaper that covered the rival Red Sox, whom McCarthy would later come out of retirement to manage) even published a note on its editorial page, saluting the skipper when he resigned from the Yankees due to health reasons in 1946.

"His success seems like proof that the best violin teacher may be himself only a mediocre fiddler," the paper noted. "...He exemplified the iron hand under the velvet glove; got rid of rowdies, prima-donnas, and clubhouse lawyers, relied little on trades and depended on results for selection and development of players. In this he was eminently successful.... The record of his team during his regime has been outstanding and something for any successor to shoot at."

Many have tried and some have come closer than others. But McCarthy's Yankees managerial mark has never been matched.

Miller Huggins Suspends Babe Ruth and Fines Him $5,000

Miller Huggins was a small man, 5'6", 140 pounds, and not the intimidating type. But he was the manager of the Yankees, which gave him a measure of impressiveness, even if the media and some in Yankees management didn't see it that way in the early part of his career.

His career was one of triumph and tragedy. Baseball historian Steve Steinberg wrote, "Miller Huggins showed that brains, savvy, and determination could beat brawn and raw talent."

Huggins became Yankees manager prior to the 1918 season after five seasons as manager of the Cardinals (four as a player/manager, capping a 13-year playing career).

Huggins' pre-Yankees managerial record was not overwhelming, but he did improve a Cardinals team by 30 wins from 1913 to 1914 and 22 wins from 1916 to 1917 and was known as a clever trader. The Yankees were in need of a similar touch after going 71–82 and finishing in sixth place in 1917.

"Sooner or later he will catch some rival outfit napping and steal away the athletes he needs to round out his own combination," one newspaperman wrote of Huggins that December. "Huggins has the trading faculty developed to an amazing degree and reckons not the advantage to the other fellow if he feels that he is benefiting himself. Too strong a faith in the ability of some of their players to make good on undeserved reputations has long been one of the Yankees most serious afflictions."

Huggins knew what he was doing, even as some trade attempts failed. He improved the team's winning percentage in each of his first four seasons as manager.

The Yankees were in need of a similar touch after going 71–82 and finishing in sixth place in 1917.

Prior to the 1920 season, the Yankees purchased a group of players from the rival Red Sox, including Babe Ruth. This was a turning point in the franchise's history.

In the wake of the Black Sox Scandal (when the 1919 White Sox threw the World Series to the Cincinnati Reds), the Yankees became the team to watch.

They won pennants in 1921, 1922, and 1923, winning the World Series in the latter season, the first year in Yankee Stadium, and finished a close second in the AL to the Senators in 1924. But they were not yet thought of as a dynasty, since they had won "only" one title in four years.

In 1925, the Yankees had a miserable season and Ruth was not playing up to this usual level, due to an ulcer that caused him to miss a significant amount of time at the start of the season. The Yankees were 15–25 when he returned.

Ruth, who had a reputation as a carouser, took advantage of the Yankees' team rules even after his return, repeatedly overindulging off the field and breaking curfew. On August 29, Huggins took action, suspending Ruth indefinitely and fining him $5,000.

"Patience has ceased to be a virtue," Huggins said. "I have tried to overlook Ruth's behavior for a while. But I have decided to take summary action to bring the big fellow to his senses."

Ruth was infuriated by the suspension, but a couple of days later, he met with owner Jacob Ruppert and apologized. Noted one reporter: "Ruth not only repented, but he broke all existing records repenting."

Ruth returned on September 7 and it was as if a switch had been flipped. For the rest of the season, he played like the best version of himself.

Ruth hit .346 with 10 home runs and 31 RBIs in his last 29 games of the season. Those had little impact on the standings, but they set the tone for a return to full form in 1926.

Huggins managed the team back to the pennant in 1926 and to World Series titles in 1927 and 1928. That is the point at which the Yankees and Ruth (who hit three home runs in the final game

MYRIL HOAG: 1ST YANKEES PLAYER WITH A 6-HIT GAME

Some of Babe Ruth's hitting prowess rubbed off on one of his replacements for a day, backup outfielder Myril Hoag.

Ruth took himself out of the lineup for a doubleheader against the Red Sox on June 6, 1934, due to what he said was an ankle injury (though some thought he was upset at teammates for making disparaging comments about his play).

Hoag was his replacement, and the Red Sox may have wished the Bambino played in Game 1.

Hoag did something never done before in Yankees history and only done twice since. He banged out six hits in a 15–3 win.

The only other Yankees to replicate Hoag's six-hit effort are Gerald Williams against the Orioles in 1996 and Johnny Damon against the Royals in 2008.

Hoag's 13-year career was otherwise modest. His other claim to fame is that he hit .320 in 25 World Series at-bats and was a member of three championship teams.

of a four-game sweep of the Cardinals in 1928) realized their full potential.

"Apparently it is hopeless to expect some other club to build itself up to the size of the Yankees," wrote Tommy Holmes of the *Brooklyn Eagle*.

Huggins was fired up.

"They had heard we were a lot of cripples, little short of pushovers," Huggins said of the Cardinals' overconfidence. "They watched us practice, noticed perhaps that a few of us limped, and that Lazzeri's throwing arm was bad but, and this is important—We seemed to be able to play a little snappy baseball."

Huggins managed the team back to the pennant in 1926 and to World Series titles in 1927 and 1928.

When one writer suggested that next year should be another dominant one, Huggins made a comment that was eerie, given what happened the next year.

"You can never tell what will happen. Maybe we will be all right and maybe we won't."

In 1929, the Yankees ran into the start of a mighty Philadelphia Athletics dynasty. Off the field, their manager suffered a tragic ending to his life. In September 1929, he died of a blood infection at age 51.

The Yankees' biggest star was devastated by the loss.

"He was the only man who knew how to keep me in line," Ruth said.

Tony Lazzeri Drives in 11 Runs in a Game

For much of his career, Tony Lazzeri played the role of second, third, or even eighth banana to the likes of Babe Ruth, Lou Gehrig, and Joe DiMaggio.

But for a period of four games, in a time in which it was thought that his best performances were in the past, there was no Yankee more prodigious in his power. And one game stands above the rest.

It is Lazzeri and not the names mentioned above, or for that matter Mickey Mantle, Don Mattingly, or Alex Rodriguez, who holds the franchise record for most RBIs in a game.

The 5'11", 170-pound Lazzeri was a San Francisco native, who blasted his way through the minor leagues. He hit 60 home runs and had 222 RBIs (in 197 games) for Salt Lake City of the Pacific Coast League as a shortstop in 1925, and the Yankees made a swap, including a payment of $50,000, to obtain his contract.

"I have made a special investigation of Lazzeri among every good baseball judge I can find and the opinion is almost unanimous that he will make good," Yankees owner Jacob Ruppert told newspaper reporters that spring.

Lazzeri more than made good. He didn't quite drive the ball like he did in the Pacific Coast League, but made a successful move to second base and showed consistent power in becoming the game's first Italian-American star.

Lazzeri is best remembered for a moment from his rookie season when he struck out against Grover Cleveland Alexander with the bases loaded and two outs and the Yankees trailing the Cardinals by a run in Game 7 of the 1926 World Series (which the Cardinals would win).

But it's not fair to Lazzeri to single out that moment, as there were plenty of glorious moments in his career.

The most notable of those came in four games on a 16-game road trip from May 21 to 24, 1936. By this time, Lazzeri's 14-year career was near its end. In fact, one story noted that he was "tagged washed up by the baseball scribes when the 1936 season started."

The first of the four games had an unfortunate conclusion. Lazzeri hit a two-run home run among his three hits as the Yankees raced out to a 9–4 advantage at the game's midpoint. But the Detroit Tigers rallied for three runs in the eighth and one in the ninth to win 10–9.

The Yankees went on to Philadelphia next and pummeled the Athletics, winning 12–6 and 15–1. Lazzeri batted eighth in both games (the 3-4-5 hitters were DiMaggio, Gehrig, and Bill Dickey), hitting a solo homer in the first contest and two two-run shots in the second.

The arms in the stands proved to be more potent than the arms on the mound for the Athletics. The *New York Times* noted that the

MOST RBIs IN GAME, YANKEES HISTORY

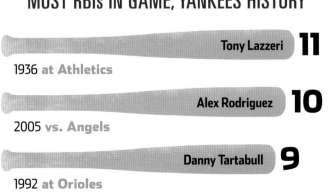

Tony Lazzeri **11**
1936 at Athletics

Alex Rodriguez **10**
2005 vs. Angels

Danny Tartabull **9**
1992 at Orioles

Athletics fans "showered the field with pop bottles, seat cushions, torn papers, fruit and vegetables, and whatever else came to hand in a rowdy outburst that has had few parallels in organized baseball."

Lazzeri was undaunted, both by his place in the lineup and by the fans' behavior. The next day, with Lazzeri again hitting eighth, he and his Yankees teammates crushed an overmatched Athletics pitching staff.

Lazzeri hit a grand slam in the second inning, a grand slam in the fifth inning, and a solo shot in the seventh inning. In the last of his six trips, he just missed a fourth home run, instead settling for a two-run triple.

The Philadelphia fans celebrated Lazzeri's accomplishments despite their team losing 25–2, as he was besieged by autograph seekers.

The Yankees finished with a franchise record for runs scored, of which Lazzeri drove in a club- and AL-record 11. He became the first player to hit two grand slams in a game, the third to hit five

JOE GORDON RECORDS 1,000 HITS FOR YANKEES IN 1,000 GAMES

One of the most fascinating statistical quirks in Yankees history is how their former second baseman, Joe Gordon, played in exactly 1,000 games for the team and had exactly 1,000 hits for them.

Gordon was a really good player, a nine-time All-Star, and 1942 AL MVP who was eventually rewarded with enshrinement in the Hall of Fame in 2009, 59 years after his final game.

Gordon won five World Series titles, four with the Yankees between 1938 and 1943. He played a big role in two postseasons, hitting .400 with six RBIs in the 1938 World Series and .500 with five RBIs (and seven walks) in the 1941 World Series.

Oddly for a player so good, it took a bizarre run of bad luck for Gordon to hit 1,000–1,000 on the nose. His Yankees career ended with a 2-for-37 slump.

MOST RBIs BY YANKEES, PRIMARY POSITION: SECOND BASE

1,157	822	617
Tony Lazzeri	Robinson Cano	Joe Gordon

home runs in two games (along with Ty Cobb and Cap Anson), and the first to hit six home runs in three games, and seven homers in four. He's the only player in major league history to drive in 15 runs in a two-game span.

It was a great day of appreciation for Lazzeri, who earned headline recognition across the country for his performance (though one Pennsylvania paper, the *Greeneville Record-Argus,* noted his performance paled in comparison to a local league player who went 7-for-7 with four home runs).

Recognition to that degree did not often come for Lazzeri, whose accomplishments were overwhelmed by those of his world-famous teammates. He battled epilepsy throughout his life and died young, at age 42 in 1946.

Eventually Cooperstown came around to recognizing the many great days in Lazzeri's career. Lazzeri was inducted into the Baseball Hall of Fame in 1991.

Robinson Cano: AL-Record 5 Straight Seasons of 25 HR by a Second Baseman

To borrow a phrase from John Sterling, dontcha know that Robinson Cano was a heck of a Yankee?

Cano is the son of former major league pitcher Jose Cano, who with his wife decided to name the family's new baby after baseball pioneer Jackie Robinson. After spending his first two seasons in pro ball trying out third base, shortstop, and second base, Cano ended up playing full-time at the position Robinson was best known for during his Hall of Fame career: second base.

He was a remarkably good player in his nine seasons with the Yankees, from when he first came up as a 22-year-old rookie in 2005 to his final season in 2013. The Yankees were fortunate that the Rangers picked another player over Cano from a list provided by the Yankees in the trade that brought the team Alex Rodriguez.

Cano began his debut season by going 2-for-23 in his first seven games, but went 13-for-22 in the next five after that and never looked back.

Cano was known for that kind of streakiness. But thankfully for the Yankees, the hot streaks came around more often than the cold ones. And the one thing in which Cano was most consistent was that he played every day. From 2007 to 2013, he averaged 160 games played per season.

He made the jump from impressive rookie to star quickly, when he hit a career-best .342 in 2006, the first of seven times that he batted .300 for the Yankees. Power came in 2009, when Cano, who

hadn't hit 20 home runs in his first four major league seasons, hit 25. He followed that with seasons of 29, 28, 33, and 27 home runs.

His five straight 25-homer seasons are the most by an American League player whose primary position was second base, one shy of the overall record held by Dan Uggla.

Cano's offensive abilities made life difficult for many major league pitchers. He racked up plenty of doubles in addition to his home runs.

"He had a Vladimir Guerrero kind of approach sometimes, meaning you couldn't get him out throwing strikes, because he didn't swing and miss," said former Red Sox pitcher Curt Schilling, against whom Cano hit .387 with four home runs. "He swung at a lot of [bad pitches], but when he did, he didn't just make contact. He hit the barrel of the bat. That's a gift."

Cano, sometimes criticized for lax play, was a good defender regardless, who won a pair of Gold Gloves, an award he frequently battled for with his Red Sox counterpart, Dustin Pedroia.

"The game came easy to him," said former teammate Aaron Small. "He used to get a bad rap that he was dogging it in the field, but he wasn't dogging it. He was that relaxed, that quick, and his hands were that good. He worked as hard as anybody."

Cano doesn't have a list of signature moments along the lines of some of his former teammates, like Derek Jeter, partly due to the Yankees losing in the postseasons in which he hit best (2007 against the Indians, 2010 against the Rangers, and 2011 against the Tigers). But he did have a few memorable hits.

Cano had a bases-loaded double in his first postseason at-bat, clearing the bases in an eventual win over Bartolo Colon and the Angels in Game 1 of the 2005 ALDS.

In 2008, Cano had the final walk-off hit in the old Yankee Stadium, a single that beat the Orioles 1–0. The Yankees closed the ballpark the next day.

In 2011, he beat Adrian Gonzalez in the Home Run Derby Finals. Cano had his father pitch to him, and credited Jose for knowing where his hot spots were.

MOST 40-DOUBLE SEASONS, YANKEES HISTORY

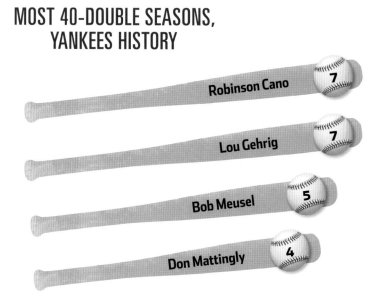

Robinson Cano — 7
Lou Gehrig — 7
Bob Meusel — 5
Don Mattingly — 4

"I don't want to say that I won the trophy," the younger Cano told the media. "I want to say that my dad has won the trophy."

In Game 1 of that year's ALDS against the Tigers, Cano had six RBIs, including a grand slam in a 9–3 Yankees win. That matched the franchise record for most RBIs in a postseason game (Bobby Richardson, Bernie Williams, and Hideki Matsui each had six).

Despite the lack of memory-making moments, Cano's collective work is what stands out.

"He was on a Hall of Fame trajectory for a very long time as a Yankee," said Ben Kabak, one of the founders of the premier Yankees fan website, River Avenue Blues.

Perhaps most notable: from 2010 to 2013, he ranked first among position players in wins above replacement, more than a full win ahead of Miguel Cabrera. In other words, you could make a very reasonable case that Cano was the most valuable player in baseball in that span, even though he didn't win that award for a particular year.

"He should have won at least one for sure," said former teammate Jorge Posada.

Posada considers Cano the most underrated Yankee he played with. Baseball historian Craig Wright goes one step further.

"In his nine years with the Yankees he had more hits, more doubles, more triples, more homers, more RBIs, more runs created, more win shares than Derek Jeter—and he was the better defensive player, too," Wright said. "But how many fans know that or would guess that? Robinson Jose Cano, that's your most underrated Yankee."

Cano left the Yankees to sign a 10-year, $240 million deal with the Mariners following the 2013 season.

Mariners fans grew anxious early in 2015 as Cano struggled like he never had before some midseason improvements. How the rest of his career plays out remains to be seen, but Cano's Yankees legacy is secure. While a Yankee, there was no reason to worry. He was always money in the bank.

2 Unlikely Heroes Help Yankees Win 2000 World Series

The 2000 Yankees roster had big-name stars that carried the team to a Subway Series against the Mets: Derek Jeter, Bernie Williams, David Justice, Paul O'Neill, Tino Martinez, and Jorge Posada.

But it was a pair of utility infielders who brought them a championship.

Jose Vizcaino was a surprise starter in Game 1 of the World Series. He hadn't started a game in the postseason to that point, but Joe Torre plugged Vizcaino into the lineup in the No. 9 spot, hoping that a contact hitter of Vizcaino's caliber would give Al Leiter trouble. Vizcaino also entered the day 10-for-21 (.476 batting average) against Leiter for his career.

Vizcaino went 1-for-3 against Leiter, but the one hit was a key one, an infield single in a two-run sixth inning that put the Yankees ahead.

More importantly, Vizcaino went 3-for-3 against the Mets bullpen.

After the Mets rallied to take a one-run lead into the bottom of the ninth inning, Vizcaino was a key part of the Yankees comeback. His single against Mets closer Armando Benitez loaded the bases for Chuck Knoblauch, who drove in the tying run with a sacrifice fly.

In the 12th inning, the bases were loaded with two outs and Vizcaino came up again.

"What do I remember about it?" Vizcaino said 10 years later. "I remember everything.

"The first thing in my mind was: This is exactly what I've been dreaming of. I knew Turk [Wendell] was going to try to get ahead in the count. He threw me exactly what I was looking for—a fastball middle-away. He threw it right in the sweet spot."

Vizcaino bailed out a teammate who popped out to the catcher by lining that pitch into left field for the game-winning hit.

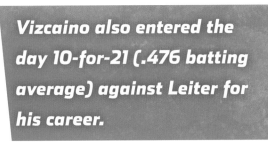

Vizcaino also entered the day 10-for-21 (.476 batting average) against Leiter for his career.

Vizcaino has a mini-shrine in his home devoted to that single. He has the baseball, his glasses from that day, and his batting gloves. He treasures that moment.

The teammate that Vizcaino bailed out that night was 35-year-old Luis Sojo, who was in his second stint with the team. Sojo was reacquired in a trade with the Pirates in early August and hit a respectable .288 the rest of the season.

It was Sojo whom Vizcaino replaced in the lineup at the start of the World Series and who was 1-for-6 in the first four games of the World Series.

The Yankees led the Series 3–1 heading to Game 5, but other than Game 2, the games were tight from start to finish.

Game 5 was no different. The score was 2–2 in the eighth inning when Torre made a switch. He pinch-hit for Vizcaino with Knoblauch, then put Sojo in the field. Sojo (via the reporting of Kevin Kernan of the *New York Post*) had told Orlando Hernandez that he would be the hero of the game. That turned out to be a great call.

In the top of the ninth inning with the score still even, Leiter struck out the first two Yankees. But then came a nine-pitch walk to Jorge Posada and a single by Scott Brosius.

Much as Vizcaino took an aggressive approach, so did Sojo. He swung at Leiter's first pitch and hit a grounder up the middle. Leiter lunged for it and missed it. The ball kept rolling toward center field. Second baseman Edgardo Alfonzo and shortstop Kurt Abbott both made desperation attempts to keep the ball in front of them.

Both failed.

There was one question left: Would Posada score ahead of the throw from center-fielder Jay Payton?

Payton's throw made it a close play, but the ball hit Posada and bounced away. That allowed Brosius to score as well, putting the Yankees up two runs.

"I figured they thought I would take the first pitch, but I was going to swing," Sojo said. "That's just what I did. I don't hit the ball hard, but it was an effective at-bat."

The Yankees won the Series on the strength of that hit.

This was a true team triumph. The Yankees may have been a team of superstars, but in these five games, every player was vital. Ten different Yankees drove in a run. None of their hitters had more than three RBIs.

Everyone on the pitching staff was noteworthy, from Roger Clemens and Andy Pettitte, who allowed five runs in a combined $21\frac{1}{3}$ innings, to David Cone, who got a huge out in Game 4, retiring Piazza to escape potential trouble in the fifth inning.

"It took all 25 guys on that team to win," Vizcaino said. "There were no egos on that team. Every day was a different hero."

2 Game-Tying HR with 2 Outs in Ninth in 2 Nights in 2001 World Series

If you were going to rank Yankees moments based on improbability, the ninth innings of Games 4 and 5 of the 2001 World Series would probably rank highest on the list.

That World Series is a special one, because the Yankees weren't just playing for themselves, but for a city devastated by the attacks on the World Trade Center on September 11.

The Arizona Diamondbacks were the team in the Yankees' way, and they dominated the first two games of the Series, winning 9–1 and 4–0. The Yankees won Game 3 by a score of 2–1 to cut Arizona's lead to two games to one, but their chances of winning Game 4 looked grim after the Diamondbacks scored twice in the eighth inning to take a 3–1 lead. The Yankees found Arizona closer Byung-Hyun Kim's submarine pitches baffling, as three straight hitters struck out in the eighth and Derek Jeter bunted into an out to lead off the ninth.

Tino Martinez blasts his two-run homer off Byung-Hyun Kim. *(Bill Kostroun)*

With one out, Paul O'Neill singled, bringing Bernie Williams up as the tying run. But Williams struck out on three pitches and the game came down to a matchup of Tino Martinez versus Kim.

Martinez was 0-for-9 in the Series to that point and 7-for-47 (.149 batting average) that postseason.

Martinez stood all the way back in the batter's box, which allowed him to get a good look at Kim, who had faced 27 batters that postseason and allowed only two hits.

"I went up there in that situation and was looking for a fastball, something over the middle of the plate I could just try to drive out, just try to take a big hack and I got ahold of it," Martinez said.

Indeed, Martinez got a powerful swing at a pitch aimed at the outside corner. Center-fielder Steve Finley raced back toward right center, but this ball was well over the fence, just shy of the first row of the bleachers. The cameras showed Martinez running the bases in a very businesslike fashion and Kim looking incredulous.

Tie game.

"I don't think anybody has gotten bigger hits or hit bigger home runs than Tino has for the six years I've been here," Yankees manager Joe Torre said.

*And the Yankees were **1-for-24** with runners in scoring position for the Series.*

Kim got out of the ninth, and after Mariano Rivera retired the Diamondbacks in order in the top of the 10th, Diamondbacks manager Bob Brenly let Kim pitch the bottom half, hoping he'd get through his third inning of work. That didn't happen.

With two outs, Derek Jeter hit his "Mr. November" home run, just after midnight, winning the game and tying the Series 2–2.

The teams met again the next night in the final Yankees home game of the season. Mike Mussina and Miguel Batista engaged in a terrific pitcher's duel, but Mussina blinked first, allowing fifth-inning home runs to Finley and Rod Barajas.

Batista and Greg Swindell held the Yankees scoreless into the ninth inning and Brenly decided to send Kim out to get the last three outs and protect a 2–0 lead.

The baseball gods had other plans.

Jorge Posada doubled to lead off the inning, but Kim recovered to get the next two outs. This put the Yankees in the same situation as the previous night, down two runs with two outs in the ninth and the tying run at the plate.

As badly as Martinez was doing entering his critical at-bat, Brosius was doing worse. He was 7-for-49 in the postseason. And the Yankees were 1-for-24 with runners in scoring position for the Series.

Brosius turned on a 1–0 pitch and cranked it toward the left-field line. It was fair by plenty and gone by plenty, tying the game.

"I have never seen anything like it," said FOX broadcaster Tim McCarver as the Yankees celebrated and the Diamondbacks consoled Kim on the mound.

Martinez said he was thinking home run when he came to the plate in Game 4. Brosius said he had no such thoughts, that he just happened to be very fortunate.

"You certainly don't want to try to make a living waiting until the 26th out to make something happen, but it's worked out the last couple of nights," Brosius said.

Kim left the game, which still had a lot of life to it. Rivera escaped a bases-loaded jam in the 11th and then the Yankees won in the 12th

RAUL IBANEZ'S TWO HR TO TIE, BEAT ORIOLES IN 2012 ALDS

Forty-year-old Yankee Raul Ibanez had one of the most clutch performances in major league history in Game 3 of the 2012 ALDS against the Baltimore Orioles.

First he pinch-hit for Alex Rodriguez and hit a game-tying home run in the ninth inning (his third game-tying home run that late in a game in three weeks).

He then hit a walk-off home run in the 12th inning. The Elias Sports Bureau noted that he became the first player to hit two home runs in the ninth inning or later of a postseason game and at age 40, the oldest player to hit a postseason walk-off home run.

"I just had a gut feeling," said Yankees manager Joe Girardi, explaining why he inserted Ibanez into the game.

Sometimes those pay off in a big way.

GAME-TYING HR IN 9TH INNING, YANKEES WORLD SERIES HISTORY

Scott Brosius	2001 vs. Diamondbacks*
Tino Martinez	2001 vs. Diamondbacks*
Tom Tresh	1964 vs. Cardinals
Elston Howard	1957 at Braves

* Yankees won game

on Alfonso Soriano's RBI single, putting the Yankees ahead in the Series, three games to two.

These two games are the only instances in World Series history in which a team was down to its last out, got a multiple-run game-tying home run in the ninth inning or later, and went on to win the game.

And though the Yankees lost the World Series in seven games, blowing a ninth-inning lead in Game 7, the Series and those two home runs are special to those who played a part in them and watched them.

"I told the players we're disappointed in the outcome but they should be very proud of what went on here," Torre said after Game 7 ended. "I certainly am proud of the way my ball club responded to the pressure. I think the people of New York got what they wanted. They saw a ball club out there that struggled at times and yet found a way to get through it. I think my ball club represented New York very well and I'm proud of them for that. I'm proud for their dedication, for their selflessness. We felt this year, we represented more than just baseball fans, [but also] the people that needed a lift."

They never gave up. That's a spirit every New Yorker can get behind.

2 Pennant-Winning Walk-Off HR

Chris Chambliss and Aaron Boone both had the same thought as they stepped to the plate just prior to the most magical of moments.

Just get a good pitch to hit. It doesn't matter when it comes or where it is. But if it looks hittable, hit it.

Heeding such thoughts had the highest possible payoff—a walk-off home run that put the Yankees into the World Series.

Chambliss capped an epic five-game ALCS with the Kansas City Royals in 1976. The Yankees and Royals were tied heading into the bottom of the ninth inning, thanks to a game-tying three-run home run in the eighth by Yankees nemesis George Brett.

Chambliss led off against Royals reliever Mark Littell. The Yankees first baseman was one of the top hitters in the AL that season. He finished fifth in the league MVP voting (teammate Thurman Munson won the award).

He entered this at-bat hot: 10-for-20 in the series, a carryover from the regular season, in which he hit .383 against Royals pitching.

Littell allowed only one home run in 108⅔ innings that season to that point. But he made a mistake to Chambliss and Chambliss made him pay, with a long drive to right field. Royals right-fielder Hal McRae gave it his best shot, but his jumping attempt at the fence came up empty-handed.

"What made me go after the first pitch?" Chambliss asked in an interview with ESPN in 2010. "Because it looked good. It was high. It was over the plate. I'm an aggressive guy so I swung at a pitch in a zone that I thought that I could get a good swing at."

Madness ensued as thousands of Yankees fans stormed the field to celebrate. Chambliss was lucky to get back to the Yankees dugout. He dodged people as he circled the bases, never actually touching home plate.

Boone was more fortunate in that he got to live out the celebration of the moment without fear.

> *Chambliss entered this at-bat hot: 10-for-20 in the series to that point.*

His turn came 27 years after Chambliss, also in an epic series against the fiercest rival, the Boston Red Sox in the 2003 ALCS. This series went seven games and it looked like the Red Sox were going to prevail in Game 7.

But the Yankees rallied from three runs down to tie against Red Sox ace Pedro Martinez in the eighth inning. Boone entered the game as a pinch-runner after the rally and then replaced Enrique Wilson at third base. Before the series began, Yankees coach Willie Randolph had told Boone that he would be a hero at some point in the series. After Mariano Rivera shut the Red Sox out for three

MOST POSTSEASON WALK-OFF HR BY TEAM

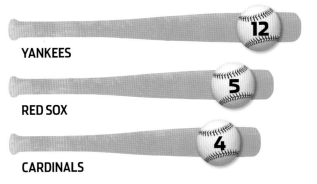

YANKEES — 12

RED SOX — 5

CARDINALS — 4

innings, Boone got his chance in the bottom of the 11th against knuckleball pitcher Tim Wakefield.

"I knew running off the field that inning, I had a feeling like I was gonna do something," Boone said. "As I'm walking up to the plate, initially I was thinking about taking a pitch. And on my way up there, I kind of changed my thought and said, 'Forget that. You've been thinking too much this series. Just go up there and get a good pitch to hit.' The first pitch was a good pitch to hit...and I got a good piece of one. When I made contact I knew almost instantly that it was gonna be a home run."

Boone was able to make the trip around the bases without fan interference, though he admits now it's all a bit of a blur to him.

MOST WALK-OFF HR BY BOONE (INCLUDING PLAYOFFS)

Aaron Boone came from a family that produced three generations of major leaguers. Aaron dominated his relatives when it came to walk-off home runs

7   Aaron

3   Bret (brother)

2   Ray (grandfather)

1   Bob (father)

Though the Yankees did not win the World Series in either season, the moments still resonate with fans. Both Chambliss and Boone regularly get approached by fans who like to reminisce about it.

They are proud of the accomplishment and embraced their role as baseball hero.

"When I see it I'm proud," Chambliss said. "I'm happy that I was part of a special moment in Yankee history."

"All of us that played ball when we were little kids, all lived out that moment in our backyard," Boone said. "To get to actually live that out on a major league field in Yankee Stadium against the Red Sox was something that...I feel really blessed to just be in that situation."

Bernie Williams Leads MLB with 80 Postseason RBIs

The turning point in Bernie Williams' career came during the 1994 season when he got a pep talk from Yankees coach Willie Randolph.

"I looked him in the eye and said, 'Bernie, do you want to be great?'" Randolph said. "He gave me a deer in headlights look. I said 'You are a great player. You can't hide when you're the center-fielder for the New York Yankees. Everyone is looking to you for greatness.' You cannot be afraid to fail and you have to want to embrace success. Bernie said to me, 'Wow, that's deep.' I said 'Bernie, it's not deep. It's the next level for you.'"

Williams reached the next level with his postseason performance, which solidified his legacy as an all-time Yankees great.

Williams was a fantastic player in the regular season, hitting .297 with 287 home runs, 2,336 hits, five All-Star selections, and four Gold Gloves. He always seemed to thrive when it mattered most, whether it be in clutch situations, or the postseason.

"He had a pretty serious competitive streak in him," said former teammate Mike Stanton.

Williams played in 121 postseason games, third-most all-time (due to playing in a three-round playoff era). He had his share of failures, but he also had some of the greatest successes. His 80 postseason RBIs are an MLB record.

"So many great things happened with Bernie Williams in center field for the Yankees," said longtime sportswriter and ESPN baseball analyst Tim Kurkjian. "The Yankees are not winning those championships unless he's there every day as a switch hitter in center field. You can't underestimate how important he was to the great Yankees teams."

Williams had a terrific first playoff run, going 9-for-21 with seven walks and five RBIs in the 1995 ALDS loss to the Seattle Mariners.

He was equally great in the 1996 ALDS and ALCS. In Game 3 of the former against the Texas Rangers, he homered in the top of the first inning and robbed a home run in the bottom of the inning. His sacrifice fly tied the game in the ninth inning. The Yankees took that game and won Game 4 on the strength of two Williams home runs.

Williams hit .467 against the Rangers in that series. He bettered that in the ALCS against the Baltimore Orioles by hitting .474. Williams earned series MVP honors, his signature moment coming in the 11th inning of Game 1 when he hit a walk-off home run. The Yankees won that series in five games to advance to their first World Series in 15 years.

The Yankees got drubbed in the first two games of the World Series by the Atlanta Braves, and it was Williams who led them back in

MOST RBIs, MLB POSTSEASON HISTORY

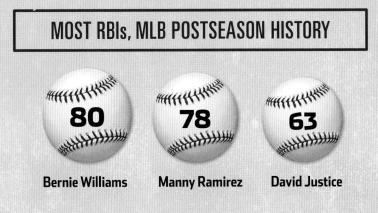

| 80 | 78 | 63 |
| Bernie Williams | Manny Ramirez | David Justice |

Game 3, with a first-inning RBI hit and a two-run home run in the eighth inning.

The intimidation factor of those two hits paid off in Game 4, when the Yankees rallied from 6–0 down to tie. With runners on first and second and two outs in the 10th inning, Braves manager Bobby Cox ordered that Williams be intentionally walked (even though he was 0-for-4 in the game). Cox's gamble failed as his reliever walked Wade Boggs to bring in the go-ahead run. That was a Series-changing moment. The Yankees did not lose again, taking the title in six games.

Williams set the tone in the 1999 postseason as well, with a six-RBI game in an 8–0 win in the ALDS opener against the Rangers. The Yankees went 11–1 that postseason, with Williams winning Game 1 of the ALCS against the Boston Red Sox with a walk-off home run. Williams and David Ortiz are the only players with multiple postseason walk-off home runs.

"When it went out, I was so surprised," said the ever-modest and usually quiet Williams.

Williams provided an image to remember with his catch of Mike Piazza's fly ball to center field for the final out of the 2000 World Series. He didn't have a hit in the first four games of that Series, but he had a pair in the final game, including a home run against Mets starter Al Leiter.

In Game 7 of the 2003 ALCS, Williams entered what looked to be his final at-bat of the year, 4-for-24 that postseason and down to

MOST RBIS IN SINGLE GAME, YANKEES POSTSEASON HISTORY

Robinson Cano (2011)	6
Hideki Matsui (2009)	6
Bernie Williams (1999)	6
Bobby Richardson (1960)	6

DID YOU KNOW?

Bernie Williams holds the Yankees record for consecutive hits. He had hits in 11 straight at-bats in 2002.

his final strike against Red Sox ace Pedro Martinez, before lining a base hit to center that scored Derek Jeter and gave the Yankees, who now trailed by two runs, some hope. Hope turned to joy in the form of Aaron Boone's walk-off home run.

And you can't fault Williams for the loss to the Marlins in the World Series. He went 10-for-25 (.400 batting average) with a pair of home runs in the six-game defeat.

Sometimes it wasn't about October. It was about getting the Yankees to October, like in 2004, when he hit a walk-off home run that clinched the AL East title in the season's final week (and gave the squad the franchise record for most home runs in a season).

"This time of year seems to bring out the best in him," manager Joe Torre said that night.

There are so many great examples of that.

THE CORE 4 (PLUS ONE)

Every good group needs a nickname and the one for the players most essential to the Yankees dynasty is the Core 4, which encompasses Derek Jeter, Jorge Posada, Andy Pettitte, and Mariano Rivera. Most Yankees fans feel that label is a little unfair to Bernie Williams, so when he's included, some refer to the group as the Fab 5 (with apologies to Michigan college basketball).

The key for this group is that they stayed together. The Yankees were well known for trading prospects to try to add established talent, or hanging on to prospects who didn't pan out.

Credit for keeping the core intact goes to general manager Gene Michael, who resisted temptation to deal any of them while George Steinbrenner was serving a suspension. Michael made his share of deals, but avoided the mistakes that had plagued the front office for the past decade.

Andy Pettitte Wins 18 Postseason Games for Yankees

You know the look.

It's the one your television zoomed in on countless times during October baseball—the icy stare that Andy Pettitte gave his catcher, glove covering all but his eyes as he looked in for the sign from his catcher.

That stare isn't indicative of who Andy Pettitte was off the field ("He's just a good dude," said his former bullpen mate, Mike Stanton), but it epitomized who he was on the mound. It helped make him into one of the most successful pitchers in postseason history.

As Tom Verducci and Joe Torre noted in their book, *The Yankee Years*, the stare was about "intense focus."

"One thing I learned about Andy," Torre wrote, "is he thought you weren't allowed to be nervous."

Pettitte's nerves of steel helped turn him into baseball's all-time leader in postseason wins with 19 (18 with the Yankees, one with the Astros).

For those who say his total is the product of three-round postseasons, it's not his fault that his teams repeatedly reached October.

And for those who nitpick and say his 3.81 ERA is high, consider the era and opposition against which he was pitching.

Pettitte was not a power pitcher, even with his 6'5", 235-pound frame. He had a good mix of pitches. But he knew how to use his frame to his advantage, throwing pitches from closer to the plate than most.

Said Stanton, "Andy was tough to come in and pitch behind because he took such a long stride—12 inches more than I could."

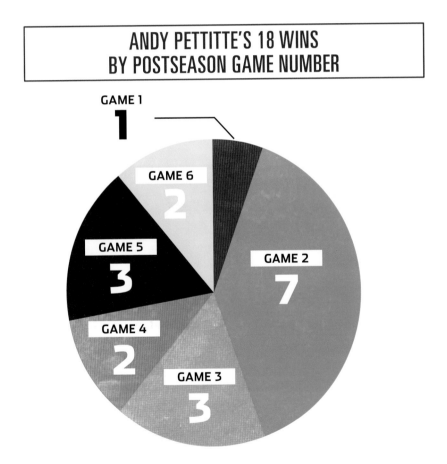

ANDY PETTITTE'S 18 WINS BY POSTSEASON GAME NUMBER

GAME 1
1

GAME 6
2

GAME 5
3

GAME 2
7

GAME 4
2

GAME 3
3

When October came around, Pettitte wasn't just tough to pitch behind. He was tough to pitch *against*.

The postseason game with which Pettitte is most identified is Game 5 of the 1996 World Series against the Atlanta Braves. With the Series knotted at 2–2 and facing 24-game winner John Smoltz, Pettitte bounced back from a 12–1 Game 1 loss and took a shutout into the ninth inning as the Yankees won 1–0, their third of four straight wins on the way to their first title since 1978.

"He's got a lot of heart," Yankees manager Joe Torre said afterward.

Pettitte's postseason identity was carved not in being the Yankees' top starter, but in being the guy who followed that guy.

"Andy Pettitte was Game 2," said *Sports Illustrated* baseball writer Joe Sheehan. "He always pitched Game 2 and he always won Game 2, no matter who the No. 1 starter was."

MOST STRIKEOUTS, YANKEES PITCHER

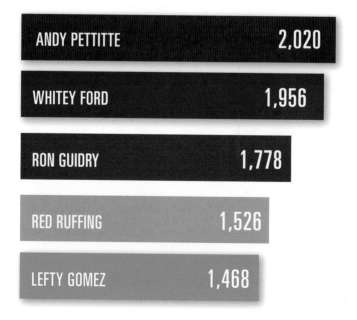

ANDY PETTITTE	2,020
WHITEY FORD	1,956
RON GUIDRY	1,778
RED RUFFING	1,526
LEFTY GOMEZ	1,468

Pettitte was second to none in Division Series Game 2s from 1998 to 2000. In two wins over the Rangers and one win over the Athletics, he combined to allow two runs in 22 innings (a 0.82 ERA), with 16 strikeouts, and one walk.

Pettitte won postseason MVP honors once. In the 2001 ALCS, he beat a Mariners team that won 116 games in the regular season twice. He opened the series with a win and closed it with a win. He held the Mariners scoreless in $14\frac{1}{3}$ innings.

The Yankees had such good bullpens that in Pettitte's second stint with the Yankees, he knew all he had to do was get into the seventh inning and everything would be alright. In his last 10 postseason starts with the team, he totaled $64\frac{2}{3}$ innings and pitched to a 2.92 ERA.

Pettitte is the Yankees' all-time leader in strikeouts (2,020) and is tied with Whitey Ford for most games started by a Yankees pitcher (438).

In 2009, Pettitte was the winning pitcher in each of the three series-clinching games. Pettitte and Derek Lowe are the only pitchers to win three series-clinchers in a single postseason. Pettitte's six series-clinching wins are the most all-time.

Pettitte wasn't necessarily at his best in the last one, in which he allowed three runs and five walks in $5\frac{2}{3}$ innings against the Phillies in the World Series. But he had carried the Yankees through a lot of big games. It was only right that they repaid the favor.

"I've had a lot of wonderful players surrounding me," Pettitte told reporters afterward.

Those players helped Pettitte through a lot of games in the regular season as well. Pettitte's Octobers are the focal point of his career, but his consistency from April to October was significant.

MOST POSTSEASON WINS
BY YANKEES PITCHER ALL-TIME

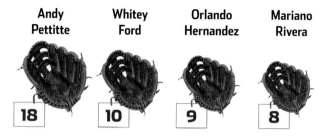

Andy Pettitte	Whitey Ford	Orlando Hernandez	Mariano Rivera
18	10	9	8

Pettitte is the Yankees' all-time leader in strikeouts (2,020) and is tied with Whitey Ford for most games started by a Yankees pitcher (438). His 219 wins and 2,796⅓ innings rank third in franchise history.

Pettitte's are great numbers, especially when you combine those with his brief stint with the Astros. His Hall of Fame case is complicated, because he was implicated for using performance-enhancing drugs by Brian McNamee (Pettitte apologized and said he used HGH to recover from an elbow injury).

If you go just by numbers, it's an interesting candidacy to debate. Some may think he comes up a little short, but if you stare at them with the intensity with which Pettitte looked at opposing hitters, certain things come into focus.

"If you have players who pitched 250 postseason innings at the level of Andy Pettitte, that's got to count a lot," Sheehan said. "There's a lot of 'championship value' in that."

Pettitte has five rings to bear that out.

Jorge Posada Becomes 3rd Yankees Catcher with 1,000 RBIs

"He brings an intensity and a passion that everyone can see. He's one of those guys, you can see the intensity coming out of his ears, coming out of his nose. When Jorge is on the field, you know he's there."

That quote, given by Joe Girardi in Jorge Posada's *Yankeeography,* sums up Posada very well.

Posada's intensity drove him to a highly successful career. There were good moments and a few rough patches, but Posada made the Yankees a better team with his presence.

Intensity was a necessity for Posada, who grew up in Puerto Rico, the son of Jorge Sr., a native Cuban who became a major league scout and desperately wanted his son to become a professional baseball player.

The skills were there, but not to the level of superstardom. Posada was a 43rd-round pick by the Yankees in 1989 and then a 24th-round pick by them in 1990 out of Calhoun Community College in Alabama. His original draft position was shortstop.

Posada tried to play as an infielder in the low minor leagues, but it was clear that his future was not at those positions. He caught part-time previously, but turned to the position full-time in 1992. It didn't come easily, but it came eventually.

"I was not a good player," Posada said of his younger days. "I wasn't the best player on any of my teams. They would stick me in right field, put me on the bench, DH, play first, play third, second, short, left field, center field. I didn't catch until later. I got better because I wanted to be in the big leagues so bad, that I didn't stop until I made it."

Posada made it to the majors for cameos in 1995 and 1996. In 1997, he apprenticed behind Girardi, then took the position over full-time the following season.

"[I was] very hard-headed," Posada said, describing himself as a young player. "Stubborn."

The breakthroughs came slowly but steadily for a couple of years, as Posada played a supporting role on the 1998 and 1999 championship teams, and then suddenly he became a star. In 2000, he hit .287 with a .417 on-base percentage and 28 home runs and was an integral part of the team's third straight World Series title.

From 2000 to 2007, Posada established himself as a top catcher. He made five All-Star teams, won five Silver Sluggers, and twice finished in the top six of the AL MVP voting.

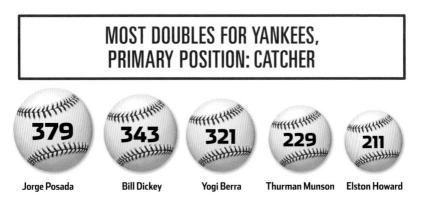

MOST DOUBLES FOR YANKEES, PRIMARY POSITION: CATCHER

379	343	321	229	211
Jorge Posada	Bill Dickey	Yogi Berra	Thurman Munson	Elston Howard

In 2001, he had two huge moments in the ALDS against the Athletics. With the Yankees down two games to none, Posada snapped a fifth-inning scoreless tie with a home run against Barry Zito. Two innings later, he was on the finishing end of "The Flip"— the no-look desperation toss from Derek Jeter that nailed Jeremy Giambi at the plate. Jeter is often lauded for his alertness on that play, but it took a turn-and-tag by Posada to get the out.

JORGE
POSADA
NEW YORK YANKEES® C

Posada originally was going to come off home plate to take the throw, but once he saw what Jeter was doing, he stayed put and managed to get the out at home on a bang-bang, close-as-can-be play, which was the turning point in a series the Yankees rallied to win.

"I saw [Giambi] out of the corner of my eye, and I just happened to catch him right on his calf," Posada said. "I was really lucky. He was out. There's a picture and I'm right on his calf and he's [got his foot above the plate]. I have the picture because there are people who don't believe he's out."

In 2003, Posada drove in 101 runs, the most by a Yankee who primarily played catcher since Thurman Munson drove in 105 in 1976. But it was two postseason RBIs that were the most memorable of his career.

The Yankees trailed the Red Sox 5–3 in the eighth inning of Game 7 of the ALCS, but had runners on second and third with one out, after three straight hits against Posada's nemesis, Pedro Martinez.

In 2001 and 2002, Martinez struck him out 18 times in 24 at-bats, but in 2003 Posada was much better, going 4-for-8 with two home runs in the regular season. He was 1-for-5 against Martinez in the playoffs.

This was an at-bat where it counted, and Posada was known for coming through when it counts. He blooped a broken-bat double to shallow center on a 2–2 pitch to tie the game. The Yankees won the game and pennant three innings later on Aaron Boone's walk-off home run.

Posada still had a few good years after that. In 2007, he hit .338, the highest batting average by a Yankees catcher since Elston Howard hit .348 in 1961.

Toward the end of his career, Posada's memorable moments became fewer, as injuries, age, and performance decline took their toll. There were quibbles with management and one day in which Posada pulled himself out of the lineup in anger.

"I would have communicated with [Girardi] more," Posada said, explaining how he would have handled things differently.

But there was still one pretty noteworthy accomplishment left. On July 23, 2010, Posada smacked an RBI double against Royals pitcher Brian Bannister for his 1,000th career RBI. He joined Yogi Berra and Bill Dickey as the only Yankees whose primary position was catcher to drive in 1,000 runs.

Five years later, when asked to pick his favorite among his many statistical accomplishments, this is the one he chose.

"It's tough to get 1,000 RBIs as a catcher," he said.

Posada knows this well. More than a statistic, he wants to be remembered for passion, fervor, and grit.

"[Remember me as] a gamer," he said. "A guy who went out there every day and wanted to win, someone who gave it 100 percent every day, even though most of the time he wasn't feeling 100 percent."

1 Yankee has Won Both AL Rookie of the Year and MVP

Thurman Munson was always impressive.

The day he was drafted fourth overall out of Kent State in 1968, Yankees scouting director John Johnson said, "He was our first choice all the way."

Upon assignment to the minor-league team in Binghamton, Munson marked his turf, letting those on the team know that he was the catcher and he wouldn't be there for long. He was good and he was confident.

He left enough of an impression to be ranked the fifth-best player to play for a Binghamton baseball team (a city that has housed pro baseball for more than 100 years) even though he played only 71 games there.

The first game Munson caught as a major leaguer was a shutout against the Oakland Athletics on August 8, 1969. Munson not only excelled behind the plate, he hit well too. He had two RBIs in his big-league debut and a home run in his second start.

Munson got a brief taste of the big leagues that season, but was back for the full course in 1970. He hit .302 with a .386 on-base percentage. Munson was the first catcher to post a batting average and an on-base percentage that high in his rookie season since Hall of Famer Mickey Cochrane did in 1925. Munson also ranked fourth in the American League in caught-stealing percentage.

He lived up to the billing of manager Ralph Houk, who in spring training 1969 said, "That guy can throw. He's got a doggone cannon on him.... I'm telling you this guy is really something. You don't see many like him."

Beyond Munson's basic stats, he excelled in three important areas that season.

1) He hit in the clutch: He batted .353 with runners in scoring position and .324 in situations that Baseball-Reference.com defined as high leverage.

"The guy was a great clutch performer," said his former locker mate, Roy White. "He was a guy you wanted to see up there. He wasn't afraid of anything."

2) He rose to the occasion: He hit .358 with a .429 on-base percentage against teams that finished the season with a winning record.

3) He closed strong: He hit .348 after the All-Star break.

Munson survived the physicality of the position to become the first American League catcher to win Rookie of the Year.

"I think a catcher holds the club together but a lot of the things we do go unnoticed," Munson said. "You take 10, 15, or maybe even 20 points off your batting average because of catching."

By 1976, the Yankees were Munson's team. Just after the start of the season, he was named the team's first captain since Lou Gehrig, coming off a year in which he drove in a career-high 102 runs. Munson bettered that with 105 RBIs that year.

DID YOU KNOW? Munson is one of three catchers with at least three straight seasons of a .300 batting average and at least 100 RBIs, along with Bill Dickey and Mike Piazza.

For the first time in his career, Munson didn't just have a good team around him, he had a great one. New additions Mickey Rivers and Willie Randolph were offensive catalysts. Staff ace Catfish Hunter and Ed Figueroa made for an excellent one-two punch atop the starting rotation.

The Yankees pulled away from the AL East pack in June and July. Munson was outstanding in that run. In one 10-game spurt in mid-July, he hit .500 (22-for-44) with 12 RBIs and no strikeouts.

MUNSON, T., *Yankees*®

TRADING CARDS
TOPPS & CO. N. Y.

As Munson continued to star, his MVP candidacy was talked up by the media. When asked about it, he put it simply and bluntly: "I want to win it."

Munson and the Yankees made the postseason for the first time since 1964 and they were challenged there by the Kansas City Royals. The teams played a classic five-game LCS best remembered for Chris Chambliss' pennant-winning home run.

But it's worth noting that Munson had a tremendous series, hitting .435 (10-for-23). He hit .529 (9-for-17) as the Yankees got swept in the World Series by the Cincinnati Reds.

Munson *did* win the AL MVP award, outpolling George Brett and Rivers. He became the first Yankee to win both the Rookie of the Year and MVP awards with the team.

"This is the greatest individual honor I've ever received in baseball," he said upon receiving the award. "It's great to know that I won it on my ability. If I had lost the award, I would have been upset. I felt I deserved to win it."

HIGHEST BATTING AVERAGE IN POSTSEASON, YANKEES HISTORY

Lou Gehrig	.361
Thurman Munson	.357
Babe Ruth	.347
Billy Martin	.333
Reggie Jackson	.328

When asked about the World Series, he spoke like a leader.

"We got beat by a great ball club," he said. "We'll be back next year."

The Yankees *were* back next year and the year after that, winning both times.

Munson was integral to the victories. He hit a huge home run to beat the Royals in Game 3 of the 1978 ALCS on a day in which Brett hit three home runs. Munson also had seven RBIs in the 1978 World Series against the Dodgers and caught the final out in the clinching game, his final World Series moment.

On August 2, 1979, Munson was killed in a plane crash, while flying home on an off day. He was only 32 years old.

Munson's funeral was held on August 6, and the Yankees played that night against the Baltimore Orioles. It's well-remembered that Munson's close friend Bobby Murcer got the winning hit in that game.

His words about Munson are well-remembered as well.

"No greater honor could be bestowed upon one man than to be the successor to this man, Thurman Munson, who wore the pinstripes with No. 15—No. 15 on the field, No. 15 for the records, No. 15 for the Hall in Cooperstown. But in living, loving, and legend, history will record Thurman as No. 1."

Elston Howard
Hits .348

As great as the Yankees are, they were not a perfect franchise in every regard.

The Yankees were among the slowest teams to integrate and there are many indications of opportunities that were passed up by owners and management out of fear, ignorance, and racism.

General manager George Weiss did a solid job in helping build a farm system as farm director and then general manager, but baseball historians have documented that Weiss was among those most aggressive at keeping black players off the roster.

The Yankees finally integrated in 1955, when International League MVP Elston Howard made the team out of spring training. Their first black player made the most of his opportunity.

Howard played 13 seasons with the Yankees and did so in a classy manner that earned him the highest level of respect from his teammates.

"He was a gentleman," said Howard's former teammate Bobby Richardson. "He could play and hit and do everything exceptionally well. He was just a really fine person as well. He had gone through a lot, in an era when segregation was still intact, yet was able to work through all that in such a way that he became the most valuable member of the ball club."

Elston Howard (second from left) was beloved by his Yankees teammates.

Howard's path to stardom was a tough one on the field in that he shuffled back and forth between positions and was moved to catcher at a time when the Yankees already had the best one in the game in Yogi Berra.

So Howard split time behind the plate, in the outfield, and at first base as part of manager Casey Stengel's platoon system. Howard's bat and glove were good enough that it was necessary to find somewhere on the field for him to play.

Howard became an All-Star in 1957 and was one for nine straight seasons. In 1958, he excelled, hitting .314 with 11 home runs. In Game 5 of that year's World Series, with the Yankees trailing three games to one against the Milwaukee Braves and clinging to a 1–0 lead in the sixth inning, Howard made a sprawling catch on Red Schoendienst's line drive and turned it into a rally-killing double play. The Yankees won the game and came back to win the Series.

When Howard first came up to the majors in 1955, Stengel said, "He needs a course in outfielding," but by the end of the Series, Stengel was highly praising of his defensive efforts.

"I'm a better catcher than I am an outfielder, but I will tell you this, if they want me to play in the outfield, then I'm a better outfielder than I am catcher," Howard said.

Howard made key contributions at the plate too. After going 0-for-his-first-10 in the first five games of the Series, Howard had two hits in each of the last two games. In the eighth inning of a tied Game 7, the Braves elected to pitch to Howard with a man on second, first base open, and third baseman Andy Carey on deck.

Howard made the Braves pay. His go-ahead hit against Lew Burdette put the Yankees ahead for good. They avenged their loss to the Braves and Burdette in Game 7 in 1957. Howard was named

HIGHEST BATTING AVERAGE IN SEASON, YANKEES CATCHER

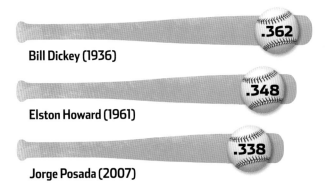

Bill Dickey (1936) **.362**

Elston Howard (1961) **.348**

Jorge Posada (2007) **.338**

the winner of the Babe Ruth Award, given by the New York baseball writers to the Series MVP.

Howard's next chance to star came in the 1960 World Series, in which he went 6-for-13 with four runs scored and four RBIs, but suffered a broken finger in Game 6 that kept him out of the lineup in the Series' decisive game.

In 1961, Howard had a fantastic season. He hit .348, the second-best batting average by a Yankees catcher in franchise history (Bill Dickey hit .362 in 1936), with 21 home runs.

In almost any other season, Howard would have been the AL MVP. But because of the greatness of that Yankees team, he placed 10th in the voting, behind four teammates—Roger Maris (who hit 61 home runs), Mickey Mantle (who hit 54), and pitchers Whitey Ford and Luis Arroyo.

Howard's recognition would come two years later, when Mantle and Maris missed significant time due to injuries. He hit a career-

PAUL KRICHELL AND TOM GREENWADE COMBINE FOR 53 YEARS OF SCOUTING EXCELLENCE

The forgotten people among those who helped to put together the various iterations of the Yankees dynasty are the scouts, those who beat the bushes to find the best talent for the team's minor-league system. The two best the Yankees ever had are Paul Krichell and Tom Greenwade.

Krichell, a friend of general manager Ed Barrow, made his mark by signing Lou Gehrig and Tony Lazzeri early in his career, landing Phil Rizzuto in a tryout camp, and convincing Whitey Ford to try pitching.

Greenwade, who played an integral role in the Dodgers' signing of Jackie Robinson, made his best discoveries by finding Mickey Mantle, Elston Howard, and Bobby Murcer, and recommending a trade for Roger Maris.

"The one thing we can't teach is desire," Greenwade once said. "I look for kids with desire."

That same trait makes a good scout as well.

high 28 home runs and played Gold Glove–winning defense in leading the Yankees to their fourth straight AL pennant.

The Yankees lost to the Dodgers in the World Series, but Howard easily won AL MVP honors, beating out Hall of Famers Al Kaline and teammate Whitey Ford. He became the first black player to win the AL MVP award.

"This has to be the greatest thrill of my career," Howard said. "My one ambition had been to become baseball's No. 1 catcher and last spring I had a feeling this could be my big year where I could put everything together.... One thing is for sure: Without the help of my teammates I could not possibly have won it."

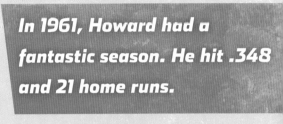

In 1961, Howard had a fantastic season. He hit .348 and 21 home runs.

"I couldn't conceive of a more merited award," said Ralph Houk, Howard's manager that season. "There is no denying Ellie was the solid man of our club. There simply would have been no replacing him had he got hurt. With both Mantle and Maris out for long stretches, it was Howard who kept us going with his hitting. And when our pitching started to wobble at the start and we had to make changes, it was Ellie's skillful handling of the young pitchers—Bouton and Downing—that again saved the day for us."

Howard's playing career lasted five more seasons, the last one-and-a-half coming with the Red Sox, who acquired him to help win the 1967 AL pennant. He became the first black coach when the Yankees transitioned him into that role when his playing days were over.

Howard died prematurely of heart failure in 1980 and his loss was a significant one. His No. 32 was retired in 1984, making him a part of Yankees history. But more than that, the ultimate tribute comes from how his friends remembered him.

"Had I had a boy, I would have wanted him to be like Elston Howard," said Howard's Negro League manager, Buck O'Neill. "Not only blacks—any kid could look up to Elston Howard."

Bill Dickey Catches 100 Games in MLB-Record 13 Straight Seasons

Catching is a profession based on pain.

Your knees and back get bent into uncomfortable positions dozens of times per day. Your fingers get mangled by foul tips and pitches in the dirt. Until recently, high-impact collisions while protecting home plate were a work hazard.

It is incredibly difficult to maintain longevity at this position. But Bill Dickey set the standard. He became the first catcher in major league history to catch at least 100 games in 13 straight seasons (three others followed: Johnny Bench, Brad Ausmus, and A.J. Pierzynski). Dickey did it while hitting at a level matched by few others.

Dickey began the legacy of great Yankees catchers, passed on to two catchers he mentored—Yogi Berra and Elston Howard, as well as Thurman Munson and Jorge Posada.

Dickey proved he could hit almost immediately. He became the Yankees full-time catcher at age 22 in 1929 and never played anywhere else.

"It's beginning to look like the New York Yankees are finally going to have catching that befits a championship club" wrote one sportswriter a month into that season. "Dickey has already shown he is a master at the mechanical end of his position and makes up for his lack of experience with the American League hitters by plenty of catching intelligence.... He also is giving evidence of being a first-class batsman."

As predictions go, that was a good one. However, Dickey, a highly modest southerner who was born in Louisiana, was not one to boast on a team that included the likes of Babe Ruth and Lou Gehrig. He was much more doer than talker.

Dickey hit .310 or better in each of his first six full seasons, with the only blemish to his ledger coming in 1932, a punch to the jaw of a base runner after a nasty collision at home plate. Dickey was suspended for 30 days and later admitted great regret for the incident. In his first game back from suspension, he went 4-for-6 with five RBIs in a win over the Chicago White Sox.

That season was the first in which Dickey got a chance to play in the World Series and he excelled, hitting .438 with four RBIs in a four-game wipeout of the Chicago Cubs. The Series is best remembered for Babe Ruth's Called Shot (which Dickey said was not Ruth predicting a home run, but rather Ruth's response to being quick-pitched), but roommates Lou Gehrig and Dickey were two of the Yankees stars.

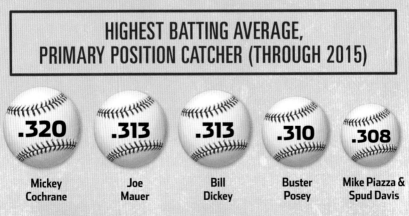

HIGHEST BATTING AVERAGE, PRIMARY POSITION CATCHER (THROUGH 2015)

.320	.313	.313	.310	.308
Mickey Cochrane	Joe Mauer	Bill Dickey	Buster Posey	Mike Piazza & Spud Davis

* Minimum 3,000 plate appearances

Dickey adapted to the ballpark he played in. He hit 135 of his 202 home runs in Yankee Stadium by taking advantage of a short porch in right field. But he had a higher batting average and hit more than 60 percent of his doubles on the road.

Dickey endured his share of illnesses and broken bones, one of which shortened his 1934 season by a month (the Yankees finished second to the Tigers) and another limited his effectiveness in his next World Series opportunity in 1936 (Dickey played through the pain and hit .120, but the Yankees beat the Giants anyway). Dickey was a huge part of that 1936 team, hitting .362 with 22 home runs and 107 RBIs.

It was the first of four straight seasons in which Dickey hit at least .300 and drove in 100 runs, coinciding with the Yankees' run of four straight World Series titles. Dickey finished in the top six of the MVP balloting each of those seasons.

"When he's around, the Yankees travel in high gear," wrote AP sportswriter Sid Feder, "and when he's missing, monkey wrenches show up all through the machinery."

JOE SEWELL STRIKES OUT 3 TIMES IN 1932

The Yankees have a lot of record holders who had great power. But they had one hitter who was the best in the business at making contact—third baseman Joe Sewell.

Sewell finished his career with 7,132 at-bats. He struck out a *total* of 114 times. He played three seasons with the Yankees and struck out 15 times in more than 1,500 at-bats.

In 1932, Sewell struck out three times in 503 at-bats, giving him the best at-bats to strikeouts ratio in MLB history.

Sewell developed his skills as a child by hitting rocks and Coca-Cola bottle caps with a broomstick handle growing up in Alabama.

"I can't ever remember when I couldn't hit," Sewell told an interviewer 45 years later.

Sewell *could* hit. He hit .312 for his career and was inducted into the Baseball Hall of Fame in 1977.

His most noteworthy game in that time was a 4-for-4 outing in Game 1 of the 1938 World Series against the Cubs. Dickey and Munson are the only two catchers to record at least four hits and be perfect at the plate in a World Series game.

By 1940, the 33-year-old Dickey was a bit beat up. He caught 102 games that season and 104 the following year, the latter of which ended with another World Series title. But his days of being a great hitter were over.

Dickey got one more moment of glory on the diamond, in 1943. His sixth-inning home run accounted for the only scoring in a 2–0 win in the clinching Game 5 of the World Series against the Cardinals, who had beaten the Yankees in the World Series the year before.

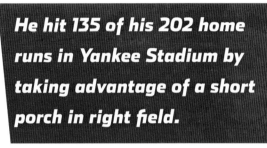

He hit 135 of his 202 home runs in Yankee Stadium by taking advantage of a short porch in right field.

Dickey served in the military during World War II and played briefly in 1946 upon his return. He managed the team for much of that season, but preferred coaching and scouting. He was inducted into the Baseball Hall of Fame in 1954 and had his uniform number retired by the franchise in a joint ceremony with Berra in 1972.

Dickey may not have been a man of loquaciousness like Berra, but he did have one famous line: "A catcher must want to catch. He must make up his mind that it isn't the terrible job it is painted and that he isn't going to say every day, 'Why, oh why, with so many other positions in baseball did I take this one?'"

The Yankees are thankful Dickey never had any such laments.

Pitcher Red Ruffing Hits 31 Home Runs

You can debate if Red Ruffing's pitching, including a 3.80 ERA due to some pre-Yankees struggles, made him worthy of induction to the Hall of Fame.

But you can't discount his skill at the plate. He is the greatest hitting pitcher in Yankees history and one of the best in major league history.

In 15 seasons with the Yankees, he hit .270 with 31 home runs and 213 RBIs in 1,475 career at-bats. Ruffing is one of those who would be thankful that the DH did not come into existence until 1973.

Ruffing was not a good pitcher prior to coming to the Yankees. His acquisition from the Red Sox in early May 1930 netted a paragraph or two in most newspapers and for good reason. At the time of the trade, he was 39–96 with a 4.61 ERA. By the end of the season, those same papers would be calling him the Yankees' staff ace.

Ruffing established early in his major league career that he was potent at the plate. A coal-mining accident had cost him four toes on one foot as a youngster and were it not for that, perhaps he would have been a full-time position player.

Ruffing was a great hitter from his first day with his new team. He drove in two runs in his Yankees debut en route to a win and hit .374 with four home runs as a Yankee that season.

Highlights from that year included a September 14 start in which he hit two doubles *and* a triple to drive in four runs in a win over the Tigers, and another start four days later against the Browns in which he hit a pair of home runs (the first of two instances in which he homered twice in a game).

But that would not be the most incredible of Ruffing's batting feats. Two others rate as more impressive by our standard.

On August 13, 1932, Ruffing not only pitched a three-hit, 12-strikeout, 10-inning shutout against the Washington Senators, but matched Washington's output with three hits, including the game-winning home run to left field in the top of the 10th inning.

The following April 14, Ruffing again delivered dramatically. This time, he hit a walk-off grand slam to beat the Red Sox 6–2. Newspapers noted that the opposing pitcher "reached a new altitude record for hurling the pitcher's glove."

RED RUFFING'S 36 CAREER HR BY TEAM

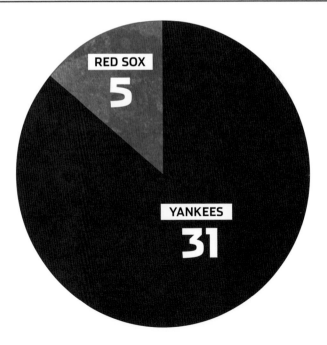

RED SOX
5

YANKEES
31

We can't confirm that, but we do know it to be the second and most recent walk-off grand slam by a pitcher in major league history (the other came in 1890 by Jack Stivetts). It's the most notable of Ruffing's 31 home runs with the Yankees.

Ruffing was able to laugh about his clout, telling reporters, "I suppose a single would have done as well, but I wanted to make sure."

The Yankees took full advantage, with manager Joe McCarthy making Ruffing a useful member of their bench on his off-days.

"My favorite Yankees stat is the record for most pinch-hits by a Yankee," said Lyle Spatz, co-chair of the Baseball Records Committee for the Society for Baseball Research. "Who do you

MOST HR BY YANKEES, PRIMARY POSITION: PITCHER

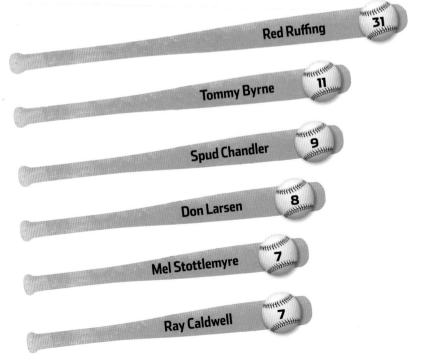

Red Ruffing 31

Tommy Byrne 11

Spud Chandler 9

Don Larsen 8

Mel Stottlemyre 7

Ray Caldwell 7

think it is? A lot of people guess Johnny Mize, Johnny Blanchard, or Yogi Berra. It's Red Ruffing [with 47]."

Ruffing is also among the Yankees standard-setters when it comes to clutch pitching. He went 7–2 with a 2.63 ERA in World Series games, as the Yankees won six of the seven Fall Classics in which he appeared.

He drove in two runs in his Yankees debut en route to a win and hit .374 with four home runs as a Yankee that season.

Ruffing hit only .176 in World Series play, but still managed his share of impressive performances. Prior to Game 2 of the 1937 World Series, he excitedly talked of trying to throw a no-hitter. He didn't quite do that, but he did pitch a complete game and had three RBIs in an 8–1 win.

Ruffing had held out until after that season began because he felt he deserved extra money because of his combination of pitching and hitting. He didn't get it, but he did get a nice measure of satisfaction that day.

"My greatest thrill? Pitching and hitting," he told reporters.

Not many could say they did both as well as Ruffing.

Lefty Gomez Goes 6–0 in the World Series

Lefty Gomez was a quick-quipping, hard-throwing Yankees pitcher known to some as "El Goofy," who excelled in the game's spotlight throughout the 1930s.

Gomez was memorable in a number of regards and always willing to have a little fun.

This ranged from his claiming to have invented a revolving bowl for tired goldfish to pausing during a World Series game to watch a plane fly overhead.

But Gomez's pitching ability matched his entertainment value, particularly in the World Series, in which he holds the record for most wins without a loss, with six.

One of Gomez's most famous quotes was, "I'd rather be lucky than good."

When it came to the Fall Classic, Gomez was both. His 6–0 mark came with a 2.86 ERA in seven starts.

He was a beneficiary of some of the Yankees' biggest offensive outbursts. But he was also adept at escaping trouble. Opponents hit .171 with runners in scoring position against him in the World Series.

In his World Series debut against the Cubs in October 1932, Gomez was so nervous that the AP reported that he sweated off four pounds during the game. His performance was one of his finest, a complete-game win in which he scattered nine hits and allowed only two runs.

"Seemed like the further I went, the better I got," Gomez said. "What did I throw? Oh, a fastball and curves mostly. Guess I was lucky. They weren't swinging when I was pitching."

Opposing manager Charlie Grimm thought Gomez was under-selling himself.

"One of the greatest pitchers I ever saw!" said Grimm, whose time as a pro ballplayer dated back to 1916. "He beats Lefty Grove with me. Why, today he was just as fast as Grove, and what control!"

Gomez's next two World Series wins came in 1936 against the Giants, with the Yankees scoring 31 runs in those two games, including a single-game record 18 in Game 2. Gomez didn't pitch particularly well, but he drove in three runs to make up for it.

MOST WINS, NO LOSSES, WORLD SERIES HISTORY

LEFTY GOMEZ	6
JACK COOMBS	5
HERB PENNOCK	5
MADISON BUMGARNER	4
MONTE PEARSON	4

Most Triple Crowns Won by Pitchers*

Sandy Koufax	3
Grover Cleveland Alexander	3
Walter Johnson	3
Lefty Gomez	2
Christy Mathewson	2
Lefty Grove	2
Roger Clemens	2

* Led league in wins, K, ERA

Two of a Kind: Lefty Gomez Triple Crown Seasons

	1934	1937
ERA	2.33	2.33
Complete Games	25	25
Shutouts	6	6

The 1937 World Series was Gomez's best, matching the caliber of his regular-season performance. In Game 1, he was matched against Giants ace Carl Hubbell and came out on top 8–1. Gomez pitched a complete game six-hitter. He also walked twice in a seven-run Yankees' sixth.

In the Series-clinching Game 5 win, Gomez again went the distance, yielding two runs and 10 hits. But he was most excited about his fifth-inning RBI single that plated the run that put the Yankees ahead for good.

"Pitching? Pitching, my eye! How about that hit I got off Melton that drove in the winning run! That's what I call hitting!" he said.

Gomez would be pleased to know that his four career World Series RBIs are tied for second-most by a pitcher, trailing only Dave McNally's six.

"I had only one weakness as a hitter...a pitched ball," said Gomez, a career .147 hitter. "I was dangerous until I swung."

Gomez recorded one more win the next season, which pushed him past former Yankee Herb Pennock and Jack Coombs for best undefeated record in World Series history. He was the recipient of some good fortune and deferred credit to Frankie Crosetti and Joe

DiMaggio, whose home runs turned a 3–2 deficit into a 6–3 victory over the Cubs.

Gomez's World Series success came alongside great accomplishment in the regular season. He became a star in his second big-league season, going 21–9 with a 2.67 ERA in 1931. It was the first of four 20-win seasons for the Yankees ace, matching Bob Shawkey and Red Ruffing for most in Yankees history.

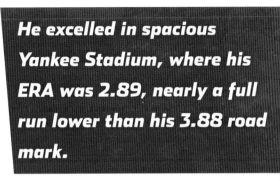

He excelled in spacious Yankee Stadium, where his ERA was 2.89, nearly a full run lower than his 3.88 road mark.

In 1934 and 1937, Gomez did something done by no other Yankees pitcher. He won what is now known as the Pitching Triple Crown, leading the American League in wins, ERA, and strikeouts. He is in elite company as one of seven pitchers who have achieved that combination twice.

Gomez was great for his era and for the situation in which he was in. He excelled in spacious Yankee Stadium, where his ERA was 2.89, nearly a full run lower than his 3.88 road mark.

He won on the strength of a dominant fastball, and though strikeout frequency was mild compared to the rate at which whiffs are accumulated now, he was capable of compiling them in relatively large quantities, twice averaging more than six per nine innings.

Gomez was a bit of a goofball but was so highly respected that he was chosen as the American League's starting pitcher in five of the first six All-Star Games. His five All-Star starts are tied with Don Drysdale and Robin Roberts for the most by a pitcher and his three

DID YOU KNOW?

Gomez holds the MLB record for most walks recorded in a shutout with 11 in 1941.

LEFTY GOMEZ YANKEES RANKS

Wins	189	4th
Innings	2,498⅓	5th
Strikeouts	1,468	5th
Complete Games	173	2nd
Shutouts	28	4th
World Series Wins	6	T–4th

All-Star wins rank as the most all-time. He also had the first RBI in All-Star Game history.

Gomez's career ended in 1943, but he kept himself connected to the game through radio shows, guest columns, a traveling salesman job with Wilson Sporting Goods, and other baseball-related work. He was married to Broadway actress June O'Dea for 56 years before he died in 1989.

Gomez was honored with induction into the Baseball Hall of Fame in 1972, a plaque in Monument Park, and has multiple awards named in his honor, including the most prestigious annual award given by the American Baseball Coaches Association.

In April of 1931, Gomez's second season, none other than Lou Gehrig said, "He has imagination, he wants to be a great pitcher and a smart pitcher. He wants to be an aviator and sometimes gets baseball confused with flying. But just the same, he has the stuff and the disposition, and two years from now, barring accident, will be the greatest left-hander in the business."

Gehrig knew of what he was speaking.

Yankee Stadium(s): Home to More Than 7,500 Games

The most majestic ballpark in baseball got the grandest of openings on April 18, 1923.

Despite temperatures described by the *New York Times* as "arctic" a record gathering of 74,200 fans made their way to the Bronx. The Yankees defeated the Red Sox 4–1, with Babe Ruth hitting the ballpark's first home run in the third inning. Both team and stadium made a big impression.

"The Yanks looked like a new team on their own ball field," wrote the *Times*. "They hustled every minute, kept their head up, and struck hard when the time came to strike.

"First impressions and also last impressions are of the vastness of the arena. The stadium is big. It towers high in the air, three tiers piled one on the other. It is a skyscraper among baseball parks."

After that kind of opening act, who wouldn't want to come back?

Fans have been flocking to Yankee Stadium(s) ever since. The team is closing in on 200 million fans in attendance at Yankee Stadium.

The Yankees reward their fans by winning there at an extraordinarily high rate.

The Yankees have won a major league best 63 percent of their regular-season home games since the park opened in 1923. In that time, the two highest home winning percentages by any team belong to the 1932 team (.805, 62–15) and the 1961 team (.802, 65–16).

Then there is October, when mystique and aura seem to carry the Yankees through. Many players, most notably Derek Jeter, have spoken reverentially of the ghosts that seem to inhabit the ballpark at that time.

The Yankees' postseason winning percentage in Yankee Stadium is almost as good as their regular-season winning percentage. The Yankees have won 62 percent of their postseason games at Yankee Stadium, playing against the toughest competition in baseball.

Home-field advantage is a big part of the ballpark's history.

The original was oddly built in that it was designed with a *heavy* bias to left-handed hitters. Right field was a short poke away, but left-center and center field seemed like miles from the batter's box (it was nearly 500 feet to straightaway center).

While lefties like Babe Ruth thrived, right-handed hitters such as Joe DiMaggio didn't fare as well power-wise. But DiMaggio was good enough that he could hit anywhere and the Yankees were good enough that they won everywhere, especially in the Bronx.

Said Major League Baseball's official historian, John Thorn: "The composition of the park and its outfield dimensions are not crazily different from the Polo Grounds or Tiger Stadium. Short down the line, very deep in the alleys and center. It was the open feeling of the stadium. The openness of the outfield and the 'wedding cake frieze' [of the grandstand] is what those of us who remember the old stadium loved."

The fan experience at the park was a remarkable one. Author Bill Ryczek wrote, "Walking through a Yankee Stadium portal for the first time and seeing the vast expanse of beautifully manicured green grass is something most people never forget."

The Yankee Stadium that you probably best remember was able to retain that, though the renovations in 1974 and 1975 did eliminate the overly monstrous outfield. Tho overhauled park thrived as a home from 1976 to 2008, because even though it could still house nearly 60,000 fans, it had an unmatched feeling of intimacy.

"You would have 50,000 fans and they were right on top of you, even during batting practice," said former Yankees reliever Jeff Nelson. "When you did well, it was the greatest place ever."

"The best thing about the previous Yankee Stadium is the simple structure of the place, particularly the way the upper decks practically hung over the first- and third-base lines," said Jason Rosenberg, editor of the fan blog, It's About the Money, Stupid. "The stadium itself wasn't a beautiful thing, comfort wise. But once you walked out of the cramped corridors, up the ramp to the seats, mercy it was a gorgeous thing."

The acoustics of that park were such that when it got loud, it got *very loud*. It could be an intimidating place for opposing players.

The previous Yankee Stadium rocked *a lot* in the 1990s and 2000s, though its regulars will tell you it roared the most when Don Mattingly homered in Game 2 of the 1995 ALDS.

"The noise that emitted was unlike anything I ever heard at the stadium," said one longtime fan, Gregg Savarese. "The eruption was heartfelt. It was actually frightening. The noise caused the stadium to shake and I was afraid it was going to fall down."

The Yankees' 10-game postseason home winning streak from 1998 to 2000 is the longest all-time.

Yankee Stadium did not come down until the new version was completed in 2009. The team closed the park in grand style, inviting back former players for a celebration, with Jeter giving the goodbye speech.

The Yankees' new home is as majestic as its old one, though some of the intimacy is missing. The upper deck is farther from the field and the ability for a fan to get close to the action is hindered by a moat separating most of the park from its most luxurious seats in the lower level.

But what fans want most from their ballpark experience is to see a winner. That season, the Yankees welcomed fans to their new home the same way they did 86 years prior—with a championship team.

NEARLY 50 MONUMENTS AND PLAQUES IN MONUMENT PARK

Sportscaster Bob Costas likes to tell the story of how as a child he cried when seeing the monuments that now encompass Monument Park, thinking that was where the team's players were buried. But this area is a tribute, not a burial ground.

The area in which the Yankees honor their past is one of the hallowed parts of Yankee Stadium. Its origin dates to the death of former manager Miller Huggins in 1929. The Yankees honored him with a monument that was within the field of play, in the deepest part of center field.

Others followed for elite Yankees, such as Lou Gehrig and Babe Ruth. When Yankee Stadium was remodeled, the monuments were moved beyond the outfield fences, hence the area in which they are housed being named Monument Park. There are currently seven monuments and more than 40 plaques.

"We loved our titles and canonize those that helped bring them," said Jason Rosenberg, editor of the fan blog It's About the Money, Stupid. "It's hard not to love it."

"They're part of the aura of Yankee Stadium," said ex-Yankees PR director Marty Appel.

Section 39 and Section 203: The Home of the Bleacher Creatures

"DEH-REK JEE-TER...DEH-REK JEE-TER!"

"HOR-HAY...HOR-HAY!"

"JOHN-EE DAY-MON...JOHN-EE DAY-MON!"

They are the loyalest of the loyal and the loudest of the loud. They are hard-core and ultraknowledgeable. They sit on the metal benches and make noise, whether it is 40 degrees and raining or 90 degrees and sunny. They love and they hate and they do so with great intensity.

They come with nicknames like Bald Vinny, Sheriff Tom, the Queen, and Walkman John. Or in some cases, they're well known enough that they don't need a nickname when they come for a cameo appearance, like former New York Giants star Justin Tuck.

They are the Bleacher Creatures. They have a special bond with the Yankees players, who respect and admire their devotion.

They originally made their home in Section 39 of the previous incarnation of Yankee Stadium. They now reside in Section 203. Their intention is the same regardless of the location—to support the Yankees in their quest for victory.

The patron saint of the Bleacher Creatures is Ali Ramirez, who has a seat reserved in his memory (he died in 1996). In the 1980s, Ramirez was one of the people who helped turn the group that sat on the benches beyond the outfield fence into a unified family.

The most popular feature for the Bleacher Creatures is the roll call.

"In the 1980s, sitting in the bleachers was tough," said Vinny Milano (aka Bald Vinny) who now serves as the group's de facto leader and owns his own business selling Bleacher Creature apparel. "There were a lot of fights. Any time there was a distraction in the bleachers, Ali would ring a cowbell. That got everybody's attention focused back to the game and cheering for the Yankees."

The original Bleacher Creatures were an intimidating group, but now most of their attention is focused in a different manner.

"[Back then] if we could get in somebody's head, especially an opposing player or fans of the opposing team, that was a huge thing for us. The intimidation factor of the old stadium was built on the reputation of the Bleacher Creatures," Milano said. "It's completely different from what we are now. Not it's all about being positive Yankees fans."

The most popular feature for the Bleacher Creatures is the roll call, in which they salute every player in the field in the top of the first inning. They yell the player's name repeatedly in different sing-song manners.

"The roll call started out of boredom," Milano said. "It was like, hey maybe we can get them to hear us. Can we get them to turn around? The players caught on and each guy has their custom response. It's a cool rapport with the players that most fans don't get with other teams. The moment of realization I had was when little kids started to come up to me to say 'I can't believe Nick Swisher turned around and saluted me.'"

The players are very much aware of the importance of roll call.

"I made my only career start in 1998," said former Yankees reliever Mike Stanton. "The Bleacher Creatures were awesome. They [chanted my name] a couple different times. It got to the point where they weren't going to stop until I acknowledged them. So I had to give them a little nod."

The Bleacher Creatures are unified by their love for the Yankees.

The awareness extends from the biggest stars to the last man on the bench. On Bernie Williams bobblehead day, Williams decided to entertain the Creatures by moving his head in a bobblehead motion when his name was chanted. And even the former Yankees captain acknowledged his biggest supporters.

"On photo day, they bring the season ticket holders out and you stand on the warning track while they bring players over," Milano said. "Derek Jeter came out, saw me, and said, 'Hey Vinny, I saw you in the *New York Post* the other day. You're looking awesome.'"

How do the Creatures decide how the chant for each player will go?

"I'll ask Walkman John [better known as John McCarthy]," Milano said. "He's the most level-headed guy. If I'm stumped, I'll ask a kid, because kids will tell you straight [if it's a good name]."

Yankees management was a little uneasy with the group's interaction at first, but grew to enjoy it. General manager Brian

FREDDY SEZ WAS THE YANKEES' NO. 1 FAN FOR 85 YEARS

The Yankees' most devoted fan was Freddy Schuman, also known as "Freddy Sez."

Freddy would walk around Yankee Stadium banging a frying pan with a spoon and encouraging others to do so. He was mostly quiet otherwise, expressing his thoughts through signs he would carry as he made his way around the ballpark. His Yankees jersey had his nickname, Freddy Sez, with the No. 1 on the back.

Freddy suffered a heart attack in October 2010 and died at the age of 85, but he is very well remembered by those who saw him in the 1980s, 1990s, and 2000s.

"Freddy was a presence," said Yankees fan and baseball historian Cecilia Tan. "He was like part of the Stadium itself. The sound of people banging on the pan was as much a part of the Stadium experience as seeing the elevated train go by in that gap in the stands in right field. Since Freddy died in 2010, in the middle of the ALCS, postseason games since then just haven't felt the same. And you'll note the Yankees haven't won since then, either."

Cashman has sat with the Creatures and helped arrange for special guests. Former players David Cone and David Wells have hung out there too.

Supreme Court justice Sonia Sotomayor may have been the most noteworthy person to be a Creature for a day.

"She was very chill," said Milano, which isn't exactly how you'd think most people would describe a Supreme Court judge. "She used to go to games by herself. I told her we had something in common. That's why I used to go to games. Come for three hours and forget your problems."

Tuck was arguably the most popular.

"Most people who come out there get overwhelmed," said Milano. "They don't know what to do. I gave [Tuck] a rundown and he said, 'Dude, I'm a Yankees fan. I already know.'"

Why do people come to the bleachers? It's a good time at a reasonable price. It may not be for everyone, but those who are regulars swear by it.

"The group of friends you sit with is a draw," McCarthy said. "I don't mind the bench thing. I don't need a cup holder at my seat. I just enjoy going to the games."

In the end, that's what it's all about. Different fans enjoy games in different ways. The Bleacher Creatures have found their perfect way to enjoy a game.

"I think we show a lot of passion," Milano said. "That's our hallmark. It's what makes us what we are."

Mel Allen Could Sum It All Up in 3 Words

The Yankees have had a grand tradition of noteworthy and popular broadcasters, including both Phil Rizzuto and John Sterling. But the pioneer was the most popular of them all—Mel Allen.

Allen, a native of Alabama, became part of the Yankees' first announcing team in June 1939. He had broadcasting experience for CBS Radio and called the previous year's World Series.

David Halberstam, a former broadcaster who wrote a book called *Sports on New York Radio: A Play-by-Play History*, described Allen as having three traits that made him a great announcer: "A deliberate speech cadence, a caring husky sound, and an infectious love of the game."

Allen was wonderful at conveying emotion through three-word bursts. There was "Hello there, everybody," his broadcast greeting, which set a tone of friendliness a listener was looking for from an announcer.

There was also "Going, going, gone!" which was Allen's home run call, a simple one that told the story for many a long drive.

And on a great play, Allen would always punctuate it with "How about that?" which was more exclamation than question.

But there was more to Allen than those phrases we remember most.

"What I liked about Mel Allen was that, above and beyond the historic catchphrases, he was an intelligent and articulate observer of the happenings below him," said Gary Gold, a Yankees fan dating back 55 years. "It was not surprising to learn then that he was a law school graduate.

"But what I *really* liked about Mel Allen was that he was the Yankees' announcer. In essence I loved the second-best sportscaster of all time because he was ours—and hated the best of all time [Vin Scully] because he was theirs [the hated Dodgers]."

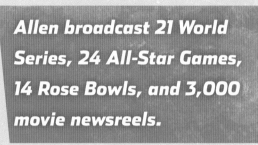

Allen broadcast 21 World Series, 24 All-Star Games, 14 Rose Bowls, and 3,000 movie newsreels.

Allen wasn't just the voice of the Yankees. He was the premier voice of the game. If there was a big baseball game, he was the national voice for it. And his work wasn't limited to just baseball. Allen broadcast 21 World Series, 24 All-Star Games, 14 Rose Bowls, and 3,000 movie newsreels.

"Nationally, Mel was everywhere," said Curt Smith, author of *The Voice*, a comprehensive biography of Allen, in an interview with GelfMagazine.com "Today, cable and free-TV networks divide voices, events, and rights. Mel thrived in a smaller universe. A broadcaster could more easily dominate. No one will ever dominate like Allen."

Allen broadcast full-time for the Yankees from 1939 to 1942 and 1946 to 1964. He was let go by the Yankees at the end of the 1964 regular season for reasons never publicly explained. Many were stunned by the news and voiced their support for Allen.

"When you broadcast for one club for 25 years, you have to be good and Mel Allen was better than good," wrote Dick Young. "He had music in his voice and the voice was of tireless muscle. He could talk for hours on end, with a resonance and a sustaining quality that was incredible."

Allen had occasional broadcasting work for the next dozen years, including stints with the Braves and Indians.

In 1977, he became the voice of *This Week in Baseball,* a syndicated baseball highlights show, where he welcomed a new audience with "Hello there, everybody."

A year later, Allen and his former broadcast partner Red Barber were named the winners of the first Ford C. Frick Award, an honor given by the Baseball Hall of Fame.

"Every day when I go to work, I want to look at [the plaque] and say 'How about that?'" Allen said in his acceptance speech.

Allen held his *This Week in Baseball* job until his death in 1996. He was also brought back to the Yankees under George Steinbrenner's

BOB SHEPPARD'S 57 YEARS AS PA ANNOUNCER

Mel Allen, Phil Rizzuto, and John Sterling may have been the voices of the Yankees, but the voice of Yankee Stadium was Bob Sheppard.

"A man of great dignity and intelligence," said ex-Yankees PR director Marty Appel.

Sheppard, whose primary job was as a speech teacher, announced everyone coming to bat from Joe DiMaggio and Mickey Mantle to Reggie Jackson and Ron Guidry to Derek Jeter and Mariano Rivera. Sheppard became a legendary figure in Yankees history because of a distinct baritone voice.

"As he would say: clear, concise, and correct," said Chris Pavia, who does a remarkable impersonation of Sheppard and organist Eddie Layton on YouTube.

After Sheppard died in 2010, Jeter requested each of his home-plate appearances be announced by Sheppard for the rest of his career.

"I grew up a Yankees fan and he was always the voice I heard," Jeter said.

It's a great tribute to the man known around the ballpark as "The Voice of God."

ownership to broadcast approximately 40 games a year through the mid-1980s.

He got one more moment of broadcasting glory, joining the Yankees crew in the booth for a game against the Red Sox on July 4, 1983.

You may recognize that as the day Dave Righetti pitched a no-hitter. The broadcast crew ceded the call to Allen, who punctuated Wade Boggs' strikeout with a "How about that?"

In 1998, the Yankees honored Allen with a plaque in Monument Park. It read:

"Mel Allen—The Voice of the Yankees, 1939–1964."

With his warm personality and signature greeting, he shaped baseball broadcasting by charismatically bringing the excitement and drama of Yankees baseball to generations of fans. He made pet phrases such as "Going, going, gone!" a part of our language and culture.

A Yankee institution. A national treasure.

"How about that?"

Phil Rizzuto Leads the Major Leagues in Sacrifices 4 Straight Seasons

The folks at the Bowman baseball card company knew what they were doing when they produced the artistic rendition for one of Phil Rizzuto's cards. They captured him in deep concentration showing off his bunting style. There's good reason for this. Rizzuto was the sport's most prolific bunter. In fact, he's still the only player to lead the major leagues in sacrifices four times...and he did it in four consecutive seasons.

Many remember Rizzuto the broadcaster more than Rizzuto the player. The former was a skilled play-by-play man for a long time, though most recall his humorous moments, such as his early departures from games to beat traffic on the George Washington Bridge.

Or they know him by the two-word phrase that he uttered regularly—"Holy cow!"

Though some may not think he ranks with the game's immortals as a player, the fact is that he's there and he isn't being kicked out any time soon.

Rizzuto, a Brooklyn native, played for the Yankees from 1941 to 1956, though he missed the 1943 to 1945 seasons due to Navy service during World War II.

His playing style didn't change. He was 5'6", 150 pounds, but he played with his heart on his sleeve.

Rizzuto played a lot, averaging 141 games over 11 years. He was a good contact hitter and a good base stealer for his era (he ranked in the top six in the American League in stolen bases eight times).

"He was a terrific player, a good hitter and he could bunt really well," said former teammate Bobby Brown.

PHIL RIZZUTO
Champion Base Ball Fielder

In Rizzuto's time, bunting was an important part of the game.

From 1949 to 1952, Rizzuto totaled 93 sacrifices, leading the majors in each season. The player who ranked second in that time span was Hall of Famer Nellie Fox. He had only 56.

"Without knowing how to bunt, I'd have never made it to the big leagues," Rizzuto said during his Hall of Fame speech in 1994.

Rizzuto also excelled on defense. If you look back at the numbers, you'll see that the Yankees pitchers overachieved through the 1940s and 1950s. They should have allowed more runs than they did based on their strikeout, walk, and home runs allowed. One of the reasons they didn't is because their defense was so steady. Rizzuto was at the center of that, at the shortstop spot.

"Nobody ever played shortstop better than Phil Rizzuto," Brown said.

Rizzuto played in nine World Series, and though he hit only .246 in them, he had a .355 on-base percentage and raised his level of play at an important time. He had a .303 batting average in World Series games in which the Yankees had a chance to clinch the Series.

In Game 7 of the 1947 World Series against the Dodgers, Rizzuto was in the middle of just about everything. His second-inning RBI single cut the Dodgers' lead to 2–1. His two-out single in the fourth inning extended a Yankees rally in which they took the lead. And in the sixth inning, he started another rally with a bunt hit and stolen base that led to an important insurance run. Appropriately, the game and Series ended with Rizzuto starting a 6-4-3 double play.

Also noteworthy: Rizzuto was playing hurt, with some of the wear and tear coming from a Jackie Robinson take-out slide earlier in the Series.

As the Yankees transitioned from being Joe DiMaggio's team to Mickey Mantle's team, Rizzuto played a major role in the club's winning ways. He placed second in the AL MVP voting in 1949 and won the award in 1950.

He copped an MVP of a different type in 1951 after the Yankees beat the Giants for their third straight title, winning the Babe Ruth Award as World Series MVP.

MOST SACRIFICES IN CAREER WITH YANKEES

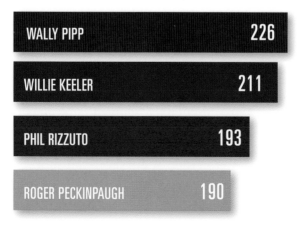

WALLY PIPP	226
WILLIE KEELER	211
PHIL RIZZUTO	193
ROGER PECKINPAUGH	190

EDDIE LAYTON PLAYS THE ORGAN AT YANKEE STADIUM FOR NEARLY 30 YEARS

If Bob Sheppard was the voice of Yankee Stadium, Eddie Layton represented the musical accompaniment.

Layton played the ballpark's organ from 1967 to 1970 and 1978 to 2003 and is credited with popularizing "Charge!" in baseball stadiums.

Layton kept the tune of songs he played intact, but added little wrinkles with timing and beat to "New York, New York" and other songs prior to games. Layton was considered an integral part of the team. He was given a World Series ring for each of the five titles the Yankees won during his tenure.

"He always knew what to play for each occasion," said Chris Pavia, who keeps Layton and Bob Sheppard's memories alive through a YouTube tribute. "He was amazing. He just brought the place to life."

The website theatreorgans.com described his style as "smooth" and rated him "among the very best Hammond organists ever."

Layton died just after Christmas in 2004. Among those who paid tribute was Yankees owner George Steinbrenner.

"Eddie Layton was a treasured member of the Yankee family and, as a gifted musician, he made Yankee Stadium a happier place," Steinbrenner said.

In that Series, Rizzuto hit .320 and batted safely in each of the six games. He had his only World Series home run in a Game 5 win. Wrote Arthur Daley of the *New York Times*: "The most important man in the lineup was the smallest man the Yankees had, Phil Rizzuto, baseball's Merlin the Magician. They could not have won without him."

"Merlin the Magician" didn't stick as a nickname, mainly because Rizzuto already had a nickname—"Scooter," which had been given to him in his minor-league days.

Scooter scooted through five more big-league seasons. He played in the triumphant Fall Classics of 1952 and 1953, hitting .316 with four runs scored in six games in the latter.

MOST DOUBLE PLAYS, YANKEES SHORTSTOPS

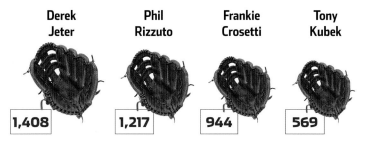

Derek Jeter	Phil Rizzuto	Frankie Crosetti	Tony Kubek
1,408	1,217	944	569

Rizzuto was released late in the 1956 season and began a second career as a beloved play-by-play broadcaster the next season. He called many memorable Yankees games and moments, including Roger Maris' 61st home run in 1961 and Chris Chambliss' pennant-winning home run in 1976.

In 1994, nearly 40 years after he'd played his final game, Rizzuto was inducted into the Baseball Hall of Fame after being elected by the Veterans Committee. In his inauguration speech, Rizzuto thanked the fans who supported him with petitions and letters to Hall of Fame voters.

"My records pale with all these Hall of Famers behind me," Rizzuto said that day. "I've been so lucky to be with the Yankees for 54 years, with the same organization."

They were fortunate to have him as well.

John Sterling:
0 Missed Games

Yankees broadcaster John Sterling is to this generation of Yankees fans what Mel Allen was to Yankees fans of the 1950s and 1960s and Phil Rizzuto was to Yankees fans after that.

He is easily identifiable because of a highly distinct voice. He is there for every game without fail. He's the voice that represents the diehard fan.

"He's the personification of Yankees pride," said Grantland baseball writer Ben Lindbergh.

What is most amazing about Sterling is that he's never missed a game since he started broadcasting for the team in 1989.

Sterling's voice is one that evokes power and authority, but off the air, he's modest about this distinction.

"I've been sick, but not enough to miss a game," Sterling said. "When you get on air, you get that adrenaline and you give it your all."

A Sterling broadcast, whether it was with his previous partners, who include Jay Johnstone, Charley Steiner, Michael Kay, or his current partner, Suzyn Waldman, is filled with high energy. It comes through when he welcomes you to the ballpark; when he calls a double play; when he calls home runs as high, far, and gone; and especially at the end of a great victory when he practically bursts out of his seat and proclaims, "Yankees win! Thhhhhe Yankeeeees winnnnn!"

"Sterling is like your favorite movie," wrote *New London Day* columnist Mike DiMauro. "You know the lines are coming. You know the inflection. But you just can't wait to hear it again."

A Sterling broadcast also comes with a high entertainment factor. The wordplay is clever on the home-run calls, as Sterling likes to add a special touch to a player's name.

"I always kidded with ballplayers' names," Sterling said in an interview with Chuck Hildebrandt of the Society for American Baseball Research. "I never knew it was going to catch on to the point where I would need a home run call for every player."

New York Magazine once broke down Sterling's home run wordplay into seven categories: rhymes ("Gardy goes yardy"), alliteration ("Bernie goes boom"), name-play ("You're on the mark, Teixeira"), foreign languages ("El capitan"), cultural references ("Curtis, you're something sort of Grandish"), Babe Ruth ("The Bamtino"), and made-up words ("Swishalicious").

> **The last assignment he recalls missing was a Nets game during the 1980–81 season due to vocal nodule surgery.**

Sterling's style has always been that of watching the game and reacting as if he were a fan. The description may not be perfect or precise, but the emotion is always there.

"I broadcast by the seat of my pants," Sterling said. "It's just expressing yourself in the English language in different rhythms. You know what I've done? I've combined my avocation with my vocation."

Said Katie Sharp, a writer for the top Yankees fan blog, River Ave Blues: "What I like most is that you really never know what you are going to hear when you listen to a John Sterling broadcast. Sure I want to know what's going on in the game when I listen on the

FIRST FULL-TIME FEMALE BASEBALL RADIO ANALYST: SUZYN WALDMAN

Suzyn Waldman is a baseball broadcasting pioneer, the first full-time, full-season female baseball broadcaster. The 2015 season was her 11th in the radio booth with John Sterling. She previously worked on game broadcasts for WPIX and YES.

"People often throw around the word 'pioneer' but in the case of Suzyn it fits," said WFAN update anchor Erica Herskowitz. "Her passion, knowledge, and ability to shut out the doubters and the haters has propelled her to the amazing success she is today."

What distinguishes Waldman from other announcers is her reporting. She can speak to players, management, and ownership about any subject from how a pitcher is properly gripping a curveball to the player's family life.

Wrote former *New York Times* writer Claire Smith, "Think about the grace, the professionalism, and the courage. These are the core of the legacy still being artfully written by Suzyn Waldman to this day."

radio. But I also want to be entertained. And there are few that do it better than John Sterling."

Sterling grew up in Manhattan in the 1940s and is old enough to remember listening to the 1947 World Series between the Yankees and Brooklyn Dodgers (which the Yankees won in seven games). Sterling had the good fortune to know exactly what he wanted to do at a young age. He told his childhood friends that he wanted to be the next Mel Allen.

Prior to being the Voice of the Yankees, Sterling broadcast for other New York teams, including the Islanders and Nets in the 1970s, and hosted a sports-talk show. He then broadcast the Atlanta Braves and Atlanta Hawks throughout most of the 1980s and also did so without missing an assignment. The last assignment he recalls missing was a Nets game during the 1980–81 season due to vocal nodule surgery.

The Yankees job came open prior to the 1989 season. He expressed interest and got the position without an audition.

"I was afraid of leaving Atlanta, but I didn't want to be an old man saying, 'I wish I'd done the Yankees,'" Sterling said.

He's done it day after day through 162 games. Those Yankees teams when Sterling first started were pretty bad, but Sterling did his best to make every broadcast interesting. That's less of a concern these days, given the Yankees grand status for two decades running.

He's also fortunate that everything has worked out as well as it has.

"There is not a day in my life that someone doesn't come up and tell me how much of a fan they are and how much they like my broadcast," Sterling said. "So that's a very nice thing. It makes me feel very good."

"I came here and the results have worked out better than I could have dreamed. I couldn't have fantasized this happening. I'm very happy."

Bobby Murcer Homers in 4 Straight At-Bats

When Bobby Murcer came up as a prospect, he was often compared to fellow Oklahoman Mickey Mantle. Though Murcer could never match Mantle's awesome power, he made his own name with big hits.

If Mel Stottlemyre was the pitcher that young Yankees fans of the late 1960s and early 1970s wanted to be like, Murcer was the hitter kids of that era idolized.

"He represented to me, the ideal of what an undersized shaggy-haired Little Leaguer could become," said baseball historian and blogger Kevin Graham. "I had his baseball card with me whenever I was on the field [tucked into my hat], and in a sense he has never left my side."

Murcer's first career home run was a game-winner in the seventh inning against the Washington Senators in 1965, with his favorite childhood player, Bobby Richardson, scoring in front of him. His last two home runs (one in 1982, one in 1983) also came in situations that put the Yankees ahead for good.

Murcer carried the Yankees offense through some of the team's toughest times. Yet the Yankees came very close to trading him to the Senators for Bronx native Mike Epstein, a power-hitting first baseman. But the deal never happened.

It turned out that Murcer had pretty good power too. His greatest individual accomplishment came when he hit four home runs in four at-bats in a doubleheader against the Indians on June 24, 1970, less than a month after the trade rumor became public.

> **Murcer finished in the top 10 in the AL MVP race each season from 1971 to 1973.**

Murcer began his barrage with a home run in the ninth inning of a loss in the opening game. In the nightcap, he homered in the first inning, homered again in the fifth inning, then homered a third time in the eighth inning, the latter a game-tying shot in an eventual Yankees victory.

"I couldn't believe it myself," Murcer said of the ovation he got after that game-tying home run. "I tipped my cap because I wanted to let them [fans] know I heard them and appreciated it."

Murcer finished in the top 10 in the AL MVP race each season from 1971 to 1973. In one memorable game at Yankee Stadium in late August 1972 against the Rangers, Murcer hit a game-tying home run in the ninth inning, one that gave him the Yankees' first cycle since Mantle had one in 1957.

"He is the best player in the American League," Mantle said when he visited the Yankees during spring training in 1973. "Everybody keeps saying he's going to be another Mantle or DiMaggio. I think he's already there."

The number 4 is significant to Murcer's Yankees career. It's the number of times he made the All-Star team and the number of different uniform numbers he wore with them (17, 1, 27, and 2).

Murcer had a penchant not just for the long ball, but for turning potential defeats into victories.

MOST RBIs IN AMERICAN LEAGUE, 1971–1973

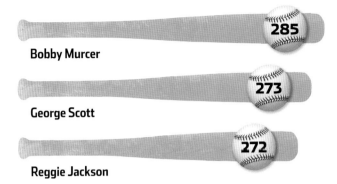

Bobby Murcer 285

George Scott 273

Reggie Jackson 272

Fourteen times Murcer came up with the Yankees trailing in the ninth inning or later and delivered a hit that either tied the game or gave the Yankees the lead.

Murcer's Yankees career spanned two stints. In the second, after spending four seasons with the Giants and Cubs, Murcer became an effective part-time player and late-game pinch-hitter.

That is why in Murcer's *Yankeeography*, former major league manager Sparky Anderson said, "He was a guy you didn't want to have up there against you with the game on the line."

Yankees fans always wanted Murcer up, never more than on August 6, 1979, with the team trailing by a run against the Orioles. That was the day of the funeral for Yankees catcher and captain, and one of Murcer's best friends, Thurman Munson, who had been killed in a plane crash four days earlier. Murcer was given the option of not playing after being among those who eulogized Munson earlier in the day. But he felt that the right thing to do was to play.

The Yankees trailed in the game 4–0, but Murcer's three-run home run in the seventh inning got them back within a run. They were still down a run with runners on second and third and nobody out in the ninth inning when Murcer came up. He lined an opposite-field, two-strike, two-run single scoring Bucky Dent with the tying run and Willie Randolph with the winning run.

"I think we felt like Thurman played a part in it, somehow, some way for him on his night," Murcer said years later. "We needed something to feel good about because it had been such a tragedy."

Murcer became beloved in his post-playing career as a Yankees broadcaster, work that lasted more than 20 years and ended with his death due to brain cancer in 2008.

Former Yankees PR director Marty Appel offered this tribute at Murcer's funeral: "He was a fan's player and he was a player's player. We rooted hard for him—not just because the rebuilding started with him, but because he was just a terrific kid, handed an oversize assignment, and he handled it with grace, with honesty, and with dignity—as he did with everything to the very end, including his final challenge."

Murcer was always very appreciative of the opportunity that he got and of the fans who supported his play. He had a lifelong respect for the franchise he grew up following while living in the Midwest.

"Being able to really live out your dream for such a long tenure and to be able to have such a long relationship with the pinstripes, you cannot get any better," Murcer said.

Reggie Jackson put it best after Murcer's death: "If there's a Hall of Fame for people, he's in it."

HORACE CLARKE BREAKS UP THREE NO-HITTERS IN A MONTH

Yankees second baseman Horace Clarke hit .251 in 1970, but there are a few pitchers who wish he'd hit just a little bit worse.

Clarke became the nemesis separating a pitcher from the game's ultimate glory. In June and July of that season, Clarke broke up *three* no-hit bids in the ninth inning—Jim Rooker, Sonny Siebert, and Joe Niekro. The last of the three was the closest call, with Clarke barely beating Niekro in a race to first after Clarke hit a grounder to the right side.

Clarke kept a noteworthy streak going for the Yankees. The Yankees went nearly 45 years between being no-hit until six Astros combined on one against them in June 2003. The 6,980-game streak was the longest in major league history until broken by the Cubs in 2009.

11 Seasons Without a Postseason Appearance Before Roy White Finally Made It

"I always thought that once I got to the Yankees, I was going to be in the World Series every year," said former Yankees outfielder Roy White.

But baseball doesn't always work out like you think it will. White had a long wait ahead of him.

The 11 years from 1965 to 1975 was one of the toughest times in Yankees history. The years represent a transition period when aging stars like Mickey Mantle and Whitey Ford retired and attempts to replace them were unsuccessful.

Changes weren't just happening on the field. The franchise went through ownership transitions as well, first to CBS between the

1964 and 1965 seasons and then to a group of investors that included George Steinbrenner in January 1973.

Only one player was a part of each season of the gap between the greatness—Roy White.

White made his big-league debut in September 1965. He went 2-for-5 as a leadoff man in his first major league start, prompting Mantle to come over to him in the dugout and say with a smile: "This game's easy, isn't it?"

> *In 1970, he became the second Yankee to have a 20-homer, 20-steal season, the first to do so since Mantle in 1959.*

The big-league game didn't come all that easily to White. Though he hit .333 in his first 14 games, he then dropped off. He hit .225 in 1966 and .224 in 1967.

"[Early in 1966] I was leading the team in home runs and RBIs and I got it into my head that I was a home run hitter," White said. "It got me into some bad habits. I'm a line-drive hitter that needs to use the whole field. I got out of the habit of trying to jerk the ball out of the park. I had a second opportunity to be a regular and things worked out better."

The 1968 season was known as the Year of the Pitcher, but for White it was the Year of the Breakout. While most hitters struggled, White thrived. His batting average jumped 43 points to .267, he placed 10th in the AL with a .350 on-base percentage, and his slugging percentage soared from .290 to .414.

The next two seasons, White was an All-Star. In 1970, he became the second Yankee to have a 20-homer, 20-steal season, the first to do so since Mantle in 1959.

Though the Yankees had decent seasons as White became an established veteran, they did not win championships. They finished at least 15 games out of first place in seven straight seasons.

ROY WHITE YANKEES RANKS
(THROUGH 2015)

Games	1,881	7th
Stolen Bases	233	5th
Sac Flies	69	T–2nd
Walks	934	8th

"That was tough to go through," White said. "A lot of people were happy to see [us] down."

Things turned around under Steinbrenner, who made Gabe Paul general manager and Paul went to work surrounding players like White with better talent. In came Willie Randolph, Catfish Hunter, and Reggie Jackson to go along with White, Graig Nettles, and Sparky Lyle. Paul also brought in former Yankee Billy Martin as manager.

In 1976, the Yankees had a championship-caliber team. White hit in the No. 2 spot in the lineup, stole 31 bases, and led the AL in runs scored, and the Yankees made the World Series for the first time since 1964, only to be swept by the Reds.

In 1977, White hit .268 and came through with a hit that marked a turning point in the season. The Yankees trailed the Red Sox by five games in late June entering a three-game series against them in the Bronx. The Red Sox had swept the Yankees the previous weekend, with Jackson and Martin getting into a fight in the dugout.

The Red Sox had a two-run lead with two outs in the ninth inning with their closer, Bill Campbell, pitching.

Campbell had allowed only one run in his last 29⅔ innings, but gave up a triple to Randolph prior to facing White.

"I came up to the plate feeling great," White said. "The first pitch doesn't break sharp and I hit it for a two-run home run. That was the one time I felt like I was going to hit a home run and it actually happened."

The Yankees won on Jackson's 11th-inning hit.

White's season-ending numbers didn't look bad on the surface, except he went through a two-month slump at the end of the season and was bumped to the bench for the playoffs and World Series. But he scored the winning run in the ninth inning of Game 5 of the ALCS against the Royals.

White got at least one hit in all 10 games that postseason.

"In retrospect, I should have been happy [that we won the World Series]," White said. "But I was angry that I didn't get a chance to play and hit."

That chance would come in 1978 after the Yankees rallied to catch the Boston Red Sox in the standings amid a tumultuous season.

White was actually traded to the Oakland Athletics, but was able to reject the trade due to his status as a veteran.

"At that time I wasn't playing, but after that I was playing regularly and had one of the better two months of my career," White said.

White played an important role behind the scenes in the Yankees' win over the Red Sox in the one-game playoff, though it was one that went unknown for a long time, until White shared the story of how Bucky Dent used White's bat to hit the game-winning home run, with Marty Noble of MLB.com.

"It was a bat I'd given to Mickey Rivers," White said. "I didn't like how it felt. When we played Boston, Bucky hadn't been going well. He used the same model, but it was a much bigger bat—35 inches, 34 ounces. I said, 'Why don't you use Mickey's bat [that I gave him]. It's the same model, but it's 34 inches and 32 ounces.' He tried it in batting practice.

"In the game, he was using that bat. It had a chip in the knob. When he fouled the ball off his ankle, Mickey asked him how come he

DID YOU KNOW?

Roy White ranks 11th all-time for most hits in Yankees history.

was using that one. Bucky said, 'I don't want to use your gamer.' So Mickey gave him his other bat and said, 'Hey, we're on the same team.'

"Mickey told that story for so long, I started to think it was his bat. But I was in Cooperstown [a few years ago] and I asked someone to find out.... He called me and said 'It was your bat.' I knew it."

White got at least one hit in all 10 games that postseason. His home run in the sixth inning of Game 4 of the ALCS against the Royals was a pennant-clincher. He scored nine runs in six games in the World Series win over the Dodgers and was neck-and-neck with Bucky Dent in the race for MVP, which Dent won with a strong Game 6.

"It was a tough, gritty team that knew how to win and played great under pressure," White said. "It was a better team than what I thought it was at the time."

White finished his career with three seasons in Japan with the Yomiuri Giants. In his post-playing career, he served as a Yankees hitting coach for three seasons in the mid-1980s and a first-base coach in the mid-2000s.

"I want to be remembered as a winner, a guy who did all the little things, and that was a team guy," White said.

And one who battled through the tough times to be a key contributor during the good ones.

Paul O'Neill's 10-Pitch At-Bat in Game 1 of the 2000 World Series

Paul O'Neill was bummed after learning that the Cincinnati Reds, a team that played only two hours from his hometown of Columbus, had traded him to the Yankees just after the end of the 1992 season.

But his father made a prediction that day and it was one that came true: The trade was the best thing that could happen to O'Neill.

Though upset at being dealt, O'Neill took a professional attitude in his new home. O'Neill became popular because of his intensity, his modesty (he was embarrassed by the size of his contracts), and how hard he played. Yankees owner George Steinbrenner nicknamed O'Neill "the Warrior" and outside of "the Sultan of Swat" that moniker may be the most appropriately given one in Yankees history.

"Paul O'Neill was the heart and soul of those Yankees teams," said former teammate Mike Stanton.

O'Neill pounded his share of water coolers in frustration, but there were plenty of memorable moments in pinstripes.

- O'Neill won the new home-team fans over quickly by going 4-for-4, with two singles, a double, and a triple in his Yankee Stadium debut.

- He hit .300 or better in his first six seasons with the Yankees. The only other Yankees to have a six-season streak of hitting .300 since the end of World War II are Bernie Williams and Don Mattingly.

- In the strike-shortened 1994 season O'Neill won the batting title by hitting .359, the highest batting average by a Yankees player since Mickey Mantle hit .365 in 1957.

- He had a three-homer, eight-RBI game against the Angels in 1995, the first Yankees player to have that many home runs and that many RBIs in a single game in the Bronx.

- Playing right field on a bad hamstring, he made a running, reaching catch of Luis Polonia's bid for an extra-base hit with two men on to end a 1–0 Yankees victory in Game 5 of the 1996 World Series. Had O'Neill not made the play, the Braves would have won the game and had a 3–2 Series lead. Instead the Yankees were winners and soon-to-be World Series champions.

- He played Game 4 of the 1999 World Series after the death of his father. O'Neill's mom insisted that his father would have wanted it that way. The Yankees won the game to complete a sweep of the Braves and their second straight World Series

MOST HR IN FINAL SEASON OF MLB CAREER, PLAYING WITH YANKEES

Paul O'Neill	2001	21
Chili Davis	1999	19
Mickey Mantle	1968	18
Tino Martinez	2005	17

title. O'Neill had gotten the winning hit against Braves closer John Rocker in the Series opener.

- He hit more home runs in the final season of his major league career than any other Yankees player. He is the only player in major league history to have a 20-homer, 20-steal season in his final big-league season.

- O'Neill played his final inning at Yankee Stadium to a standing ovation with the sellout crowd repeatedly chanting his name in the ninth inning of Game 5 of the 2001 World Series.

Paul O'Neill made big plays for the Yankees both with the bat and with the glove.

HIGHEST BATTING AVERAGE BY YANKEES PLAYER, SINCE END OF WWII

Mickey Mantle	1957	.365
Paul O'Neill	1994	.359
Mickey Mantle	1956	.353
Don Mattingly	1986	.352

O'Neill's most memorable postseason plate appearance came with one out in the ninth inning in Game 1 of the 2000 World Series against Mets closer and Yankees nemesis Armando Benitez.

The Yankees trailed 3–2 to their crosstown rivals. O'Neill's turn took slightly more than five minutes and 10 pitches. He fell behind in the count 1–2 but stayed alive by fouling off four two-strike offerings, even though he was unable to catch up to Benitez's near 100-mph heater.

On 3–2, Mets catcher Todd Pratt set a target down around O'Neill's ankles. Benitez kept the ball low, but missed outside for ball four.

O'Neill did his job by getting on base, and his teammates brought him around. He scored the tying run on Chuck Knoblauch's sacrifice fly. The winning run scored in the 12th inning on Jose Vizcaino's single.

Derek Jeter won World Series MVP honors, but you could make a pretty good case for O'Neill too. He hit .474 with nine hits and three walks in the five-game triumph. He didn't hit a triple in the regular season, but had two that led to runs in that Series.

In short, he did everything it took to win, even though he didn't necessarily get the glory.

That's what warriors do.

Hideki Matsui Has 6 RBIs in Game 6 of the 2009 World Series

Hideki Matsui wielded a bat in a manner that made pitchers uncomfortable, because his slashing swing was so quick, so well-suited for putting the ball in play, and so potent. It was a swing that produced one of the great performances in Yankees' World Series history.

"Matsui was pure strength," said a former rival, outfielder Doug Glanville. "He had a strong base, grip of steel, matched with an uncanny ability to get the barrel down directly to the ball. He hit some balls that had so much backspin that it looked like it would start its own tornado."

Matsui starred for the Yomiuri Giants from 1993 to 2002, winning three MVP awards, and was immensely popular in his native Japan. He signed a three-year $21 million contract with the Yankees in December 2002 and came with a reputation for durability and power. In his final season in Yomiuri, he slugged a career-best 50 home runs in 500 at-bats.

Matsui was 28 on Opening Day 2003 and in the prime of his career, and it didn't take him long to show that his skills would translate well to the States. He wasn't quite the rock star he was in Japan, but he was embraced by Yankees fans of all nationalities.

Matsui endeared himself to them by hitting a grand slam in his Yankee Stadium debut against the Minnesota Twins. He played in every Yankees game in each of his first three seasons, eventually extending a consecutive-games streak spanning Japan and the major leagues to 1,768 games. In those first three seasons in the Bronx, he hit .297, totaled 70 home runs, and drove in at least 100 runs each year.

One thing that made Matsui great was that he was a difficult hitter to get out in a clutch situation.

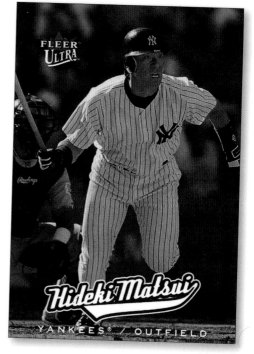

Baseball-Reference.com defines "late and close" situations as those in the seventh inning or later with the batting team tied, ahead by one, or the tying run at least on deck. From 2003 to 2005, Matsui posted a 1.044 OPS in late and close situations.

The five players who ranked better were the game's best hitters—Barry Bonds, David Ortiz, Todd Helton, Carlos Delgado, and Albert Pujols.

Matsui's 82 hits in "late and close" situations were 21 more than the Yankees player with the next-most in that span, Jorge Posada with 61.

Matsui also thrived in postseason play. His .312 batting average and .933 OPS in the postseason are the highest of any Yankees player from 1995 to the present.

Among Matsui's highlights was a pair of five-RBI games, including one of three five-hit, five-RBI games in postseason history, against the Red Sox in the 2004 ALCS. However, it was his last postseason game for which he is best remembered.

By 2009, Matsui was 35, and though he could still hit, injuries limited him to a DH-only role in the World Series against the defending-champion Phillies.

In the sixth inning of a tied Game 2 against Pedro Martinez, Matsui reached down for a two-strike curveball and hooked it about five rows deep into the right-field stands. The Yankees' win evened the series 1–1.

In Games 3 through 5, Matsui made cameos as a pinch-hitter. His pinch-hit home run in Game 3 padded a lead as the Yankees won two of three games to come back home leading 3–2.

To that point in the Series, Matsui was 5-for-9 with two home runs. But he wasn't done.

With Martinez on the mound again in Game 6, Matsui came up in the second inning with a man on first base. As the crowd chanted "Who's your daddy?" at Martinez (in reference to comments Pedro made earlier in his career about the Yankees' success against him), Matsui worked an 0–2 count to 3–2 and got a fat fastball over the middle of the plate. Phillies catcher Carlos Ruiz hung his head as soon as Matsui completed his swing. This one hooked into the second deck.

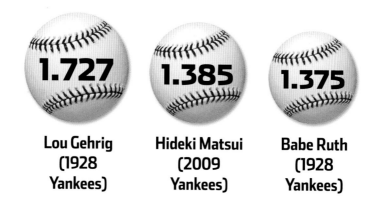

HIGHEST SLUGGING PERCENTAGE IN A SINGLE WORLD SERIES, ALL-TIME

1.727
Lou Gehrig
(1928
Yankees)

1.385
Hideki Matsui
(2009
Yankees)

1.375
Babe Ruth
(1928
Yankees)

JOHNNY DAMON STEALS TWO BASES ON ONE PLAY IN 2009 WORLD SERIES

Johnny Damon is what you might call a two-face.

There is the scraggly bearded, long-haired enemy who struck the grand slam that killed off the Yankees' postseason dreams in Game 7 of the 2004 ALCS.

And there is the clean-shaven veteran, whose heads-up baserunning maneuver was the key to an important triumph.

Damon had four respectable seasons in the Bronx, but saved his best for last, with a memorable play.

With Game 4 of the 2009 World Series tied in the ninth inning, Damon singled with two outs. The Phillies shifted their defense with Mark Teixeira up and Damon took advantage. He stole second and when he noticed that third base was uncovered, he beat Pedro Feliz in a sprint to the bag.

Two batters later, Alex Rodriguez doubled Damon home and the Yankees went on to win to take a 3–1 Series lead.

Damon hurt his calf in the third inning of the Series-clinching game, his final one with the Yankees. But he left his mark on the Bronx, one far superior to any other for which he would have been remembered.

Matsui got another shot at Martinez in the third inning with the bases loaded and two outs. Again, he fell behind 0–2, but Martinez couldn't put him away. Martinez tried to go up top with a fastball, but the pitch hung where Matsui could whack it on a line into center field for a two-run single.

By the fifth inning, Martinez was out of the game, but the Yankees and Matsui kept coming. FOX announcer Tim McCarver warned of a dangerous pitch coming on 3–1 with Matsui up and two men on base, and he was prescient. Matsui slammed a breaking ball from reliever J.A. Happ on one hop off the right-center field wall, bringing in two more runs.

The six RBIs tied former Yankee Bobby Richardson's record for most RBIs in a World Series game (a mark since matched by Albert Pujols), and are the most by a player in the clinching game of a

World Series. The Yankees won Game 6 by a score of 7–3 for their 27th World Series title. Matsui's .615 batting average, the fourth-highest ever in a World Series, earned him MVP honors.

Matsui played three more seasons with the Angels, Athletics, and Rays but did not play in another postseason game. His final postseason numbers—a .312 batting average with 10 home runs and 39 RBIs in 56 games—were illustrative of his performance in the spotlight.

Matsui did get to fulfill one final wish. He signed a one-day contract with the Yankees, allowing him to retire in pinstripes.

"I've always aspired to be a member of the New York Yankees and to have been able to do that for seven years, every day for me was just an absolute joy," Matsui said at his retirement press conference.

Not just for him, but for so many fans as well.

Hank Bauer's Record-Setting 17-Game World Series Hitting Streak

The batter with the longest hitting streak in World Series history was once referred to as "a flop" by the media during the postseason struggles of his younger days.

We don't think Hank Bauer looked upon that term too kindly. Perhaps it served as motivation for future performance.

Bauer is the Joe DiMaggio of the World Series. His 17-game hitting streak in the Fall Classic is a mark unmatched more than 50 years after his retirement.

Bauer is one of the unsung stars of the 1950s Yankees dynasty. Known by the nickname "The Bruiser," he was a modestly potent right-handed batter who played alongside Mickey Mantle and was a three-time All-Star and five-time recipient of MVP votes. Bauer was a member of seven World Series–winning teams in a career that spanned from 1948 to 1961.

He was also a war hero, having earned two Bronze Stars in the Marines in World War II. Bauer's toughness was evident on the field (sportswriter Jim Murray once said "his face looks like a closed fist") and off the field (he was accused of punching someone, though never charged, in what became known as "the Copacabana incident").

"He used to get on me at second base," said former teammate Bobby Richardson. "When I turned a double play, I had a habit of getting rid of it fast, but not throwing the ball really hard to first base. He got behind me and said, 'Throw the ball hard. You throw like a girl.' When he said it I started throwing a little bit harder and quicker."

But though Bauer was a good player, the sum of his early October performances was not great. He was a combined 7-for-57 in his first four World Series.

"I seemed to be hitting the ball well, but somehow there were fielders catching it everywhere I looked," he said, explaining his early troubles.

Bauer had only a few hits, but some of the ones he had were quite important.

His three-run triple in the sixth inning of Game 6 of the 1951 World Series was the decisive hit in the clinching game over the Giants.

He also made a terrific sliding catch of a line drive for the Series' final out with the tying run in scoring position.

LONGEST HITTING STREAKS BY YANKEES, WORLD SERIES HISTORY

Hank Bauer	1956–1958	17*
Derek Jeter	1996–2000	14
Reggie Jackson	1977–1981	12
Billy Martin	1955–1956	11
Yogi Berra	1953–1955	11

* Longest all-time

After going 1-for-18 in the 1952 World Series, Bauer's fortunes began to shift in 1953. He had six hits and six runs in a six-game win over the Dodgers, a Series that ended when he touched home plate after Billy Martin's walk-off single in Game 6.

Bauer missed parts of the 1955 World Series (in which the Dodgers finally beat the Yankees) with a thigh injury, but did manage two hits in Game 1 and three hits in Game 6. It foreshadowed his future performance.

Each of the next three years, the Yankees made the World Series and the Series went the distance. Bauer started all 21 of those games and had at least one hit in 19

He was a combined **7-for-57** *in his first four World Series.*

of them. His 17-game hitting streak spanned from the first game of the 1956 World Series through the third game of the 1958 World Series, during which he hit .316 with six home runs and 16 RBIs.

In 1956, Bauer had one of the two Yankees' RBIs to support Don Larsen in his perfect game against the Brooklyn Dodgers in Game 5. The next year, his go-ahead home run in the seventh inning of Game 6 against the Braves provided the run the Yankees needed to win.

The 1958 World Series rematch against the Braves was Bauer's last and best Fall Classic appearance. Reggie Jackson may have been "Mr. October," but Bauer turned in a performance that was Jackson-worthy.

Bauer homered in three straight games, something only two other Yankees had previously done in a single World Series (Hall of Famers Lou Gehrig and Johnny Mize) and that only Jackson would do since.

Bauer led the team past the Braves with a .323 batting average, four home runs, and eight RBIs. On three different occasions in the Series, he had a hit that gave the Yankees the lead.

Though Hank Bauer had a 17-game World Series hitting streak, his longest regular-season hitting streak was only 15 games.

With the Yankees trailing two games to none against the defending champs, Bauer fought through a sore wrist and took matters into his own hands. He drove in four runs—two with a single and two with a home run—in a 4–0 win.

Bauer's go-ahead hit that day gave him eight in his World Series career. That's tied with Yogi Berra, Goose Goslin, and David Justice for third-most, trailing only Ruth's 11 and Gehrig's 10.

"I don't know where we would have been without him," Yankees manager Casey Stengel said afterward.

Without Bauer, the Yankees might not have won the last three games of the Series to beat the Braves 4–3, returning the title of baseball's best team to the Bronx.

After the 1959 season, Bauer was traded to the Athletics in a multi-player deal that netted his right-field replacement, Roger Maris. Bauer played two seasons with the Kansas City Athletics, and became their manager after retiring in 1961.

Bauer was known as a disciplinarian as a manager, and for the most part, his teams responded. They won more than 90 games three times in eight seasons, and his 1966 Orioles team won the World Series.

Post-baseball, Bauer owned a liquor store and became a regular at Yankees Old-Timer's Day events. He died in 2007.

"Nobody was more dedicated and proud to be a Yankee," Yogi Berra said in mourning his longtime friend. "He gave you everything he had."

He certainly was no flop.

Dr. Bobby Brown Hits .439 in the World Series

Dr. Bobby Brown's recollections of his baseball-playing past are so sharp and so vivid even as he enters the ninth decade of his life.

"I remember the pitches I did hit and the pitches I didn't hit," said the 90-year-old Brown during a 2015 phone interview. "Sometimes I wake up at night and I can see them.

"If you were a hitter who had any sense at all, you could figure out what you were looking for. If a guy threw a fastball for strikes 80 percent of the time, and a curve 50 percent, and a change of pace 30 percent, you knew you were going to get the fastball. I made contact a lot. I struck out 88 times in my career. I could always hit the thing."

Brown is the best World Series hitter that the Yankees have ever had. He hit .439, second-best of anyone who had at least 40 World Series plate appearances.

When I pointed out that the only player with a higher average (David Ortiz, .455) could dip below Brown if he makes the Series again someday, Brown laughed.

"I didn't want to say that," he said. "I'll let you say it."

Brown played in four World Series in his eight major league seasons and the Yankees won all four. In fact, the Yankees went 9–1 in the 10 World Series games that Brown started.

Brown, who hit .279 with a .367 on-base percentage in the regular season, often played an integral role. In his first World Series, in 1947 against the Brooklyn Dodgers, Brown pinch hit four times. He had three hits and a walk and drove in three runs. In the decisive Game 7, he had a pinch-hit double against Hal Gregg that tied the score in the fourth inning. The Yankees took the lead two batters later and never looked back.

> *In fact, the Yankees went 9–1 in the 10 World Series games that Brown started.*

"He threw a ball on the outside part of the plate," Brown said. "I thought it could have been a ball, but it was hittable. I hit a line drive to left. There was a tremendous roar. It's the first time I ever really listened to the crowd. They had nearly 72,000 people there that day. I knew where my folks were sitting, and I could see a hat being thrown up in the air. It was my dad's hat. He was throwing it up, catching it and throwing it up again."

By 1949, Brown became a starter and again made a notable impact on a championship series. He went 6-for-11 with five RBIs batting fifth behind Joe DiMaggio in the three games he started. Brown only hit in the fifth slot nine times that season (he usually hit sixth or third), but Casey Stengel made a smart move to slot him fifth for the World Series.

In Game 4, Brown made the Dodgers pay for intentionally walking DiMaggio, crushing a three-run triple to extend a Yankees lead from 3–0 to 6–0.

The next day, in Game 5, Brown went 3-for-4 with two RBIs. He had a first-inning RBI single to give the Yankees a 2–0 lead and then hit another triple. This one salted away a Series-clinching 10–6 win.

Brown joined an illustrious list of players who hit multiple triples in a World Series lasting four or five games. The names include Lou Gehrig and Paul O'Neill.

"That's pretty good company," Brown said. "But they weren't in medical school either."

Ah yes, there's a reason we know him as Dr. Bobby Brown. While playing for the Yankees, Brown planned to become a doctor.

"I wish I could have spent my winters like everyone else did, trying to improve my baseball skills," Brown said. "But I couldn't do that."

One time, Brown was reading a textbook for exams he knew he would have to take once the season ended. His roommate, Yogi Berra, was reading a collection of Superman comic books. They both put their books down at the same time.

HIGHEST WORLD SERIES BATTING AVERAGE, YANKEES HISTORY

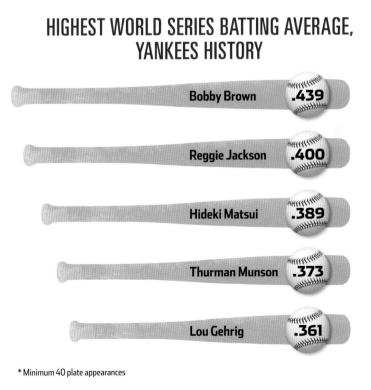

Bobby Brown	.439
Reggie Jackson	.400
Hideki Matsui	.389
Thurman Munson	.373
Lou Gehrig	.361

* Minimum 40 plate appearances

HIGHEST WORLD SERIES ON-BASE PERCENTAGE, YANKEES HISTORY

.500 Bobby Brown | .500 Reggie Jackson | .497 Babe Ruth | .483 Lou Gehrig | .483 Hideki Matsui

"Man, I love those Superman comics," Berra said to Brown, who he then asked, "How did your book turn out?"

Brown was smart enough to chuckle at that question and was sharp enough to continue pounding opposing pitchers in key spots. He still remembers his batting average in the 1950 World Series (.333) as the Yankees swept the Phillies in four games, three of which were decided by one run.

Brown's final World Series appearances came in 1951, when he went 5-for-14 in a win over the New York Giants. It's not a base hit he remembers, but a blown call by the umpires that cost him a hit (one that would have pushed his average to .463).

"I knew Sal Maglie had a great curveball, but he threw me a fastball down the middle and I was a fraction of a second late," Brown said. "Willie Mays went back on it. The ball hit his glove, hit the ground, and landed in his glove. They called me out. My dad nearly jumped out of the second deck after he saw it. We had six umps and none saw it. I should have gotten credit for it. I'm still mad. I wasn't looking fastball on that pitch. I think I could have hit it out of the park."

Brown's baseball career ended in 1954, as he followed his passion of becoming a cardiologist, a field in which he excelled. Brown returned to baseball many years later as an interim executive for the Texas Rangers and then American League president from 1984 to 1994. He lives happily now in retirement in Fort Worth, Texas, and still gets around regularly both to vacation and to share stories of his big-league days.

There are so many elements to Brown's story from his sports success to his days as a doctor, to the 19 months he spent in Korea and Tokyo treating injuries during the Korean War. His lifesaving skills are a part of a legacy that began when he and college teammate Robert McClean saved the life of a radioman whose plane crashed while on patrol over the Pacific Ocean.

Brown is remembered as a hero for that rescue.

For his baseball time, he likes to remember that he was a tough hitter, but one who is also very thankful.

"I was able to get through four World Series and not do something that was so extremely bad that they would remember me for decades," he said. "That was a big relief."

But how does Brown want to be remembered?

"I played damn well for a medical student," he said. "I'll tell you that."

1947 Yankees Win
19 Straight Games

As you would expect, the longest winning streak in Yankees history is a story of baseball excellence.

But you don't win 19 games in a row simply by being good. You need to catch a few breaks along the way.

The 1947 Yankees won 19 straight over a 19-day stretch in June and July.

At the time, the streak tied the 1906 White Sox for the longest by an American League team. It is now one shy of the AL mark of 20, set by the 2002 Oakland Athletics.

The Yankees were 39–26 and in first place by 4½ games when the streak began with a 3–1 win over the Washington Senators. They were 58–27 with a double-digit hold on first place after the streak ended with an 8–0 loss to the Detroit Tigers.

How dominant were the Yankees?

During the streak, they outscored their opponents 119–41 and out-homered them 17–3. The Yankees scored more runs in the first eight games of the streak than they allowed in the entire 19-game stretch. They never trailed in 13 of the games and were behind at the end of only 17 innings.

But the streak was not all about dominance. It's one that would be forgotten if not for a couple of memorable games that extended the run.

Win No. 9 is a prime example. This one came against the St. Louis Browns in the first game of a 15-game road trip.

Yankees reliever Joe Page entered the game in the seventh inning with the score tied 3–3 and kept it that way through the ninth.

But Page didn't win the game just on the mound. He won it at the plate as well, clubbing a home run off the Sportsman's Park roof in the ninth inning to break the deadlock. It was the second and last home run of his major league career.

The 16th consecutive victory came in the second game of the Yankees' third road doubleheader in a four-day stretch, a 2–1 triumph over the Indians.

What made this one special was that starter Bill Bevens, who entered the day 3–8 with a 5.12 ERA, outdueled future Hall of Famer Bob Feller. The score was tied in the ninth inning until third baseman Billy Johnson tripled in the winning run.

LONGEST WINNING STREAK, YANKEES HISTORY

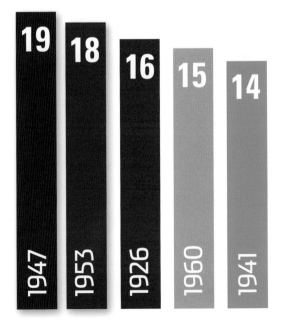

19 — 1947
18 — 1953
16 — 1926
15 — 1960
14 — 1941

Johnson was one of seven position players who played in every game of the streak, as catcher Yogi Berra was the only one to take a breather (understandable, given the number of doubleheaders). Not surprisingly, Joe DiMaggio was the team's top hitter, batting .375 with 17 RBIs. Right behind him was Tommy Henrich, who hit .350 with 16 RBIs. Allie Reynolds went 4–0 with a 1.77 ERA to lead the starting pitchers.

> **During the streak, they outscored their opponents 119–41 and out-homered them 17–3.**

Page's performance out of the bullpen was vital to the streak's length. He was the 1947 Yankees version of Mariano Rivera. Page had two wins and three saves and allowed three runs in 15 innings in six relief appearances.

The Yankees were actually a hot team before the streak began. They won 12 of 15 games prior to the streak's start, making the overall stretch 31 out of 34.

Over the rest of the season, the Yankees were more ordinary than extraordinary, and they didn't need to be the latter since they'd built up a double-digit league lead. They went 39–31 in their last 70 games to finish 97–57, easily winning the AL pennant.

Bevens became famous for nearly throwing a no-hitter against the Dodgers in the World Series, but he lost his bid and Game 4 of the Series with two outs in the ninth inning on a two-run double by Cookie Lavagetto.

DiMaggio and Berra were shut down by Dodgers pitching, hitting a combined .200, leaving it to others to carry the offense. Such support came from the likes of outfielder Johnny Lindell, who went 9-for-18 with five walks and seven RBIs.

The big story of the Series was the pitching of Page, who pitched four innings of relief to save Game 1 and five scoreless innings in relief to win Game 7 (a day after getting routed for four runs in Game 6).

SNUFFY STIRNWEISS WINS BATTING TITLE, LEADS RACE FOR ONE DAY

Second baseman Snuffy Stirnweiss had good timing. We don't just say that in describing the hitting approach that led to him leading the AL in hits, triples, and stolen bases in 1944 and 1945.

We're referring to how he won the 1945 AL batting title with a .309 batting average.

Stirnweiss won by finishing with a flourish. He had 19 hits and hit .475 in his last nine games of the season, raising his batting average by 12 points. He finished at .308544, which was .000087 better than rival Tony Cuccinello. Stirnweiss led the race for only one day: after the final day of the regular season.

That's not all Stirnweiss won. He played on three Yankees teams that won the World Series and was an everyday player on the 1947 team.

Though the 1947 Yankees were a great team, they have never been thought of in the discussion of the franchise's *greatest* teams. An analysis of every pennant winner from 1901 to 1993 by statistician/economist Harry Hollingsworth ranked the 1947 squad 58th overall and 16th-best in Yankees history. The 1947 team often gets overshadowed by the dynasty that spanned 1949 to 1953.

But for 19 days, they were the best the Yankees have ever been.

Lee Guetterman Throws 30²/₃ Consecutive Scoreless Innings to Start 1989

If you were going to guess which pitcher has the longest scoreless streak to start a season in Yankees history, you'd probably go through 100 names before you got to the right answer.

You could start with Whitey Ford and Mariano Rivera, but their best scoreless streaks were in the postseason. Ron Guidry isn't the answer. Neither is Lefty Gomez or Allie Reynolds or Mel Stottlemyre or Orlando Hernandez.

The record belongs to an oft-forgotten Yankee—lanky lefty Lee Guetterman.

The 1989 to 1992 seasons were a dark time in Yankees history—four straight sub-.500 years. There weren't many highlights, but one of the notable accomplishments was Guetterman's 30²/₃ innings scoreless run at the start of 1989.

Guetterman threw in the low 90s and relied on sinker location for his success. He had a decent season with the Mariners in 1987, but after being traded to the Yankees, he spent most of the season in the minor leagues and made only 20 appearances in 1988.

Guetterman saw that the Expos had a rookie pitcher named Randy Johnson who resembled the 6'8" Guetterman in size, but was able to throw 100 mph.

So Guetterman searched for a way that he could increase his fastball velocity. He changed his workout routine to build up lower-body strength, which allowed him to get more on his pitches.

"I was facing guys in spring training and I was noticing that my fastball was a lot crisper," Guetterman said. "People were telling me, 'Did you know you hit 94 [on the radar gun] today?' Prior to that year, I'd never hit 94 before in my life."

Lee Guetterman During Scoreless Streak (April 6–May 20, 1989)

IP:	$30^2/_3$
Hits:	20
Runs:	0
K–BB:	14–6

Guetterman opened the season as one of the last men in the bullpen. But after four successful appearances in losses and a couple of rough outings by closer Dave Righetti, Dallas Green gave Guetterman the chance to close. He got two saves in three days.

The streak stood at eight scoreless innings and it began to pick up a little steam. Guetterman wasn't a one-out lefty specialist. He was a former starter who could give his relief appearances some length. The scoreless streak spanned 19 appearances and in 12 of those, he got more than three outs.

Guetterman notched six saves and three holds during the streak, which stretched into late May.

"It takes everybody to make something like that happen," Guetterman said. "The defense came up real strong behind me. I had the confidence of, 'Hey, I'm here [on the mound], you're out,' and it didn't matter who I faced."

Guetterman got the satisfaction of throwing 2⅓ scoreless innings to pick up a save in Seattle against the Mariners team that had traded him a year-and-a-half before.

> *"People were telling me, 'Did you know you hit 94 [on the radar gun] today?' Prior to that year, I'd never hit 94 before in my life."*

On May 23, one newspaper headline asked "Who Is Lee Guetterman and Why Is He on a Roll?" and proclaimed "Watch Out Orel Hershiser" in reference to Guetterman being halfway to breaking the scoreless streak record that the Dodgers pitcher had set the season before.

As it turned out, Hershiser had nothing to worry about. Guetterman allowed a home run to Chili Davis in the ninth inning the next day against the Angels, part of a five-run outburst that ended the streak.

But that didn't stop Guetterman from having the best season of his career. Even now, as someone who had an 11-year career (parts of four with the Yankees), who owns and manages rental properties and runs a Christian education facility in Tennessee, he still remembers the streak fondly.

"Even after the streak broke, [my success] continued," Guetterman said. "Things fell my way. They could have easily gone in a different direction. Those who are prepared are able to answer when opportunity knocks. I did everything I could to prepare to be there when the opportunity came and I was able to capitalize on it."

Jack Chesbro Wins 41 Games in 1904

When we speak of the unfortunate nature of October '04 in Yankees history, we must clarify what we mean. The pain and suffering that Yankees fans went through in 2004 was one whose origins date back 100 years.

The 1904 season featured a great pennant race in which the key figure was the most prolific single-season winner in modern major league history (which began in 1900), Hall of Fame pitcher Jack Chesbro.

It is Chesbro who put Yankees baseball (then Highlanders baseball, as that was the franchise's original nickname) on the map in its second season in the city.

The 30-year-old right-hander, known as "Happy Jack," was the city's first pitching star. He set a modern mark with 41 victories that year.

Chesbro's 1904 season got off to a great start as he beat the defending World Series champion Boston Americans (later known as Red Sox), 8–2, hitting a home run off Cy Young to help his own cause on a cold, snowy day.

Chesbro sometimes took matters into his own hands with his hitting or baserunning. He started the season with a record of 15–3 and a batting average of .322.

Overall, he had his best offensive season, finishing at .236 with 17 RBIs. On July 16, 1904, he beat the Tigers with a walk-off steal of home. It was his only stolen base of the season.

But it was on the mound that Chesbro had his greatest glory. He had spent the off-season coaching baseball at Harvard with his teammate Willie Keeler and discovered a new variant of the spitball he threw. It's one that even wowed major league umpires.

He set a modern mark with **41 victories** *that year.*

"I have stood back of the plate for a good many years, but I never saw a thing like this ball," said umpire Bill Carpenter. "It generally goes over the outside corner for a strike, but it is the hardest ball for an umpire to judge that I have ever seen pitched. If it bothers the umpire, it is easy to see how troublesome it must be to a batter."

Chesbro won 14 consecutive decisions in one stretch before having his streak snapped by Boston in early July.

In the midst of his streak, his former manager with Pittsburgh, Fred Clarke, told a reporter, "Chesbro was always a good pitcher.... I never saw him looking as well as he does right now, so it's not to be wondered at that he is twirling such wonderful ball."

MOST WINS IN SEASON, YANKEES HISTORY

Jack Chesbro	Carl Mays	Al Orth
41	**27**	**27**
(1904)	(1921)	(1906)

DID YOU KNOW?

Chesbro won 41 games in 1904. The 1904 Washington Senators won only 38 games as a team.

Chesbro attributed his most recent success to a solid work ethic.

"I'm lucky because I go out and hustle," he said. "Any man with any ability at all can be one of the lucky ones if he digs into the work. It's always the fellow who loafs that kicks about his luck."

The Highlanders and Americans were in an ultra-tight race for the pennant and as the season went along, Highlanders manager Clark Griffin tried to ride his best pitcher to a championship.

Chesbro started consecutive games four times in September and October, including twice in the last dozen games of the season. He ended up making 51 starts and his $454\frac{2}{3}$ innings were the most in the sport that year by nearly 50.

He ended up making 51 starts and his $454\frac{2}{3}$ innings were the most in the sport that year by nearly 50.

The season came down to a five-game series between the two teams, with three wins needed from either to take the championship. Chesbro won the first game 3–2, but was routed in the second and the Highlanders lost the third as well, putting them in desperation mode needing two wins in the final-day doubleheader.

Chesbro pitched for the third time in four games in the opener and was given a 2–0 lead through five innings. But Boston tied it with two runs in the seventh, setting up a tension-filled final inning.

In the top of the ninth inning, the Americans put a man on third with two outs and he scored when Chesbro threw a pitch that was high and wild. The Highlanders failed to score in their half, giving the pennant to Boston.

"Never have I seen a man feel worse over the loss of a game than did Jack Chesbro," baseball writer Tim Murnane told the *Syracuse Post-Standard* more than two months after the game.

Chesbro took the loss hard, but it is a long-standing legacy that Chesbro left behind, even though he could never duplicate his extraordinary performance. His win-loss record and ERA total were average over the five remaining years of his career (66–67, 2.83).

Chesbro was inducted into the Hall of Fame in 1946 and his records are viewed as unbreakable.

"We should never say never," said Lyle Spatz, the co-chairman of the Baseball Records Committee for the Society for American Baseball Research, "but Chesbro's 41 wins, 51 starts, and 48 complete games.... We're not going to see that again."

Slow Joe Doyle Opens His Career with 2 Shutouts

The late 19th century and early 20th century were the Golden Age of baseball nicknames. There were players named Cannonball Crane, Icebox Chamberlain, and Phenomenal Smith.

Judd Bruce Doyle, a pitcher for the Highlanders from 1906 to 1910, had a nickname specific to his pitching style. The one given to him was "Slow Joe."

That sounds a little mean unless you know the whole story. Doyle is someone who would have fit in well in the game more than 100 years after he played it.

"The reason [for the nickname] was because he did things to purposely be slow on the mound," said Slow Joe's granddaughter, Mary Lou Doyle. "He would kick dirt out of his cleats, or walk around the mound. He would be slow on the mound to throw off the batter [and his timing.]"

As sportswriter C.E. Van Loan noted: "He is as deliberate as a third-avenue car on an uphill grade. He works as if he had all the time in the world in front of him."

Doyle's methods worked in a manner unprecedented by any Yankees pitcher before or since. He is the only pitcher in franchise history to start his big-league career by throwing two consecutive shutouts. He's one of eight pitchers to do that in major league history.

"That the young man is a pitcher of unusual quality was quickly shown," wrote the *New York Times* the day after his debut, when he shut out the Indians. "He is cool, deliberate in his movements, steady, and has a varied assortment of deliveries."

After his next start, the paper noted, "The ridiculous efforts of several of the opposing batsmen to gauge his delivery caused much merriment."

Doyle's success lasted for a few seasons. His major league career was done after he posted a 7.23 ERA in eight appearances in 1910.

RUSS VAN ATTA GETS 4 HITS, PITCHES SHUTOUT IN MLB DEBUT

Sometimes the first moment on the big stage is the very best one. Such is the case for Russ Van Atta, who was not frazzled by pressure and distraction.

Van Atta debuted on the mound with the Yankees on April 25, 1933, on the road against the Washington Senators. He was 26 years old and we're guessing his maturity helped him through this one as much as the Yankees offense, which banged out 21 hits in a 16–0 win.

Four of those were by Van Atta, who hit a solid .256 in 90 at-bats over three seasons with the Yankees.

Van Atta also pitched very well, mowing down a Washington Senators team that averaged 5.6 runs per game that season and beat out the Yankees to win the American League pennant.

However, Van Atta's terrific day was secondary to something else that happened during the game—a pair of brawls. The first was the result of a hard take-out slide at second base. The second came when Ben Chapman, ejected from the game, left through the Senators dugout and punched an opposing player in the face. There were not just ejections, but arrests of five fans who got involved in the fighting.

Van Atta was not among those, as he sat in the dugout to protect himself after initially wanting to join the fray. He ended up pitching a five-hit shutout.

Doyle does have one other claim to fame. His likeness appeared in the T–206 baseball-card set made most famous by the million-dollar Honus Wagner card.

One of Doyle's cards from that set includes an error, as he is confused with Larry Doyle and listed as a National Leaguer. Only a handful of those cards exist and those that do are said to be worth $100,000.

As such, Doyle is a known figure to Yankees historians and Yankees legends.

"I was a concierge at a hotel in Philadelphia and I met a lot of ballplayers," said Mary Lou Doyle. "Yogi Berra would stay there. I had breakfast with him once and I said, 'Yogi, have you ever heard of my grandfather?' And Yogi knew who he was because of his shutouts and his baseball card."

> *"He is as deliberate as a third-avenue car on an uphill grade. He works as if he had all the time in the world in front of him."*

There is one other story of note on Doyle found in his file in the Baseball Hall of Fame Library in Cooperstown. A clipping from 1933 includes the tale from sportswriter Ford Frick of a game the Highlanders were trailing in the seventh inning. But they staged a rally and Doyle was due up at bat, but no one could find him. Finally a teammate did.

Doyle was lying on a tarp along the right-field line, fast asleep.

Alex Rodriguez's 4 Clutch Hits in the 2009 Postseason

Alex Rodriguez has played just about every role imaginable as a major league player.

He is the most overdramatic and most polarizing player of his generation. He has played the role of hero and villain, megastar and goat, moral mess and the redeemed. His talent rivals that of baseball's all-time legends, but there will always be questions about its legitimacy because of how it was tarnished.

There were the $252 million and $275 million contracts, the steroid allegations and subsequent suspensions, his relationship with his teammates, with Derek Jeter, his reported marital infidelities, his vanity, and his greed. There's no shortage of topics and no shortage of comments from Rodriguez on the many moments that have stained his reputation.

And yet, he's one of the greatest baseball players of all time. He ranks among the all-time leaders in home runs, RBIs, total bases, and hits. He entered 2016 ranked 12th all-time among position players in wins above replacement, which measures all aspects of value. The two players sandwiching him are legends—Ted Williams and Lou Gehrig.

"Some people say he's a terrible legend," said ESPNNY.com Yankees beat writer, Andrew Marchand.

On the field, what dogged Rodriguez was his lack of postseason success. But he was finally able to shed that part of his reputation with one memorable October.

Rodriguez's postseason struggles date back to the Yankees blowing a 3–0 ALCS lead to the Red Sox in 2004. Rodriguez went 1-for-his-last-15 in the series and was mocked for a play in which he tried to slap the ball out of Red Sox pitcher Bronson Arroyo's hand in Game 7.

Over the next three years, Rodriguez won two MVPs and had one of the greatest seasons in franchise history (he had 54 home runs and 156 RBIs in 2007), but it was diminished because he'd been branded with the choker's label in the postseason. He went 7-for-44 with one home run in three ALDS losses, including a loss against the Tigers in 2006 in which he was dropped to the No. 8 spot in the lineup for the series finale.

In 2007, it was expected that Rodriguez would opt out of his contract, but the manner in which he did so, with his agent Scott Boras leaking the news during the final game of the 2007 World Series, was viewed harshly by baseball fans and Yankees ownership.

Rodriguez was able to not only apologize his way out of the situation, but to negotiate a 10-year, $275 million deal with the Yankees that included marketing provisions for when Rodriguez approached and set baseball's all-time home run record. At that

ALEX RODRIGUEZ IN POSTSEASON

	2004 ALCS G4–2007	2009
Games	17	15
BA	.148	.365
HR	2	6
RBI	3	18

time, reaching those numbers seemed realistic, even as Rodriguez aged.

The start of the 2009 season brought multiple issues. One was hip surgery that sidelined Rodriguez for the first month of the season. The other was the revelation that Rodriguez tested positive for steroids in 2003. Rodriguez had long been suspected of PED usage, but repeatedly insisted that he'd played the game clean since becoming a Yankee.

"I know that I am in a position where I have to earn my trust back," Rodriguez said. "And over time, I am confident that, at the end of my career, people will see this for what it is—a stupid mistake and a lesson learned for a guy with a lot of baseball to play."

The news didn't help Rodriguez's reputation, but he heard cheers from Yankees fans when he homered on the first pitch he saw upon his return, and what happened in that postseason made a lot of fans very happy.

Rodriguez went into the playoffs determined not to put pressure on himself, to swing at strikes and avoid chasing pitches out of the strike zone. So long as he did that, good things would happen.

Such was the case in Game 2 of the ALDS, when Rodriguez came up in the ninth inning representing the tying run against Twins closer Joe Nathan and crushed a 3–1 pitch far over the fence in right center. The Yankees won in extra innings on Mark Teixeira's walk-off homer.

"This whole year I'm playing with no expectations," Rodriguez said. "I'm going out and having fun and doing the best that I can."

After hitting .455 in a sweep of the Twins, Rodriguez was just as good against the Angels, hitting .429 in the ALCS. In Game 2, the Yankees trailed by a run when Rodriguez came up in the bottom of the 11th. Angels closer Brian Fuentes did the smart thing, pitching Rodriguez away on 0–2, but A-Rod managed to muscle the ball to right field, just over the fence to tie the game. The Yankees won that game in 13 innings and won the series in six games.

In the World Series against the defending champion Phillies, Rodriguez again made a huge impact. He went 0-for-8 with six strikeouts in the first two games, leading some to fear he was back to his old ways. Those concerns were allayed in Game 3, when his at-bat turned the game around.

The Yankees trailed 3–0 in the fourth inning with one man on base against Phillies ace Cole Hamels when Rodriguez was late on a pitch, but hit a fastball off the wall by the right-field foul pole.

MOST RBIs IN SINGLE POSTSEASON, YANKEES HISTORY

18
Alex Rodriguez (2009)

15
Scott Brosius (1998)

15
Bernie Williams (1996)

14
Cecil Fielder (1996)

14
Reggie Jackson (1978)

After a closer look, it was clear that the ball actually hit a camera just beyond the right-field fence. This became the first home run awarded via instant replay in World Series history. That blow gave the Yankees momentum. They went on to win 8–5.

"[That's] a big hit for us because it really got us going," Yankees manager Joe Girardi said. "He has been so good for us in the playoffs. Alex has been a great player for a long time. He's one of the reasons—he's a big reason we're at this point, what he did in the first two series. He has been patient, and he has not tried to do too much."

They won the next night as well, when Rodriguez snapped a ninth-inning tie with a double against Phillies closer Brad Lidge that scored Johnny Damon.

"There's no question, I have never had a bigger hit," Rodriguez said.

Suddenly, Rodriguez was Mr. Clutch.

ALEX RODRIGUEZ GETS HIT NO. 3000, A HR

In 2015, Alex Rodriguez returned from a year-long PED-related suspension and another hip injury determined to salvage his reputation. In doing so, Rodriguez reached three notable milestones.

He passed Willie Mays for fourth place on the all-time home-run list, joined Hank Aaron as the only players to record 2,000 RBIs since that became an official stat in 1920, and joined the 3,000-hit club in a memorable manner.

Rodriguez reached that milestone in the same way that Derek Jeter did, with a home run, this one against Tigers pitcher Justin Verlander. The ball was caught by Zack Hample, who eventually returned it to Rodriguez and the Yankees for a $150,000 donation to charity.

Hample had previously said nasty things about Rodriguez on social media, but had a change of heart in deciding to return the ball.

Rodriguez made light of that by saying, "I have a PhD in saying some dumb things over the years."

The Yankees not only won the World Series, but A-Rod was arguably the team's postseason MVP, hitting .365 with six home runs and 18 RBIs.

"I always found the postseason stuff frustrating, because if you gave him enough opportunities, he'd be just fine in the postseason," said Grantland baseball writer Ben Lindbergh. "In 2009 when he was great, that was a vindication."

Alas the good times would not last either on the field or off. Rodriguez returned to his struggling ways in the postseason and was even pinch-hit for in the 2012 ALDS and ALCS.

The latest version of Rodriguez is attempting to rewrite his legacy in the final years of his career, after more controversy, including a year-long PED-related suspension in 2014.

Regardless of what happens over the next couple of seasons, you can count on this: There will be plenty of conversations on plenty of different subjects revolving around him.

"He's one of those iconic players who will be discussed forever," Marchand said.

Acknowledgments

A first book requires a lot of work and a lot of help, and I want to make sure I thank everyone who helped a lot in making this work.

Thank you to Adam Motin, Jesse Jordan, and the rest of the staff at Triumph Books for giving me the opportunity to be a part of this project, and to Jayson Stark both for helping make the connection that led to this relationship, and for guidance along the way.

Thanks to some fellow writers and researchers for their advice and/ or help, including Jerry Crasnick, Jim Caple, Tim Kurkjian, Jonah Keri, Trent McCotter, Buster Olney, Greg Prince, Dirk Lammers, Steve Wulf, Steve Rushin, Anthony McCarron, Danny Knobler, John Schenkman, Tim Sullivan, and John Thorn.

Thanks to those I interviewed for talking and e-mailing, often about topics that they had discussed many times before. I hope those interviews were able to provide some fresh perspectives. Thanks to the PR staffs at the Dodgers, Mariners, Giants, and Yankees for their help in securing interviews. Also thanks in that regard to Jacob Pomrenke and C. Paul Rogers of the Society for Baseball Research, and Steve Cook of the Greatest 21 Days blog.

Thanks to my bosses, past and present, at ESPN Stats & Information—Craig Wachs, Jeff Bennett, Nick Loucks, Ben Keeperman, Michael Protos, Noel Nash, and Edmundo Macedo, along with all of my colleagues in SIG who come up with brilliant baseball notes every day. Also, thanks to David Kull, Matt Marrone, David Schoenfield and the rest of the editing staff at ESPN.com for giving me the opportunity to write for the site.

Also special thanks to the Elias Sports Bureau, whose past work proved highly valuable; the staff at the Baseball Hall of

Fame Library, where I made a one-day visit; and the websites Newspapers.com and Newslibrary.com, which were vital resources for this work, as was the *New York Times* online archives.

A couple of publicly available websites were immensely helpful. Baseball-Reference.com was a treasure trove of numbers, many of which found their way into the text by searches through their Play Index. Baseball-Almanac.com had dozens of great notes and quotes. Retrosheet.org was also very helpful.

I put together a team of "helpers" to assist in proofreading the book. Two deserve a special shout-out for going above and beyond, Katie Sharp and Greg Newman. Katie was diligent and asked smart questions, making sure I'd covered every necessary angle within a chapter (and she suggested a few of the "Did You Knows"). Greg focused on making my writing style the best it could be, with suggestions that tightened the text and resulted in a more efficient, reader-friendly work.

Others who assisted with edits or chapter suggestions included Gregg Savarese, Pat Coleman, Dan Braunstein, Jason Southard, Tristan Cockcroft, and Chris Barnett.

Thanks to James Gregorio for handling the details on my first book contract.

And lastly, thanks to my family—my parents, Richard and Donna, and my sister, Lisa—for their support in all my endeavors.

Sources

Between February and October of 2015, I conducted interviews and had e-mail exchanges with Patrick Bohn, Dr. Bobby Brown, Tristan Cockcroft, Kevin Connors, Mary Lou Doyle, Doug Glanville, Gary Gold, Vernona Gomez, Kevin Graham, Lee Guetterman, Ron Guidry, Toni Harsh, Erica Herskowitz, Kevin Hines, Jay Jaffe, Ben Kabak, Steve Karsay, Tim Kurkjian, Ben Lindbergh, Andrew Marchand, Don Mattingly, John McCarthy, Jeff Nelson, Graig Nettles, Vinny Milano, Chris Pavia, Jorge Posada, Jeff Quagliata, Willie Randolph, Tim Raines, Bobby Richardson, Dave Righetti, Bill Ryczek, Gregg Savarese, Curt Schilling, Katie Sharp, Joe Sheehan, Aaron Small, Claire Smith, Lyle Spatz, Mike Stanton, John Sterling, Cecilia Tan, John Thorn, and Roy White.

Below is an essay-by-essay list of sources utilized. Dates and authors are included when available.

Dominance: 27 World Series Titles
"Giants Lost Title Because They Were Outclassed." *Oakland Tribune*, October 16, 1923, Page 45.

Colonel Jacob Ruppert Buys Babe Ruth for $125,000
"Jacob Ruppert one of 3 Hall Inductees." *Associated Press*, December 3, 2012.

"Evening World's Own Sports History." *Evening World*, December 27, 1919, Page 8

Hettinger, Ty. "The Impartial Rooter." *Bridgeport Telegram*, December 27, 1919, Page 18.

Macbeth, W.J. "Ruth Delighted to Play with Yankees Says Message from Huggins to Ruppert." *New York Tribune*, January 7, 1920, Page 16.

Runyon, Damon. "Hornsby is Worth $70,000 to Any One Team These Years." *Pittsburgh Daily Post,* December 27, 1919, Page 9.

"See Trustees Guiding Yankees." *Brooklyn Daily Eagle*, January 16, 1939, Page 12.

Levitt, Daniel. SABR Bioproject: Jacob Ruppert, http://*SABR.org/Bioproject.*

Babe Ruth's 60 HR in 1927
"Ruth falters during early season." *The Times Signal*, April 24, 1927, Page 9.

"Fans think movie work has hurt Babe's optics." *Appleton Post-Gazette*, May 11, 1927, Page 12.

"Babe Ruth Hits 3 More Homers." *Scranton Republican* (AP), September 7, 1927.

Drebinger, John. "Yanks Break Even; Ruth Hits 3, Gehrig 1." *New York Times*, September 7, 1927.

"Ruth Crashes 50th but Yanks Succumb." *New York Times*, September 11, 1927.

"Babe Ruth Accused of Striking Cripple." *New York Times*, September 13, 1927.

"Babe Clouts 54th as Yanks Win Both." *New York Times*, September 19, 1927.

"Ruth's 56th Homer Wins Game in Ninth." *New York Times*, September 23, 1927.

Gustkey, Earl. "60 Years Later It Remains a Symbol of Greatness: 60." *Los Angeles Times*, September 30, 1987.

BabeRuth.com

Lou Gehrig Plays in 2,130 Consecutive Games
"Sports Chatter." *Fitchburg Sentinel,* September 29, 1923, Page 8.

"Gehrig's Four Consecutive Home Runs in Game Tie Old Record."
Indiana Gazette (International News Service), June 4, 1932, Page 7.

Cross, Harry. "Gehrig's 2 Homers Beat Senators, 11–7." *New York Times*, July 24, 1925, Page 9.

Grayson, Harry. "Gehrig, Unlike Ruth, Insists He Never Tries for Homers." *The News-Herald*, June 1, 1938, Page 9.

Holmes, Tommy. "Lou Gehrig Gamely Took on Death Fight."
Brooklyn Eagle, June 3, 1941, Page 13.

Talbot, Gaylo, "Doubtful if Lou Gehrig's Record String Would Have Been Broken by Joe McCarthy." *Corsicana Daily Sun* (Associated Press), May 3, 1939, Page 10.

"Gehrig's Choice as Most Valuable Almost a Sweep." *Brooklyn Eagle* (Associated Press). October 12, 1927, Page 20.

MoreGehrig.Tripod.com

Wally Pipp: Two-Time AL HR Champ
Bufger, Bozeman. "Angel Aragon Proves Silver Lining on Yankees Clouded Pennant Chances." *The Evening World.* August 16, 1916, Page 10.

Menke, Frank G. "Menke's Daily Sporting Letter." *Kingston Daily Freeman.* February 5, 1915, Page 7.

"Pickler Pipp." *Houston Post*, June 24, 1917, Page 15.

Spatz, Lyle. "SABR Bioproject: Wally Pipp."

1927 Yankees: .714 Win Percentage
"Johnson Elated Over 4 Straight." *Brooklyn Eagle*, October 9, 1927, Page 35.

Harrison, James. "Lazzeri's 3 Homers Save Day for Yanks." *New York Times*, June 9, 1927, Page 30.

Heller, Karen. "On Being Not Nothingness." *Philadelphia Inquirer*, May 10, 1998.

Hinton, Ed. "NASCAR has its 1927 Yankees." *Chicago Tribune*, June 13, 2007.

Holmes, Thomas "Pirates Have Good Chance Against Yankees." *Brooklyn Eagle*, September 25, 1927, Page 42.

Kieran, John. "Sports of the Times." *New York Times*, June 9 1927, Page 33.

"Yankees smother Harris' Senators." *Ogden Standard-Examiner* (Associated Press), July 5, 1927, Page 10.

1939 Yankees Hit 13 HR in Doubleheader
Bohn, Terry, SABR Bioproject: Lynn Nelson, http://*SABR.org/ Bioproject*.

Effrat, Louis. "Yankees Show Little Enthusiasm For Baseball Under Floodlights." *New York Times*, June 28, 1939.

Effrat, Louis. "Yankees 13 Homers in Two Games Blast Records." *New York Times*, June 29, 1939.

"Yanks' Homer Riot Slap at Night Ball." *Brooklyn Daily Eagle,* June 29, 1939, Page 21

Lieb, Frederick G. "Precedent-Smashing Yankees Hailed as Team of the Century." *The Sporting News,* October 12, 1939, Page 3.

Spink, J.G. Taylor. "Three and One." *The Sporting News,* October 12, 1939, Page 4.

Joe DiMaggio's 56-Game Hitting Streak
Cohen, Lou. "Hitting's My Job Shrugs DiMaggio." *Brooklyn Eagle*, July 3, 1941, Page 1.

Curtright, Guy. "Uggla's hitting streak halted at 33 games."*MLB.com*, August 14, 2011.

Ferguson, Harry. "Today's Sport Parade." *The Times* (UPI), July 3, 1941.

Gould, Stephen Jay. "The Streak of Streaks." *New York Review of Books*, August 18, 1988.

Witten, Josh. "Streaking: Joe DiMaggio and Probability." *Science 20.com,* October 28, 2009.

Tom Hetrick interview with Joe DiMaggio, file maintained by Society for American Baseball Research, February 7, 1980.

The Mike Wallace Interview: Bob Feller, August 4, 1957, ABC-TV.

Baseball-Almanac.com

DiMaggio, Keller, Henrich Form the First 30-HR Outfield
Graham, Frank. "Yank Rookie from Newark may get Selkirk's Post." *The Daily Mail* (Associated Press), March 18, 1939, Page 21.

James, Bill. "The New Bill James Historical Baseball Abstract." Free Press, New York, 2001.

Kirksey, George. "Tom Henrich's Hustling Aids New York Yanks." *Bradford Evening Daily Record*, September 18, 1941, Page 14.

Rogers, Thomas. "Charlie Keller, 73, an Outfielder and Slugger for Yanks in the 40's." *New York Times*, May 24, 1990.

"Yankees Sold on Keller, Rookie of the Year." *Brooklyn Eagle*, February 25, 1939, Page 10.

"If We Can Improve Yanks, We'll Do It." *The Sporting News*, October 12, 1939, Page 1.

Tom Henrich death notice, *Dayton Daily News*, December 2, 2009.

Mickey Mantle's 1956 Triple Crown: .353, 52, 130
Kelly, Dick. "Spotlight on Sports." *The Daily Mail*, April 18, 1956, Page 22.

"Mickey Mantle's 10 Longest Home Runs." *TheMick.com*

Mickey Mantle and Phil Pepe. *My Favorite Summer, 1956,* Doubleday, New York, 1991.

Mickey Mantle hits 18 World Series HR
"I had to hit a homer." *Fresno Bee*, October 11, 1964, Page 41.

Roger Maris Hits 61 HR in 1961
Drebinger, John. "Yankees Set Back Tigers in Tenth on Mantle's Second 2-Run Homer." *New York Times*, April 27, 1961, Page 15.

"Maris Has Edge on Mantle; 27 More At-Bats in 90 Tilts." *The Sporting News*, July 26, 1961, Page 8.

"Maris Getting Closer." *Decatur Review* (Associated Press), July 26, 1961, Page 34.

"'Red-Necked Roger' Finds Fame Hard To Cope With." *Newport Daily News* (Associated Press), August 17, 1961, Page 16.

"Homer Interrupts Debate in Senate." *Janesville Daily Gazette* (Associated Press), August 17, 1961.

Fraley, Oscar. "Today's Sport Parade." *The Daily Republican,* August 17, 1961.

"My Chances Better Now, Maris Says." *Ogden Standard-Examiner* (UPI), August 17, 1961, Page 14.

Parish Prayers Offered for Maris's Cause." *Troy Record* (AP), September 13, 1961, Page 20.

"Roger Maris Glad to Lose Pressure and Aim At Series." *Terre-Haute Star* (Associated Press), September 21, 1961, Page 25.

"Frick Sticks to Ruling on Bid for Babe Ruth's Mark." *The Post-Standard* (Associated Press), September 15, 1961, Page 14.

Nichols, Ed. "Shore Sports." *The Daily Times*, September 14, 1961, Page 14.

Reichler, Joe. "Babe's Ghost Catches Up with Maris in HR Bid." *Cumberland Evening Times* (Associated Press), September 16, 1961, Page 6.

Reichler, Joe. "Yanks Slugger Assured of Financial Bonanza." *The Daily Mail* (Associated Press), September 27, 1961, Page 16.

Baseball-Almanac.com

Derek Jeter's Perfect 3,000ᵗʰ Hit

Coffey, Wayne. "It's the Ultimate Jeterian Feat." *New York Daily News*, July 10, 2011, Page 54.

Pearson, Jake; Abramson, Mitch; McShane, Larry. "Classy Fan Returns Ball to Yank Hit King." *New York Daily News*, July 10, 2011, Page 2

11/1/01, 12:04 AM—Derek Jeter Becomes Mr. November
Fenn, Lisa. "Derek Jeter remembers his walk-off HR." *ESPNNY.com*, October 28, 2010.

1996 Yankees Win 4 Straight from Braves in World Series
Yankeeography, David Cone. 2006

Giannone, John. "A Yanks Cone-Back." *New York Daily News,* October 23, Page 57.

Harper, John. "Cone's 6th Sense Tired, But He Knew He'd Get McGriff." *New York Daily News*, October 23, 1996, Page 60.

Kriegel, Mark. "Leyritz Gets 2nd Chance." *New York Daily News,* October 24, 1996, Page 74.

Lupica, Mike. "Yankee Doodle Andy; Kid Lays Down The Lore." *New York Daily News*, October 25, 1996, Page 76.

O'Connor, Ian. "Here's Paul Giving His All." *New York Daily News*, October 25, 1996, Page 78.

Zack, Bill. "Error of Their Ways." *Chattanooga Times Free Press,* October 25, 1996, Page 1.

1998 Yankees Win 125 Games (Most of Any Team)
Botte, Peter. "Clueless in Seattle, Moyer, M's Maul Yanks." *New York Daily News,* April 7, 1998, Page 79.

Lefkow, Mike. "Brosius Confirms He'll be a Yankee." *Contra Costa Times*, November 12, 1997.

Yankeeography: Moment of Glory, Scott Brosius, 2015.

30-Year-Old Brian Cashman Named Yankees GM
Brown, Tim. "Watson deals himself out `Surprised' Steinbrenner names Cashman as GM." *Newark Star-Ledger*, February 3, 1998.

Hoch, Bryan. "Cashman signs 3-year deal to continue as GM." *MLB.com,* October 10, 2014.

Mariano Rivera: 42 Saves in Postseason
Blum, Ronald. "Exit Sandman: Rivera bids farewell to Bronx." *Associated Press,* September 27, 2013.

Miller, Scott. "Mariano Rivera: Birth of the cutter was 'gift from God." *CBSSports.com,* July 14, 2013.

Simon, Mark. "What to Watch For: Mariano Rivera Goes for 601." *ESPNNY.com,* September 15, 2011.

The 66-Pitcher Bridge to Mariano
Interviews with Jeff Nelson and Mike Stanton.

David Robertson Retires 25 Straight Hitters in Bases-Loaded Situations
Boland, Eric. "Robertson pulls off the great escape." *Newsday,* October 11, 2009, Page A93.

Kane, Colleen. "White Sox closer David Robertson keeps calm, moves on from Yankees days." *Chicago Tribune,* March 8, 2015.

Kernan, Kevin. "Joba II: With A Twist." *New York Post,* June 15, 2008.

Verducci, Tom. "How a Danish tech company is revolutionizing pitching data." *Sports Illustrated,* April 12, 2011.

Whitey Ford's 33 Straight Scoreless Innings in the World Series
Brannon, Jason. "Saving Chairman Whitey." *Rob Neyer's Big Book of Baseball Lineups,* 2003, Touchstone Books, New York.

Drebinger, John. "Ford Gives Four Hits, Richardson Has Grand Slam—70,001 See Yankees Win." *New York Times,* October 9, 1960, Page S1.

Drebinger, John. "Yanks Beat Reds a Third Time, 7–0; Ford Sets Record." *New York Times,* October 9, 1961, Page 1.

"Calm Southpaw Hero of Victors is Noted as "Pitcher's Pitcher." *New York Times,* October 5, 1961.

Whitey Ford Hall of Fame Induction Speech, August 12, 1974.

"Whitey Ford Interview – Times Talk." Hosted by Brandon Steiner, March 12, 2009, YouTube.com.

Spud Chandler's .717 Winning Percentage
Heinz, W.C. "Spud Chandler Reached Top Despite Only Average Ability." *Milwaukee Journal,* April 10, 1948, Page 2.

Reggie Jackson's 3 HR on 3 Pitches in Game 6 of 1977 World Series
Jackson, Reggie, & Lupica, Mike. *Reggie.* 1984, Ballantine Books, New York.

McMane, Fred. "Jackson Does It All For Yanks 2–0 Win." *The Daily Messenger,* September 15, 1977, Page 8.

Nissenson, Herschel. "Round Two Goes to Yankees, 2–0." *Nashua Telegraph,* September 15, 1977, Page 23.

Rothenberg, Fred. "Yanks Come Together." *The Times*, October 19, 1977, Page 23.

Reggie Jackson interview with *CBS This Morning*, October 11, 2013.

1977 World Series Game 6, ABC TV, announcers: Keith Jackson, Howard Cosell, Tom Seaver. October 18, 1977.

SportsCentury: Reggie Jackson, ESPN. 2000.

Ron Guidry's 25 Wins in 1978
Chass, Murray. "Guidry fans 18 Angels for Yankees mark and wins No. 11 without loss, 4–0." *New York Times,* June 18, 1978, Section 5 Page 1.

Grunwald, David. "Yankee Ron Guidry, The Superstar who Almost Quit." *Lakeland Ledger,* April 1, 1979.

"Top 25 Yankee Stadium Moments: No. 25 Guidry strikes out 18." YES Network.

McCaffrey, Eugene V. and McCaffrey, Roger A. *Player's Choice.* 1987, Facts on File Publications, New York.

Yankeeography: Ron Guidry, YES Network. 2003.

Pete Sheehy Works for Yankees in Parts of 7 Decades
Interview with Ron Guidry

"Yankees' Sheehy dies." *New York Times*, August 14, 1985.

1978 Yankees Overcome 14-Game Deficit to Win AL East
"Quote/Unquote" *The Childress Index*, July 11, 1978, Page 9.

Chass, Murray. "Reggie Jackson Penalized 5 Days, $9,000." *New York Times*, July 19, 1978, Page A1.

Chass, Murray. "Owner Stunned by Manager's Outburst." *New York Times*, July 24, 1978, Page C1.

Smith, Claire. "After 22 Years, the Goose Goes Home." *New York Times,* April 25, 1995.

Interview with Bucky Dent and Mike Torrez, YES Network, posted online February 13, 2015. Youtube.com.

Catfish Hunter's $1 Million Signing Bonus
Kelly, Matt. "Catfish Hunter signs Free Agent Contract with New York Yankees." *BaseballHallofFame.org.*

Graig Nettles Makes 4 Great Plays in a World Series Game
Interview with Graig Nettles, March 29, 2015.

1978 World Series Game 3 (Announcers: Joe Garagiola and Tom Seaver), NBC TV Network. Youtube.com.

Bock, Hal. "Dodgers Praise Graig Nettles." *The Spokesman Review* (Associated Press), October 15, 1978.

Grimsley, Will. "Nettles Devours Hot Shots." *Iola Register* (Associated Press), October 14, 1978.

Yankeeography: Graig Nettles; YES Network, 2005.

Sparky Lyle's 57 Saves of 6-Plus Outs
"Down to One, Yanks Win 6–4." *Associated Press*, October 9, 1977.

"Royals Believe in Lyle's Style." *Associated Press*, October 9, 1977.

Durso, Joseph. "Yanks Trade Cater for Lyle, Star Red Sox Relief Pitcher." *New York Times*, March 23, 1972, Page 57.

O'Boyle, Bill. "Former Yankee great Sparky Lyle addresses Friendly Sons." *Albany Times-Union*, March 13, 2015.

Rich Gossage's 100 MPH Fastball
"Gossage Cashes in with Yankees." *Lebanon Daily News* (UPI), November 23, 1977, Page 48.

Chass, Murray. "Gossage; Reliever Hitters Fear." *New York Times*, July 3, 1980, Page B7.

Saunders, Patrick. "Goose's intimidating style forged early." *Denver Post*, January 9, 2008.

George Brett: 220 Games Against Yankees, Every One was a Battle
The Greatest League Championship Series, Major League Baseball Productions, 1994.

Chass, Murray. "Brett Homer Nullified so Yankees Win." *New York Times,* July 25, 1983, Page 1.

Martin, Dan. "Royals success brings Brett back to old rivalry with Yankees." *New York Post*, October 1, 2014.

"Text of League President's Ruling in Brett Bat Case." *New York Times,* July 29, 1983.

Dave Righetti Sets MLB Record with 46 Saves in 1986
Interview with Dave Righetti, March 10, 2015.

Chass, Murray. "Righetti Gets Relief Role." *New York Times,* February 18, 1984.

Pennington, Bill. "Righetti Saves Day, Sets Mark." *The Record,* October 5, 1986, Page 4.

Don Mattingly Hits .343
Interviews with Don Mattingly, Joe Sheehan.

Rickey Henderson's 1985 Season Was Worth 9.9 WAR
Axisa, Mike. "Past Trade Review: Rickey Henderson." *River Avenue Blues,* February 9, 2012.

Chass, Murray. "This is Rickey Henderson: Speed that Terrorizes." *New York Times*, December 16, 1984.

NYSportsSpace.com Message Board. "Funny Rickey Henderson Quotes." November 24, 2007.

"Lunch with a Legend: Dave Winfield." ESPN 98.7 FM, April 30, 2010.

Guy Zinn Steals Home Two Times in One Game
"Yankees climb out of last place again." *New York Times,* August 16, 1912, Page 7.

Yankees Sign Dave Winfield to 10-year Contract
Anderson, Dave. "We'll See How Good I Am Now." *New York Times.* December 16, 1980, Page C15.

Noble, Marty. "Winfield puts Yanks First." *Newsday*, June 30, 1987, Page 116.

Skipper, Doug. SABR Bioproject: Dave Winfield, http://SABR.org/Bioproject.

"Lunch with a Legend: Dave Winfield" ESPN 98.7 FM, April 30, 2010.

George Steinbrenner Turns a $10 Million Investment into Billions
"New Yankee owners see clear sailing." *Tucson Daily Citizen* (Associated Press), January 4, 1973, Page 45.

Rich Gossage Hall of Fame speech. July 27, 2008,

Interviews with Andrew Marchand, Steve Karsay.

Steve Trout comments at 2015 SABR convention.

Forbes magazine team valuations, *Forbes.com.*

Merron, Jeff, "The List: Steinbrenner's worst." *ESPN.com* (date unknown).

Yogi Berra Won 12 World Series as a Yankees Player and Coach
"Money Guys? Yep, Yanks Have Access." *Gastonia Gazette* (Associated Press), September 17, 1955, Page 13.

Daley, Arthur. "Short shots in Sundry Directions." *New York Times* March 27, 1947, Page 36.

Grimsley, Will. "Stengel Praises Kucks and Berra." *The Daily Tar Heel* (Associated Press), October 11, 1956, Page 6.

Wilks, Ed. "Yankees Still Have Old Homer Magic." *Gastonia Gazette* (Associated Press), September 17, 1955, Page 13.

Williams, Joe. "Stengel Likes Yankees Chances in Flag Race." *New York World-Telegram,* March 26, 1949.

Baseball-Almanac.com.

Don Larsen Throws a 97-Pitch Perfect Game in the World Series
"Impact of Possible Perfect Game Didn't Hit Don Larsen Until Ninth." *The Decatur Herald*, October 9, 1956, Page 13.

"Mother Fails to See Son in Big Day." *The Morning Herald*, October 9, 1956, Page 12.

Coffey, Michael. *27 Men Out: Baseball's Perfect Games*. 2004, Simon & Schuster, New York, Page 61.

Klopsis, Nick. "56 years later, Don Larsen and Yogi Berra reminisce about perfect game." *Newsday*, October 8, 2012.

McIntire, Doug. "Doug's Dougout." *The Morning Herald*, October 9, 1956. Page 12.

Reichler, Joseph. "Perfect Game was Top Thrill for Babe Pinelli." *The Times Record*, October 9, 1956, Page 27.

Smits, Ted. "No Arguments Tainted Game." *The News-Palladium (Associated Press)*, October 9, 1956. Page 12.

A 300-to–1 shot comes through
"Predicts Perfect Tilt, Wins Wager." *Beckley Post-Herald* (Associated Press), October 9, 1956, Page 10.

2 Perfect Games in 14 Months

"Yankees 4, Twins 0." *Associated Press*, May 18, 1998.

Blum, Ronald. "Twins spectators for Wells' perfect game." *Associated Press*, May 18, 1998.

Blum, Ronald. "Cone defines 1990s Yankees." *Associated Press*, July 19, 1999.

Botte, Peter. "All the Pieces of a Perfect Puzzle." *New York Daily News*, May 18, 1998, Page 58.

Botte, Peter. "A Striking Moment: Molitor K." *New York Daily News*, May 18, 1998, Page 58.

Dubow, Josh. "Yankees 6, Expos 0." *Associated Press*, July 19, 1999.

Dubow, Josh. "Larsen relives Yankees history." *Associated Press*, July 19, 1999.

Olney, Buster. "Rarest Gem for Yankees' Wells: A Perfect Game." *New York Times*, May 18, 1998.

Allie Reynolds Pitches Two 2 No-Hitters in 1951

Drebinger, John. "Bomber Ace Victor at Cleveland, 1–0." *New York Times*, July 13, 1951.

Drebinger, John. "Yankees clinch flag Aided by Reynolds No-Hitter." *New York Times,* September 29, 1951.

Smith, Claire. "Allie Reynolds, Star Pitcher for Yankees is Dead at 79." *New York Times*, December 28, 1951.

Smith, Dick. "Reynolds Tosses No-Hitter to beat Tribe, 1–0." *The Massillon* (OH) *Evening Independent (Associated Press)*, July 13, 1951, Page 16.

Talbot, Gayle. "Allie Reynolds Hurls Second No-Hitter." *Bridgeport Telegram* (Associated Press), September 29, 1951.

"Reynolds drove Teammates Wild in No-Hit Job." *Brooklyn Eagle*, July 13 1951, Page 12.

Interview with Lyle Spatz.

Mike Mussina's 8²/₃ Perfect Innings
Interview with Jeff Quagliata, Mike Stanton, Patrick Bohn.

Yankeeography: Mike Mussina, 2009.

Highlights from Mike Mussina's near-perfect game: Carl Everett's hit, YouTube.com.

Highlights from Mike Mussina's 20th win in 2008, YouTube.com.

Heuschkel, David. "A Near Moose: One Out from Perfect Game." *Hartford Courant,* September 3, 2001, Page C1.

Olney, Buster. "Mussina Misses Yankees 4th Perfect Game by One Pitch." *New York Times,* September 3, 2001.

Weinberg, Neil. "Obsessing over Perfection." *HardballTimes.com,* July 31, 2014.

Orlando Hernandez Wins His First 8 Postseason Decisions
1998 ALCS Game 4 pregame press conference transcript, ASAPSports.com

Brown, Daniel. "Champion Yankees Stay Cool under Pressure. Williams, El Duque Bolster Remarkable 1st Round Resumes." *San Jose Mercury News,* October 15, 2001.

30 for 30: Brothers in Exile, ESPN Films, 2014.

Roger Clemens Gets Win No. 300 with Yankees
Botte, Peter and Goldiner Dave. "Bye Boomer – and Hi, Rocket – Yankees Give up Wells for Clemens." *New York Daily News,* February 19, 1999, Page 5.

McCarron, Anthony. "Roger Wins 300th Game; Mister Milestone Adds 4,000th K." *New York Daily News,* June 14, 2003, Page 48.

Wilstein, Steve. "Clemens playoff performance redefines his career." *Associated Press,* October 15, 2000.

Phil Niekro Also Got Win No. 300 with Yankees
"Niekro wins 300th without his knuckler." *Miami Herald,* October 7, 1985, Page 1D.

Aaron Small's 10–0 Miracle
Interview with Aaron Small.

Cook, Steve. "Interview: Part 1-4, Aaron Small." *The Greatest 21 Days* (Greatest21Days.com), November 30 – December 3, 2014.

Joe Torre Manages Yankees to 4 Titles in 5 Years
Goldstein, Richard. "Frank Torre, Inspiration to a Yankees Manager, Dies at 82." *New York Times*, September 13, 2014.

Klapisch, Bob. "Joe Torre takes his rightful place in Cooperstown today." *The Record*, July 27, 2014.

Madden, Bill. "Crowning of a Puppet." *New York Daily News*, November 3, 1995, Page 76.

Madden, Bill. "The Book on Torre." *New York Daily News,* November 3, 1995, Page 77.

O'Connor, Ian. "Joe Is in Why of the Storm." *New York Daily News*, November 3, 1995, Page 74.

"Inquiring Photographer: What's Your Opinion of Joe Torre Being Hired Yesterday to Manage Yankees?" *New York Daily News*, November 3, 1995, Page 78.

Joe Torre's Hall of Fame speech. July 27, 2014.

Mel Stottlemyre Wins 9 Games to Help 1964 Yankees Win Pennant
Radio broadcast, Game 7 of 1964 World Series, Yankees vs. Cardinals. NBC Radio. (Announcers: Phil Rizzuto, Joe Garagiola.) October 15, 1964.

Berardino, Mike. "Yankee Staff's Ace May Be Stottlemyre." *Orlando Sun-Sentinel,* October 18, 2004.

Koppett, Leonard. "Sports of the Times." *New York Times,* September 22, 1964.

Koppett, Leonard. "Talk of the Series." *New York Times*, October 16, 1964.

Lipsyte, Robert. "Double Play: Getting the Ball from Second to First is Half the Battle." *New York Times,* October 16, 1964.

Moriarty, Tim. "Rookie Gives Yanks Big Lift." *Bridgeport Post* (UPI), September 9, 1964.

Reichler, Joseph. "Yankees Have Trouble in Hitting, Hurling." *The St. Petersburg Va. Progress-Index* (Associated Press), August 12, 1964, Page 16.

Ryczek, Bill. "My Favorite Player: Mel Stottlemyre." *TheNationalPastimeMuseum.com.*

Willie Randolph: 1,000 Walks, 1,000 Double Plays

Anderson, David. "The Yankees' Rookie Second Baseman." *New York Times,* May 25, 1976, Page 53.

Durso, Joseph. "Yanks Send Bonds to Angels for Pair and Medich to Pirates for 3 Players." *New York Times,* December 12, 1975, Page 49.

Interview with Willie Randolph and Don Mattingly.

Brian Doyle Hits .438 in 1978 World Series

Willie Randolph. press conference at Yankee Stadium, 2015 Oldtimer's Day.

Billy Martin Is Hired and Fired 5 Times

Berkow, Ira. "Sports of the Times: Rubbernecking on Billy Day." *New York Times*, August 11, 1986.

Brown, Frank. "Yankees' Martin pulled own trigger." *Southern Illinoisian* (Associated Press), July 25, 1978, Page 13.

Chass, Murray. "Yankees Oust Martin as Manager, Replace Him with Howser." *New York Times*, October 29, 1979, Page A1.

Grimsley, Will. "Martin out as NY Manager at End of Season." *The News-Palladium* (UPI), June 28, 1978, Page 11.

Richman, Milton. "Stengel still a Billy Martin supporter." *Ottawa Journal* (UPI), July 29, 1975, Page 24.

Richman, Milton. "Yankees nearly fire Martin." *The Lowell Sun* (UPI), July 24, 1977, Page 30.

Sandomir, Richard. "Thousands Pay Final Respects to Martin." *Los Angeles Times,* December 30, 1989.

"Billy Martin Coming Home to Become Yankees Manager." *Naples Daily News*, August 3, 1975, Page 17.

"Billy Martin Admits He's Unorthodox." *The Van Wert Times*, August 4, 1975, Page 9.

"Billy Martin returns to manage Yankees again." *The Paris* (Texas) *News*, June 19, 1979, Page 10.

"Yankees ax finally falls: Martin's out, Berra's in." *The Providence Journal-Bulletin,* December 17, 1983, Page B2.

"Martin gets broken arm fighting Whitson in bar." *Los Angeles Times* (Associated Press), September 23, 1985.

"I'm Not Gonna Change, Martin Insists." *San Jose Mercury News* (Associated Press), October 23, 1987, Page 8E.

Casey Stengel Wins 5 World Series Titles in First 5 Years as Yankees Manager

Interview with Toni Harsh. June 30, 2015.

Hand, Jack. "Stengel to Pilot Yankees for Next Two Years," *Syracuse Post-Standard* (Associated Press), October 13, 1948, Page 14.

Holmes, Tommy. "Yankees Deserve That Big Salute." *Brooklyn Eagle.* October 10, 1949, Page 11.

Peterson, Leo. "Stengel Man of Honor in Yankees Conquest," *Brooklyn Eagle*, October 10, 1949, Page 11.

Yankees Score 55 Runs in 1960 World Series … and Lose!

Effrat, Louis. "Yankees Say Turning Point was Grounder that Hit Kubek: Double Play Ball Cited by Stengel." *New York Times,* October 14, 1960, Page 37.

Joe McCarthy's 1,460 Wins in 16 Seasons

"I'd jump off Brooklyn Bridge to Nip Cubs in Series – McCarthy" *The Sporting News*, October 23, 1930, Page 1.

"Baseball Loses One of Its Greatest Figures." *Berkshire Evening Eagle,* May 27, 1946, Page 10.

"Joe McCarthy's 10 Commandments of Baseball." Reprinted at Baseball-Almanac.com.

James, Bill. *The Bill James Guide to Baseball Managers*, New York: Scribner, 1997.

Miller Huggins Suspends Babe Ruth and Fines Him $5,000
"Look Out For Big Deals By Yank Leader." *The Evening Review,* December 28, 1917, Page 10.

"Suspend Babe Ruth, $5,000 Fine: Home Run King has Misbehaved, Charge." *The Decatur Daily Review* (Associated Press), August 30, 1925, Page 8.

Corum, M.W. "Ruth Begs Pardon of His Pilot." *The Times Herald,* September 2, 1925, Page 8.

"Victorious Yanks Sing Battle Cry." *Reading Times* (Associated Press), October 10, 1928, Page 14.

Holmes, Thomas. "Babe's Three Home Runs Bring Series Nightmare to Merciful Conclusion." *Brooklyn Daily Eagle*, October 10, 1928, Page 26.

Tony Lazzeri Drives in 11 Runs in a Game
Avery, Leslie. "Lazzeri Drives in 11 Runs in One Day." *Santa Ana Register* (UPI), May 25, 1936*.*

Dawson, James P. "Yanks Annex Two, Fans in Near Riot." *New York Times,* May 24, 1936, Page 24.

Dawson, James P. "Yanks Overwhelm Athletics, 25 to 2." *New York Times,* May 25, 1936, Page 113, 117.

Harrison, James R. "Ruppert Impressed by Yankees' Work." *New York Times,* March 15, 1926, Page 27.

"Sport Notes." *Greeneville* (PA) *Record-Argus*, May 25, 1936, Page 5.

Robinson Cano: AL-Record 5 Straight Seasons of 25 HR by a Second Baseman
Browne, Ian. "Yes we Cano: Derby win is a family affair." *MLB.com,* July 12, 2011.

Interview with Jorge Posada, Aaron Small, Curt Schilling.

2 Unlikely Heroes Help Yankees Win 2000 World Series
Simon, Mark. "Vizcaino's heroics an amazing story." *ESPNNY.com,* October 2, 2010.

Kernan, Kevin. "RBI Hero Sojo Savors Moment." *New York Post,* October 27, 2000, Page 118.

2 Game-Tying HR with 2 Outs in Nnth in 2 Nights in 2001 World Series
Postgame press conference transcripts for Gamez 4, 5, and 7, via ASAPSports.com.

2 Pennant Winning Walk-Off HR
Fenn, Lisa. "Chris Chambliss remembers his walk-off home run." *ESPNNY.com*, October 21, 2010.

Fenn, Lisa. "Aaron Boone remembers his walk-off home run." *ESPNNY.com*, October 16, 2010.

Bernie Williams Leads MLB with 80 Postseason RBIs
Interview with Tim Kurkjian, Jorge Posada, Willie Randolph and Mike Stanton.

Lupica, Mike. "Yankees make Texas twist; With season on brink, Bombers use their ninth live." *New York Daily News*, October 5, 1996, Page 38.

Rocca, Larry. "Marching on: Down 3–0 early, Bernie wins it in the 10th." *Newsday*, October 14, 1999, Page A88.

Walker, Ben. "Yankees, Williams, clinch AL East in dramatic fashion." *USA Today*, October 1, 2004.

Andy Pettitte wins 18 Postseason Games for Yankees
Gergen, Joe. "Andy's Simply Magnificent." *Newsday*, October 25, 1996, Page A93.

Giannone, John. "Yankee Doodle Andy." *New York Daily News*, October 25, 1996, Page 77.

Rumberg, Howie. "Pettitte helps Jeter, Rivera and Posada to title." *Associated Press,* November 5, 2009.

Torre, Joe and Verducci, Tom. *The Yankee Years.* Anchor Books, New York, 2009.

Jorge Posada Becomes 3rd Yankees Catcher with 1,000 RBIs
Simon, Mark. "15 Minutes with Jorge Posada." *ESPNNY*.com, May 11, 2015.

1 Yankee Has Won Both AL Rookie of the Year and MVP
Durso, Joseph. "Snyder Drafts Pitcher for Montreal." *New York Times*, June 7, 1968, Page 44.

Pepe, Phil. "High Drama in Murcer Goodbye to Munson." *The Sporting News*, August 25, 1979.

Vecsey, George. "Yanks Bow; Orioles Win, 5–2 on Circuit Drives." *New York Times*, March 15, 1969, Page 43.

Weinstein, Matt. "Thurman Munson took advantage of time in Binghamton." *Binghamton Press & Sun Bulletin*, August 28, 2014.

"Munson is Yanks MVP leader." *Kingston Daily Freeman*, September 16, 1976, Page 15.

"American League Rookie Honors to Yank Catcher." *The Daily Courier* (UPI), November 25, 1970, Page 5.

Elston Howard Hits .348
Yankeeography: Elston Howard, 2004.

Interview with Bobby Richardson.

Clary, Jack. "Howard Catch Top Play on Defense." *The La Crosse Tribune* (Associated Press), October 7, 1958, Page 14.

Daley, Arthur. "What About Elston Howard?" *New York Times* April 1, 1955, Page 35.

Drebinger, John. "Howard of Yanks Named American League's Most Valuable Player." *New York Times*, November 8, 1963, Page 50.

Effrat, Louis. "Stengel Calls Improved Defense Key to Yanks' Stirring Series Comeback." *New York Times*, October 10, 1958, Page 37.

Rosengren, John. "Elston Howard became the Yankees Jackie Robinson 60 Years Ago" SI.com, April 13, 2015.

Tan, Cecilia. SABR Bioproject: Elston Howard, http://*SABR.org/Bioproject*.

Paul Krichell and Tom Greenwade Combine for 53 Years of Scouting Excellence

Kreuz, Jim. SABR Bioproject: Tom Greenwade, http://*SABR.org/Bioproject*.

Levitt, Daniel. SABR Bioproject: Paul Krichell, http://*SABR.org/Bioproject*.

Vitullo-Martin, Julia, and Moskin, J. Robert. *The Executive's Book of Quotations*. Oxford University Press, New York. 1994.

Bill Dickey Catches 100 Games in MLB-record 13 Straight Seasons

Burr, Harold. "Bill Dickey Is Last to Admit He Is Going To Be Great Catcher." *Brooklyn Daily Eagle,* June 16, 1929, Page 38.

"Dickey of Yankees is Out for Season." *New York Times*, September 11, 1934, Page 26.

Feder, Sid. "Dickey takes Babe's Place as Pace-Setter for Yankees." *The Day*, June 11, 1938, Page 8.

Laufer. "Brushing Up Sports." *The Times Herald*, May 25, 1929, Page 14.

Sherman, Ed. *Babe Ruth's Called Shot,* Lyons Press, Guilford, CT, 2014.

Wancho, Joseph. SABR Bioproject: Bill Dickey, http://SABR.org/Bioproject.

Baseball-Almanac.com.

Joe Sewell Strikes Out 3 Times in 1932
Archived interview: Joe Sewell with Walter Langford, June 26, 1982, from the Society for Baseball Research Oral History collection.

Archived interview: Joe Sewell with Eugene Murdock, August 8, 1977, from the Cleveland Public Library Digital Gallery collection.

Interview with John Thorn.

Pitcher Red Ruffing Hits 31 Home Runs
Brandt, William E. "Homer by Ruffing Wins for Yanks, 1–0." *New York Times*, August 14, 1932, Page 37.

Burr, Harold. "Wanted to Make Sure of Hit, So Ruffing Clouted Home Run." *Brooklyn Daily Eagle*, April 15, 1933, Page 10.

Drebinger, John. "Ruffing's Homer Wins for Yankees." *New York Times*, April 15, 1933, Page 17.

Ferguson, Harry. "Rufus the Red and Col. Jake Have Merry Time After Victory." *Brooklyn Daily Eagle*, October 8, 1937, Page 20.

Mercurio, John. *New York Yankees Records.* Harper Collins Publishers, New York, 1989, Page 64.

"Ruffing Pulls Fiction Stunt as Yanks Win." *Lubbock Morning Avalanche,* September 19, 1930, Page 2.

"Ruffing Seeks No-Hitter." *New York Times,* October 7, 1937, Page 32.

Lefty Gomez Goes 6–0 in the World Series
Brandt, William E. "Pitching of Gomez Impresses Grimm." *New York Times,* September 30, 1932, Page 22.

"Gomez Loses Four Pounds." *New York Times,* September 30, 1932, Page 22.

McGowen, Roscoe. "Terry, Far From Depressed, Relies on Fitzsimmons to Spike Yanks' Guns Today; Luck Has Changed, Gomez Confesses." *New York Times,* October 3, 1936, Page 11.

McGowen, Roscoe. "Pitcher is Elated Over Timely Blow." *New York Times,* October 11, 1937, Page 15.

"Ruth sees Gomez as Star of Future." *Coshocton Tribune,* April 18, 1931, Page 6.

E-mail exchange with Vernona Gomez.

Yankee Stadium(s): Home to More Than 7,500 Games
"74,200 see Yankees Open New Stadium, Ruth Hit Home Run," *New York Times,* April 19, 1923, Page 1.

"Topics of the Times." *New York Times*, April 20, 1923.

"Red Sox Fan Brands Yankee Stadium as A.L. Frankenstein." *The Sporting News*, March 15, 1964.

Ryczek, Williams. "My First Game: Yankees v. Tigers." *National Pastime.com.*

Section 39 and 203: The Home of the Bleacher Creatures
Interviews with Vinny Milano, John McCarthy.

Freddy Sez Was the Yankees No. 1 Fan for 85 Years
Interview with Cecilia Tan.

Mel Allen Could Sum it All Up in 3 Words
Mel Allen entry, *Wikipedia.com.*

Interview with Gary Gold.

Bialik, Carl. "A Voice Above All Others." *GelfMagazine.com*, April 2, 2007.

Borelli, Stephen. *How About That! The Life of Mel Allen,* Sports Publishing LLC, Champaign, 2005.

Halberstam, David J. *Sports on New York Radio: A Play-by-Play History*, Masters Press, Chicago, Ill. 1999.

Young, Dick. "Kell reported in line for Yank radio job." *New York Daily News*, October 24, 1964.

Phil Rizzuto Leads the Major Leagues in Sacrifices 4 Straight Seasons
Interview with Dr. Bobby Brown. June 5, 2015.

Phil Rizzuto. Baseball Hall of Fame speech, July 31, 1994.

Baldassaro, Lawrence. SABR Bioproject: Phil Rizzuto, http://SABR. org/*Bioproject*.

Burr, Harold. "Dodgers Flung 27 Tossers at Yankees." *Brooklyn Daily Eagle*, October 7, 1947, Page 11.

Daley, Arthur. "A Last Backward Look." *New York Times,* October 11, 1951, Page 45.

Rose, Murray. "Phil Rizzuto Sparkles in Spite of Body Aches." *Bridgeport Telegram,* October 7, 1947, Page 14.

Eddie Layton Plays the Organ at Yankee Stadium for Nearly 30 years
Interview with Chris Pavia.

"Longtime Yankee Stadium organist Layton dies." *Associated Press*, December 27, 2004.

John Sterling: 0 Missed Games
Interview with Katie Sharp, John Sterling.

DeLessio, Joe. "The Seven Types of John Sterling Home Run Calls." *New York Magazine*, April 6, 2011.

DiMauro, Mike. "Sterling's a Rare Gem, Don'tcha Know?" *The Day*, October 10, 2011.

Hildebrandt, Chuck. "Working the Game: An Interview with John Sterling." Sabrmedia.org.

First Full-Time Female Baseball Radio Analyst: Suzyn Waldman
Interview with Erica Herskowitz.

Dudek, Duane. "Yankees broadcaster Suzyn Waldman in a class by herself and 'distressed' about it." *Milwaukee Journal Sentinel,* May 8, 2014.

Laurilia, David. "Prospectus Q&A: Suzyn Waldman." *BaseballProspectus.com*, April 25, 2011.

Smith, Claire. "Baseball Around The Horn." *DiamondInq.blogspot. com*, July 2, 2006.

Bob Sheppard's 57 Years as PA Announcer
White, Paul. "Derek Jeter Kept Bob Sheppard's Voice Alive." *USA Today,* July 11, 2010.

Bobby Murcer Homers in 4 Straight At-Bats

"Any Day Now: Murcer for Epstein." *Associated Press*, May 27, 1970.

"Monumental Mr. Murcer (For That Day At Least)." *Associated Press,* June 25, 1970.

Long, Gary. "Comparisons Are Growing Old." *Miami Herald,* March 18, 1973.

Orioles vs. Yankees broadcast, ABC TV, August 6, 1979.

Yankees organization statements on the death of Bobby Murcer, July 12, 2008.

Yankeeography: Bobby Murcer. YES Network. 2003.

Graham, Kevin. "A history of baseball in 100 objects. No. 1 A Bobby Murcer baseball card." *Baseballrevisited.wordpress.com,* January 26, 2012.

Marty Appel eulogy for Bobby Murcer.

Horace Clarke Breaks up Three No-Hitters in a Month
"Six Astros pitchers combine to no-hit Yankees." *Associated Press*, June 13, 2003.

Durso, Joe. "Clarke Foils Bid on One-Out Single." *New York Times.* July 3, 170, Page 17.

11 Seasons Without a Postseason Appearance before Roy White Finally Made It
Noble, Marty. "White, Yanks invisible man, hard to miss." MLB.com, June 22, 2011.

Interview with Roy White.

Paul O'Neill's 10-pitch At-Bat in Game 1 of the 2000 World Series
O'Neill, Paul with Rocks, Burton. "Me and My Dad." Harper Collins, 2003, Page 97.

Myril Hoag: 1st Yankees Player with a 6-Hit Game
King, Bill. "Babe Ruth's Feelings Are Quite Badly Hurt." *Freeport Journal Standard* (Associated Press), June 7, 1934, Page 17.

Hideki Matsui has 6 RBI in Game 6 of the 2009 World Series
Interview with Doug Glanville, March 10, 2015.

Hank Bauer's Record-Setting 17-Game World Series hitting streak
Hand, Jack. "Yankees Notch 14th World Series Title as Giants Run out of Miracles." *Kingston Daily Freeman* (Associated Press), October 11, 1951, Page 26.

"Lucky to Make Catch, Bauer; Giants Praised." *Kingston Daily Freeman,* October 11, 1951, Page 26.

Bauer, Hank with United Press. "Bauer Thanked the Lord for Mighty Triple." *Brooklyn Daily Eagle,* October 11, 1951, Page 29.

Reichler, Joseph. "Spahn, Ford in Opener is Repeat." *The La Cross Tribune* (Associated Press), October 1, 1958, Page 16.

Smits, Ted. "Bauer Admits He Likes Money." *The La Crosse Tribune* (Associated Press), October 5, 1958, Page 13.

"Bauer Accused of Belting Man In Club Brawl." *Herald-Journal*, May 17, 1957, Page 16.

Johnny Damon Steals Two Bases on One Play in 2009 World Series
Olbermann, Keith. "World Series Smartest Plays," *MSNBC,* November 3, 2009.

Stark, Jayson. "Damon Steals the Show in Game 4." *ESPN.com,* November 1, 2009.

Dr. Bobby Brown Hits .439 in the World Series
Freeze, Ken. "Kingfisher Crash off San Francisco," Check-six.com.

Interview with Bobby Brown, June 5, 2015.

1947 Yankees Win 19 Straight Games
Dawson, James P. "Page's Homer with 2 out in 9th Brings 4–3 Triumph to Yankees." *New York Times*, July 11, 1947, Page 18.

Hollingsworth, Harry. *The Best & Worst Baseball Teams of All-Time.* 1994, Shapolsky Publishers, New York.

Lee Guetterman Throws 30²/₃ Consecutive Scoreless Innings to Start 1989
Interview with Lee Guetterman, March 10, 2015.

"Who is Lee Guetterman and Why is He on a Roll?" *Houston Chronicle,* May 23, 1989.

Jack Chesbro Wins 41 Games in 1904
"New York Team Outplays the Boston Champions by 8 to 2." *New York Times,* April 15, 1904, Page 5.

"15,000 see New York defeat Collins' boys." *Boston Post*, April 15, 1904, Page 4.

"Powell Got Revenge and Howell Suffered." *New York Evening World*, June 20, 1904, Page 9.

"Happy Jack on Being Lucky." *New York Evening World,* July 2, 1904, Page 8.

"Chesbro's New Ball a Puzzler." *New York Evening World,* July 12, 1904, Page 9.

"Highlanders in Tenth." *New York Tribune,* July 17, 1904, Page 6.

"Shakes Hands of Old Friends." *The Syracuse Post-Standard*, December 12, 1904, Page 3.

McElereavy, Wayne SABR Bioproject: Jack Chesbro, http://SABR. org/*Bioproject.*

Slow Joe Doyle Opens His Career with 2 Shutouts
Van Loan, C.E. "Yankees Beat White Sox in Duel of Slow Pitching." *New York American,* August 12, 1909, Page 5.

"Americans Win Twice from the Clevelands." *New York Times,* August 26, 1906. Page 6.

"Americans Take Two." *New York Times*, August 31, 1906. Page 7.

T206museum.com.